the Luftwaffe over Brum

FORWARD

the
Luftwaffe
over Brum

Birmingham's Blitz from a Military Perspective

Steve Richards

The Luftwaffe over Brum:
Birmingham's Blitz from a Military Perspective

Steve Richards

ISBN 978-0-9563708-3-9

First published in 2015
Second printing (revised) 2017
Third printing 2019
Richards Publishing
48 Longmore Road
Shirley, Solihull, B90 3DY, UK
e-mail: motorwaycoaches@tiscali.co.uk
www.birminghamair-raids.co.uk

© Stephen Gordon Richards

Printed by Charlesworth Press, Wakefield, WF2 9LP

Half title page: **A representation of the Birmingham Coat of Arms.**

Opposite title page: **The scene in the Bull Ring 10th April 1941 following the previous night's major attack.** Mirrorpix/Birmingham Mail

Title page: **The Junkers Ju 88 was arguably the best of the German bombers used in the blitz on Birmingham.** EN-Archive

Opposite page: **In the raid of 9/10th April 1941, the east window of St Martin's Church was destroyed. The replacement window, pictured here, has a theme of healing and restoration. The lower part shows citizens of Birmingham in their wartime clothes; the main part of the window shows eight of Christ's healing miracles.** Gary Price Photography

CONTENTS

AUTHOR'S PREFACE

Like many of my generation who grew up in the 1950-1960s, I was regaled with stories told by my parents relating their experiences while living through the Blitz. My mother especially, who lived in Warley, Smethwick, waxed lyrical. She was of senior school age throughout the Blitz period. Her most dramatic account was of a German bomber which crashed in nearby Hales Lane, and how one of the German crew landed by parachute on the roof of a house opposite her home.

In the late 1990s, when helping one of my own teenage daughters with a school project about the Second World War, we decided to attempt to compile a list of air attacks on Birmingham. The three volumes of *The Blitz Then and Now* were diligently studied. It was there that we found a reference to the bomber of which my mother had spoken so often. It was a Heinkel He 111 of German bomber unit KG27 which, so it was said, had been brought down by a Defiant night fighter flown by Flt Lt Deanesly. This was most exciting. However, in the months that followed, I continued my own investigations which caused me to doubt that this particular RAF pilot was, indeed, responsible for the demise of the Heinkel.

In March 2012, my wife came across a reference on the internet suggesting that a pilot named Bodien had brought down a Heinkel over Birmingham on the night in question. With this lead we were able to source combat reports, squadron ORBs (Operations Record Books) and even personal letters written by Bodien, which left no doubt that he, and not Deanesly, had shot down the Heinkel. This was contrary to much published local history, both in print and on the internet.

I determined to write a short account of this incident which occurred on the night of 9/10th April 1941. As I did the research I felt constrained to expand the project to cover all air attacks on Birmingham during the spring of 1941. As the reader will see, I subsequently

threw off all restraint and went for all air attacks against Birmingham, from the Zeppelin raids in the First World War through to the last raid on 23rd April 1943. For my purposes 'Birmingham' includes the neighbouring local authorities of Bromsgrove, Oldbury, Smethwick, Solihull, Sutton Coldfield, Walsall and West Bromwich.

From the outset the focus has been the military aspect as it related to Birmingham's experience of the Blitz. *The Luftwaffe over Brum – Birmingham's Blitz from a Military Perspective* is very much a story of the German Air Force ranging virtually unopposed over the city and the gradual ascendancy of the Royal Air Force, as it strove to get to grips with the night intruders. For those wishing to read accounts from the civilian perspective, there is material on the internet and Carl Chinn's book *Brum Undaunted*, which has many personal reminiscences of Brummies. In addition, Alton Douglas has put together two pictorial books, *Birmingham at War Vols 1 and 2*, which cover similar ground.

Whilst the larger portion of this volume is a chronological account of military operations, I have not ignored the civilian experience. Part One is what may be termed a microcosm, detailing the story of one German raider and its impact on civilians in a Birmingham suburb. The sub-article *The Horrors of Bombing* also gives graphic illustrations of what the civilians of Birmingham suffered.

As in my other books, full use of footnotes has been made so as not to break the flow of the text with supplementary detail. Furthermore, there are numerous sub-articles which are presented as text boxes. These cover subjects closely related to the main narrative but which the reader may wish to treat as stand-alone features or just pass over.

The revisions to this 2017 printing amount to a small number of changes to the text and a few additional images.

Important Note

As the story unfolds, numerous individual aircraft are referred to. Each aircraft is identified by its serial/works' number and/or, in the case of German aircraft, by its unit markings. In the case of RAF aircraft, this is either a letter followed by four digits or two letters followed by three digits e.g. Spitfire P8010 and Mosquito DD629. German aircraft are identified by the last four digits of their *werke nummer* (w/n), (i.e. when translated, works'/ production number), where known and also by their unit markings e.g. Heinkel He 111 (w/n 2877) carried the unit markings G1+KL.

Steve Richards,
Solihull, England, October 2017

The scene in John Bright Street following the major attacks of November 1940, which resulted in the deaths of more than 750 people.
Mirrorpix/Birmingham Mail

PART ONE

SWEET AND SOUR
VICTORY

A Boulton Paul Defiant prepares for another
night operation. Simon Parry

SETTING THE SCENE

Birmingham suffered its first air raids in August 1940. By the second week of April 1941, the Luftwaffe had attacked Birmingham and its suburbs on around 60 occasions but, during the early months of 1941, raids had eased considerably. However, on the nights of 9/10th and 10/11th April the Luftwaffe returned with a vengeance. It is the first of these two April attacks, and one German raider in particular, to which we will give our initial attention. In this first chapter let us begin the story by setting the scene with a combination of historical fact and intelligent imagination. Here, all essentials are historically accurate, only the thoughts and conversations of individual people and their immediate environs are imagined.

Right: **Uffz Rudolf Müller poses in his flying suit in front of a Heinkel He 111.** Rudolf Müller/ The Quinton Local History Society

Below: **Fw Werner Strecke at the rear end of a Heinkel He 111.** Rudolf Müller/ Peter Kennedy

Below right: **Fw Egon Grolig (left) together with Rudolf Müller on a visit to the seaside.** Rudolf Müller/ Peter Kennedy

**Dinard, Northern France
17:45-01:00 hours (local time)
9/10th April 1941**

It is the late afternoon of Wednesday 9th April 1941 and the location is Dinard airfield in Northern France. The place is a hive of activity: armourers are carefully winching high explosive bombs and canisters of incendiaries into the bomb bays of Heinkel He 111 aircraft; technicians are checking the radio-navigational aids; on one aircraft a couple of low-ranking men in shirt sleeves are diligently cleaning the transparent canopies; in another a rigger sits in the pilot's seat operating the rudder pedals and control-column, checking for free movement; near at hand bowsers wait to deliver fuel to each machine – fuel which will power their two Daimler-Benz DB601 engines. Somewhere an engine bursts into life as a mechanic waits expectantly to see if his labours of the past six hours have been in vain or not.

One Heinkel carries on its fuselage side the identification codes '1G' and 'KM' painted on each side of the German cross (1G+KM).[1] Standing by this aircraft's starboard propeller is 23-year-old Unteroffizier (Uffz) Rudolf Müller. He is in conversation with one of the men waiting to start pumping fuel into the wing tanks. What amount of fuel will give them a reasonable safety margin whilst keeping the all-up-weight as low as possible? Müller feels unable to tell this man that the night's operation is to Birmingham, but these ground-crew have a knack of getting to know mission details and the 2,600 litres of fuel to be delivered to the aircraft on this day make it obvious that the target is not on England's southern coast or even London. Satisfied that all is in hand, Müller makes to extract a packet of cigarettes from his tunic pocket, looks across at the fuel bowser, hesitates, changes his mind and then walks off in search of his observer/ navigator.

He finds Feldwebel (Fw) Egon Grolig sitting on a canvas chair outside one of the administra-

A Heinkel He 111 of KG27 painted in a night scheme. It is seen here in a camouflaged dispersal at an airfield in northern France.
ww2.com

tion huts. He has his right leg propped up on an empty upturned ammunition box and is using his thigh to support a writing pad. Müller assumes his fellow airman is writing a letter home. Being 27 years old, Grolig is considered the 'old man' of the crew and Müller respects his maturity preferring to run through each upcoming mission with him. They are soon engrossed in airmen's talk – speeds, heights, weights, timings and navigational issues etc. Neither of them is especially apprehensive about the planned mission. Since the Luftwaffe turned from daylight raids to night bombing, losses were only 1-3%, so they shared the common attitude 'It won't happen to us'. With their discussion concluded, Müller strides off with the intention of taking a nap before having a pre-flight meal.

At around 00:30 hours (local time) the crew of 1G+KM congregate at their aircraft. When Müller and Grolig arrive, clumping in their heavily fur-lined boots, Fw Werner Strecke is already in the aircraft warming up his *FuG 3* wireless set and *Lorenz* receiver. Meanwhile, the flight engineer, 25-year-old Helmut Häcke, is enthusiastically conversing with the chief mechanic who is old enough to be his father. They stand under the wing sharing their mutual satisfaction concerning the DB601 motors and wonder how the latest He 111 (the 'H' variant) is doing with the Junkers Jumo engine. Part of their unit is already equipped with the new variant. By all accounts demand for the DB601, which also powers the Luftwaffe's Bf 109 and Bf 110 fighters, had outstripped the ability to produce them; hence the necessity for the newer bombers to switch to a different powerplant.

A quarter of an hour later, Müller and his three fellow crew members strap themselves into their seats and don their sweat-impregnated helmets, checking that the intercom is functioning satisfactorily. The unit to which they belong is the 4th *Staffel* of the operational group (*Gruppe*) designated II/KG27. For the mission in question, the *Gruppe* is contributing eleven He 111 aircraft, which are just a small part of the Luftwaffe attack heading for Birmingham this night. A total of 282 German bombers is involved, consisting of Heinkel He 111 and Junkers Ju 88 aircraft. The attack is arranged so that bombers continually arrive over the target area for a period spanning a number of hours. Bombs have already dropped on the city before Müller's aircraft has even left the ground.

281 and 283 Hales Lane, Warley, Smethwick, Staffordshire
17:00-18:00 hours BST, 9th April 1941

Doreen buttons up her blouse while she checks her hair in the dressing table mirror. In the reflection she sees her mother carefully adjusting the wedding dress on its coat hanger before hanging it up on the picture rail.

Mother and daughter chat happily about the big day, now just a fortnight away. Things have certainly taken a turn for the better since their move from London.

The two women agree to see what they can do about the Anderson shelter before getting the tea ready. It has flooded again and although they haven't used it for quite a while now, better to be safe than sorry. Setting about the task, wearing wellington boots, they start bailing using a bucket and an old washing-up bowl. The work is

Note

1 The aircraft was a Heinkel He 111P (*werke nummer* (w/n) 1555), which had been built under contract by Norddeutscher Dornier in March 1939. As for the code letters on the fuselage, see page 44. In all likelihood, the only code letter clearly visible would have been the aircraft's identity letter 'K' painted white, the other codes being virtually obscured by the supplementary black distemper camouflage application.

unpleasant with the brown water smelling stale and earthy. Doreen is inside passing the part-filled vessels up to her mother. It isn't long before water has sloshed over the top of her wellingtons and brown stains are appearing on her apron. After ten minutes the women give the thing up as a bad job.

Next door the two Smart boys, Albert (junior) and Brian, are in the garden. School is now finished until after Easter. Their mother is in the kitchen helping her two-year-old nephew Malcolm to finish the remains of his rice pudding. While the bab, who is perched in his high-chair, is deciding whether he has finished, his Aunty Doris is casting half an eye over yesterday's newspaper. She muses, 'Will the news ever get better? Rommel's Afrika Korps seem unstoppable in Libya; the German Air Force has been wreaking havoc in Belgrade – wherever that is; U-boats are sinking lots of ships in the Atlantic, but at least the RAF has been giving some back with large numbers of our bombers blasting Kiel.'

Things haven't been easy for the Smart family over the past few years. It all started with the death of their two-year-old niece, Margaret. Then Mary and Alfred had another baby, Malcolm, but tragedy struck again when Mary died. Mother and daughter share the same grave in the nearby Uplands Cemetery. After that Albert and Doris, together with the two boys, moved into 283 Hales Lane to live with Albert's brother Alfred and little Malcolm.

Doreen Hanson and her mother Amy who lived at 281 Hales Lane.
via Peter Kennedy

Doris folds up the newspaper. The war seems a long way off to her. She has things to do – Albert and Alfred will be in soon and she hasn't even begun to get their meal ready. The toddler has lost interest in his food but he has done well enough, as well as her own boys did at that age.

She looks out of the kitchen window. Her teenage boy is keeping his younger brother occupied with a balsa wood model plane. She notices Amy and Doreen in the next-door garden walking back to the house. They are clad in wellingtons and carrying a bucket and bowl…

915 Sqn (barrage balloon) HQ, Cadbury Lido, Rowheath, Bournville, Birmingham
21:00-01:00 hours BST 9/10th April 1941

The solid sounding bell of the Bakelite telephone rings out. It is one of two telephones sitting on the duty officer's desk. One is connected to the GPO exchange, but this one is part of the network used by No.6 Balloon Centre. The man picks up the receiver and is given the brief message, 'Air raid warning yellow'. The time is 21:14 hours. Five minutes later the telephone rings again, 'Air raid warning purple'. It sounds a third time and the duty officer snatches it up on the second ring. 'Condition red'; an air raid is imminent. He looks at the clock on the wall, 21:36 hours.

The raid has been in progress for half an hour and now an order from RAF Wythall, no doubt issued by Wing Commander (Wg Cdr) Gell himself, states that all balloons are to fly at 4,500 feet. The duty officer leans across the desk to pick up the list of balloon sites and their contact telephone numbers. There are about three dozen of them scattered around the Kings Norton, Bournville and Selly Oak areas. He will have his work cut out for the next 20 minutes or so while he passes on the instruction. Does the low height indicate that the 'Brylcreem boys' will be up in force and need to be given a clear piece of sky?

Explosions can now be clearly heard and some are preceded by a frightening whistle – very close. It is now nearly midnight and a call comes in from sister unit 914 Squadron. One of their balloon sites (No.25) in West Heath has had three high explosive bombs explode nearby, the blast of one of them overturning the winch, but the balloon continues to fly. No injuries to personnel.

The duty officer prints a fresh heading in the squadron operations record book – 10th April. His first two pencil entries read:

00:55 E Flight report delayed-action bomb in the vicinity of Site 3.
01:00 Delayed-action bomb in vicinity of SHQ (Squadron Headquarters).

Too bloody close.

RAF Wittering, Northants
22:00-01:00 hours BST 9/10th April 1941

Sergeant (Sgt) 'Harry' Bodien strains his eyes in an effort to pick out the Defiant aircraft he can hear taxying along the perimeter track. He gives up. The black camouflage paint, set against the dark tree-line some 400 yards distant, defeats him. Still, he has only just left the sergeants' mess, a well-lit establishment concealed behind the thick blackout curtains. The dispersal hut, lit by just two red lamp bulbs, will enable his night vision to function within half an hour.

'B' Flight has already got some aircraft airborne and with the way things are developing it looks like 'A' Flight might get a crack at the Huns too. He had planned to write to his sister Vina this night. There were some exciting things to tell her: his commission is now more or less a foregone conclusion since she had arranged the loan of £60 for him to cover the cost of the uniform; then there is all the 'gen' on the squadron's successes last night. 151 Sqn is really coming into its own. The letter will wait – maybe tonight he can get another confirmed German bastard to his credit to join the one he got a couple of months earlier.

As Bodien approaches the dispersal hut he is glad that his gunner for this 'Fighter Night' operation is the young New Zealander Dudley Jonas. He'd been crude with Jonas that night in February when they'd brought down the Do 17 which had crashed just 10 miles from the 'drome. On that occasion Bodien had felt some anxiety about the 19-year-old sergeant air-gunner who, at that time, had only flown 18 hours, never at night, never seen a Hun nor fired Browning guns. Would the kid panic? But the colonial had put up a good show.

The Boulton Paul Defiant is not a fighter aircraft that the pilots would choose to fly. Some of the chaps on the squadron are flying Hurricanes and one of them, Richard Stevens, has been particularly successful with the Hurricane at night. Nevertheless, there is no denying that if you can latch on to a Hun, then the four guns in the Defiant's turret are enough to bring down a German bomber.

When he enters the hut, the red hue reminds him of a photographic darkroom. Other 'A' Flight chaps are already there. Among them is Sgt Jack Staples and his gunner Sgt Parkin.

There is excitement in the air. Evidently Flight Lieutenant (Flt Lt) McMullen, together with his gunner Sgt Fairweather, have brought down a Ju 88 near Bramcote. This is a place familiar to them all, as the squadron was based there before moving to Wittering earlier in the year. McMullen's a lucky sod, 'B' Flight was up first last night and he got an He 111 then.

Yesterday Bodien and Staples had a night off and went into Peterborough, while 'B' Flight was mixing it with the Huns over the Coventry area. It was after one in the morning by the time he and Staples had turned in, only to be roused

Henry Erskin Bodien better known as 'Harry' or 'Snowy'.
Courtesy of Amanda Low

90 minutes later. They had been wanted down at dispersal as there was a chance that they would be needed, but the weather duffed up and so they'd returned to bed.

Someone gives a nervous cough and Bodien's thoughts return to the present. For the umpteenth time he looks at his watch. It is just coming up to one in the morning of 10th April. The telephone rings and Staples picks up the receiver. He gives a couple of nods. They're off. Bodien gives Jonas an encouraging slap on the shoulder as they each jostle to get out of the door.

Sergeants Bodien and Jonas with their Defiant night fighter. Note the skull motif below and behind the exhaust stack. Courtesy of Amanda Low

SWEET VICTORY?

The take-off time of Bodien and Jonas was formally logged as 01:10 hours 10th April. Staples' aircraft was hot on their heels. The 'Fighter Night' operation was to patrol over the Birmingham area. Bodien's patrol height was to be 13,000 feet. The weather was very good, with excellent visibility and a nearly full moon. Cloud was 5/10ths at about 3,000 feet, but such cloud would not be problematic. With the balloon barrage in place no aircraft would deliberately fly at such a low altitude.

Bodien's Defiant I (serial number N3387) bore the squadron code letters 'DZ-E'. It was using the radio call-sign 'Steeple 6'. It soon became apparent that radio communication for Bodien and Jonas was going to be a problem on that sortie. Only button 'D' was working on the radio, which did permit communication with his base at Wittering. The intercommunication set allowing speech between himself and his gunner and vice-versa failed completely, although it is not clear at what point during the flight this failure occurred. The radio equipment would have been working a few hours earlier, as the crew had

taken the aircraft up for a routine 25 minute night-flying air-test. This was intended to highlight such problems. The technology, however, based as it was on valves and crystals, was relatively new and prone to being temperamental.

Shortly after 01:30 hours, while patrolling the city in an anticlockwise direction, Bodien heard over the radio that Jack Staples had shot down an enemy aircraft. He knew that his friend had been allocated a patrol height of 1,000 feet less than his own. Almost immediately Bodien sighted a Heinkel He 111 moving at approximately 180 mph about 450 yards away at 13,000 feet. The German was flying in a north-easterly direction near Birmingham. Bodien wheeled after him.

It was the sudden manoeuvre that alerted the gunner Jonas to the fact that something was afoot (presumably the intercom was unserviceable at this point). Bodien closed in to about 200 yards and from dead astern but slightly lower. Jonas fired his guns for three to four seconds. Still keeping lower than the Heinkel, Bodien positioned Jonas on the bomber's starboard beam and his gunner opened fire again, this time for about eight seconds and from a range of 30 yards. Both of the Defiant's crew saw two or

This 151 Sqn Defiant (N3328) DZ-Z is noteworthy for its 'sharksmouth' artwork.

Sgt 'Harry' Bodien in Defiant (N1791) DZ-K.
Courtesy of Amanda Low

An air-to-air view of Heinkel He 111 1G+KN belonging to 5 *Staffel* KG27. Simon Parry

School children from
Bristnall Hall Senior
Boys School pose with
their local barrage
balloon which belonged
to 911 Sqn.
BirminghamLives

three objects fall from the German bomber. They
assumed crew members were baling out, but it
is almost certain that these were bombs being
jettisoned – perhaps parachute mines.

The Heinkel dived steeply to the left followed
by the Defiant, 300 yards behind. At 8,000 feet
the German aircraft levelled off and once more
Bodien drew alongside, enabling Jonas to put in
a long burst of fire from 90 yards. One of Jonas'
four guns stopped working, no doubt due to
overheating caused by the long and continuous
burst of fire. By now the bomber's starboard
engine was glowing. The aircraft peeled off to
the left and dived steeply towards the ground,
pursued by the Defiant in an equally steep dive.

* * *

Müller's Heinkel He 111 arrived over the southern outskirts of Birmingham shortly after 01:30
hours (local time). After leaving Dinard they
would have taken a course which crossed the
Dorset coast.

The first that Müller's crew knew about the
proximity of an RAF fighter aircraft was when
bullets from Jonas' Browning guns started slam-
ming into the underside of the bomber. Egon
Grolig got into a prone position in the nose in
order to operate the machine gun. A devastating
burst of fire from the Defiant's turret shattered
parts of the heavily glazed nose, destroying
instruments and killing Grolig.

In an attempt to rid himself of the fighter,
Müller dropped his bombs in order to lighten the
aircraft, then turned and dived to the left. He
vainly tried to make sense of the instruments.
Having lost 5,000 feet he levelled off. More bullets poured in and the starboard engine was on
fire. Once more the Heinkel half rolled to the left,
going into a near-vertical dive from which it
appears to have recovered and then assumed a
spiral descent earthwards. Müller was now
down amongst the balloons which were suspended by their lethal steel cables. The Heinkel
struck one belonging to 915 Sqn, which was
moored at site 17 in Ridgacre Road, Quinton.
Shortly afterwards a piece of burning debris
dropping from the aircraft is believed to have
been the cause of a row of houses in Balden Road

half rolled and went down beside him but saw the Balloons go by so left him in his dive and concentrated on getting out of the balloons. At 8000 I levelled off and ran my finger round my collar because I dont like balloons. Then I noticed that my guns were stationary to the port so though my gunner was dead or wounded.

Got home as quick as possible and told them to have the blood cart on the tarmac. As soon as I stopped had a look in the turrett. No gunner —

Went up to Opps and gave them the gen — got the crash confirmed — a Heinkel III K. Then my gunner rang up from a place in Birmingham called Kings Norton — he said he thought I was dead and had Baled out He's the same gunner as I had for my Dornier.

The score that night was 4 and one probable.

catching fire, which resulted in the death of 75-year-old Sarah Davies at number 211 and 3-year-old Anthony Smith at 213.

It was time to evacuate the aircraft and Müller gave the order over the intercom but, like Grolig, Helmut Häcke was already dead, leaving only Werner Strecke to receive the order. Extricating himself from his seat, Müller found that his foot was trapped under one of the damaged pedals. He succeeded in getting his leg out of his flying boot, but removing the roof hatch was a struggle, resulting in bloody hands. Hampered by his parachute, he tried to push himself through the hatch, but with the aircraft in descent the slipstream kept on pushing him back. Somehow he made it. As he fell away from the doomed bomber, Müller gave his full attention to making sure that he was well clear of the stricken machine before pulling the parachute's rip cord.

Strecke also was successful in baling out, though what exit he used when jumping from the Heinkel is not known. Judging from the locations where the two Luftwaffe airmen landed, it would seem that the pilot jumped first.

* * *

As the two Luftwaffe fliers struggled to cope with their plight, the RAF Defiant crew were also experiencing alarm and confusion. Having followed the Heinkel in its near-vertical dive, Bodien soon found himself down amongst the barrage balloons. Realising the hazard, he broke off in a frantic effort to regain height. He could not breathe easily until he had reached the safe height of 8,000 feet. Colliding with one of the invisible balloon cables would almost certainly have brought his small fighter down. Later, relating the incident to his sister Vina, he wrote with some degree of understatement, 'At 8,000 feet I levelled off and ran my finger round my collar, because I don't like balloons.' It was then that he noticed that the guns in the turret were station-

ary and pointing out to port. When not in action, the guns in the turret would point rearwards so as not to interfere with the trim of the aircraft. Bodien concluded that Jonas must be dead or wounded, or passed out from the affects of the 'G-force'. He radioed base, requesting an emergency homing course and asking that the 'blood cart' (ambulance) meet them on the tarmac. He landed back at Wittering at 02:10 hours and, with what must have been trepidation, climbed from his cockpit to inspect the turret. It was vacant.

Jonas, alarmed at the severity of the dive into the balloon barrage, assumed that his pilot was dead or wounded. Pointing his guns sideways, he was able to slide the turret's door – located behind him – and push himself out backwards, tumbling clear of the aircraft. His parachute opened successfully. Later, he reported that he had seen the Heinkel spiralling down, resulting in a huge explosion on the ground.

Jonas floated to earth and landed uninjured. The 19-year-old must have been shaken, but he was soon in safe hands and found himself a guest at a barrage balloon unit – 'E' Flight of 915 Squadron – located near to where he landed in Kings Norton. A message was passed to SHQ at Cadbury Lido. From there Wittering was contacted to assure them that their man was safe. The call was recorded at 02:10 hours, the same time that Bodien was staring into the vacant turret over at Wittering!

The German air attack on Birmingham and its suburbs had been devastating. There were many messages passing between civilian and military sites, as they sought to keep one another abreast of the developing situation. One such confused and inaccurate communication was passed on to Jonas, informing him that the Heinkel had crashed on to houses in Castle Bromwich killing 12 civilians. He took this erroneous message back to Wittering when he returned there a couple of days later.

* * *

Just minutes after Jonas had his feet on terra firma, Müller was floating over Quinton. As he came near to the ground, it was obvious to him that he would be landing in a built-up area. In fact he dropped into a smart residential neighbourhood. Barston Road is laid out in a 'U' shape and Müller found himself in the roadway[2]. In addition to his lacerated hands and heavy bruising to his leg, Müller now had a slight injury to his knee. Initially, he was apprehended by civilians and then a policeman arrived who administered first-aid and gave him some cigarettes. The policeman described Müller as a short, dark youngster of about 20, who could speak no English. In an interview conducted during July 2002, Müller recalled, 'People arrived within two or three minutes. They were more afraid of me than

I was of them. As soon as the Home Guard came, they disarmed me. I had inflated my air-suit[3], which was the reason why I appeared heavier than I actually was.'

Wearing only one boot, Müller was escorted by the Oldbury Home Guard to the Danilo Cinema[4], which served as their post. No doubt he was given more cigarettes and a mug of tea before the police arrived to take him to Piddock Road police station in Smethwick. Müller claimed that he was strip-searched, but that survival rather than escape was uppermost in his mind.

* * *

Fire-watcher, Les Bannister, and a colleague were on duty in The Oval, Smethwick. The Oval was part of a council housing estate built shortly before the war. The road was a continuous loop on a steep incline. Bannister was only a matter of yards from his home – number 38 – when the two fire-watchers were alerted to a parachute descending above them in the moonlight. Fearing that it was a parachute mine, they dived to the ground, Bannister denting his white steel helmet. In fact it was Strecke who was to have a slightly more alarming landing than that of his pilot.

Strecke landed on the front elevation of the roof of number 33 The Oval, the home of the Scrannage family. Will Scrannage was out firewatching but his wife, Ethel, was in the shelter with a neighbour and they heard a strange swishing sound followed by a bump on the roof and tiles being dislodged. The parachute of the airman had entangled around the chimney. Strecke and a number of broken tiles slid down on to the top of the bay window. A crowd soon gathered in the road as ARP wardens and Home Guard members sought to get the hapless German down onto the ground. Strecke may have felt safer on the roof, as the crowd below was awash with excitement and some hostility. Shouting and aggressive gestures were tempered by others seeking to calm the situation. Those vested with authority restrained the crowd and took charge of Strecke's rescue and arrest. Once the parachute was freed, he dropped to the ground. Strecke raised his arms in surrender, even before removing his parachute harness. He had injured his foot in the landing and soon his now-removed flying boot had become the trophy of a girl named Tina Hughes, who was gleefully telling everyone, 'I've got his boot, I've got his boot!'.

Warden Simmons, along with Home Guards Chadney and Davies, led another unevenly shod airman away. Warden Thomas Packer, who lived in nearby Goodyear Road, was at the local ARP post when Strecke was brought in. Packer said, 'He had an injury to his foot and limped. He was a smart looking man and gave his age as 22. He was not armed and offered no resistance.'

An extract from a letter dated Saturday 12th April 1941 from Bodien to his sister Vina, describing the time immediately after he had disengaged from Müller's Heinkel.

An RAF air-gunner in his cramped Defiant turret. Simon Parry

Probably Dudley Everard Charles Jonas who enlisted in the Royal New Zealand Air Force as an air-gunner in July 1940. He embarked on the Mataroa sailing for England and was attached to 151 Sqn. Courtesy of Amanda Low

Notes

2 Years later, it was said that Müller dropped on to the rear garden fence of number 12 where it backed on to number 68, giving both households justification for claiming the airman had landed in *their* garden!
3 Presumably the equivalent of the RAF Mae West buoyancy aid.
4 Later the Quinton Classic.

While gratefully dragging on his cigarette and clutching an enamel mug of tea, the young German tried to explain to Packer, in broken English, that two more crewmembers were still in the aircraft. In an attempt to describe what had happened, he said, 'Machine gun – balloon cable – bad luck – glad'. The arrest and escorting of the prisoner to ARP post H4-Warley had taken but a few minutes. A message from H4, timed at 01:43 hours, was written and then sent to Control. It read, 'Plane crashed, parachutist baled out, brought to the post, send military or police escort.'

Later, like Müller, Strecke was taken to Piddock Road police station, but kept separated from his pilot. Here an initial interrogation was quickly arranged. The most senior local RAF officer was Squadron Leader (Sqn Ldr) Norman Mawle.[5] Superintendent Challinor's teenaged son Gerald, with his School Certificate German,

was seconded to act as interpreter. Werner Strecke was reasonably co-operative. He asked Gerald if he was going into the forces and he replied that he was awaiting call-up into the RAF. The German gave the English lad his own mascot, a little pair of black and white plastic-like dogs. Gerald thought that Rudolf Müller came across as a typical Nazi, a product of the Hitler Youth who, despite his badly bruised leg and painful knee, attempted to click his heels as he gave the 'Heil Hitler!' Nazi salute in the doorway. 'Come in here,' growled Sqn Ldr Mawle, clearly unimpressed. 'I'll give you bloody "Heil Hitler."'

An ambulance, with medical orderlies and a guard, was dispatched to collect Strecke from Piddock Road police station and take him to 5 Balloon Centre headquarters at Sutton Coldfield, which was the local RAF establishment temporarily responsible for dealing with the

Who's Going to Pay for the Damage?

Many hundreds of thousands of properties in Great Britain and the contents thereof were damaged to a greater or lesser extent as a result of the war. But who footed the bill? This is a subject that receives scant attention in books describing the Home Front during the Second World War. Insurance companies which offered cover for both properties and contents, excluded from their policies damage due to Acts of War.

By 1939, home ownership stood at 31%, council housing accounted for 14% and the balance was in the hands of landlords. Inner-city areas were home to the working classes, who lived in rented accommodation, much of which had been built in the 19th century. The suburbs had grown between the wars and it was here that home ownership was flourishing.

Prime Minister Winston Churchill described being at Margate at an early stage in the Blitz. Having sheltered in a tunnel during an air raid, he emerged to survey the damage. A small hotel had been reduced to 'a litter of crockery, utensils and splintered furniture'. He was moved when he saw how the proprietor, his wife and staff were in tears. Where was their home? Where was their livelihood? He later wrote: 'Here is a privilege of power. I formed an immediate resolve. On the way back in my train I dictated a letter to the Chancellor of the Exchequer [Kingsley Wood] laying down the principle that all damage from the fire of the enemy must be a charge upon the state and compensation be paid in full and at once. Thus the burden would not fall alone on those whose homes or business premises were hit, but would be borne evenly on the shoulders of the nation'.

The Exchequer and the Treasury were very concerned about the potential liabilities involved. Churchill's ideal of immediate compensation and repair to less seriously damaged properties was not met and caused the Prime Minister some frustration. However, a complex and thorough scheme was put in place in the space of months. It was estimated that the average repair bill for a damaged house would be £50. It was acknowledged that any compensation scheme would have to set a limit of a £500 pay-out for any given claim whilst the war was in progress.

Presumably, where war-essential properties were involved, different rules applied.

The war damage compensation scheme was to be one of the success stories of the war and the immediate post-war period. In October 1940, when the Battle of Britain was in its closing stages and the Blitz under way, the Prime Minister announced that a comprehensive war damage scheme would be inaugurated at once.

As a result, in December 1940, the Chancellor of the Exchequer introduced the Bill which became the War Damage Act, 1941. As he, Kingsley Wood, said on 17th December 1940, the Bill was an instrument of justice and an act of social solidarity, spreading the burden of the war damage over the whole community.

Not dissimilar to today's Council Tax, compulsory contributions were required from all property owners and these payments were matched by contributions from government. When the Bill was introduced, it was revealed that contributions from property owners were to be based on the value of properties as at 31st August 1939. Put simply, the contribution was by five one-yearly payments, each equating to 0.5% of the capital value of the property. Payments were due each 1st July, commencing in 1941. These payments were to cover damage sustained from the outbreak of war until 31st August 1941. It was assumed that if the war continued beyond that date, revisions to the amounts would need to be made. With the diminishing of air raids following the attack by the Germans on the Soviet Union, no adjustment to contributions appears to have been deemed necessary.

A typical example for a large, semi-detached house in Hall Green, in south Birmingham, may be cited, it having a Rateable Value (i.e. Annual Value) of

£30, a demand for £3 was issued in July 1941 i.e. 2s in the £1 or 10%. This demand would be repeated for a further four years, thus making a total contribution of £15. As the Annual Value equated to 5% of the property's Capital Value, then total contributions were 2.5% of the Capital Value (which in this case would have been £600). At the outbreak of war, there were nearly 1.4 million home-owners with mortgages. By producing proof of payment in respect of their war damage contribution, home-owners were entitled to a rebate from their mortgage lender.

The aim of the scheme was to provide compensation in respect of war damage to buildings and other immovable property, including fixed plant and machinery.

The term War Damage was defined as damage occurring (accidentally or not) as a result of direct enemy action. It also included any damage resulting from precautionary measures, with regards to enemy attack, such as demolition by Civil Defence personnel.

The War Damage Commission, under the leadership of its first chairman, Malcolm Trustram Eve, set about its formidable task. Arrangements were made to deal with the various notifications of damage which came flowing in. Sixteen regional offices were set up and technical staff were located in local offices, supplemented at the peak period by the use of private professional firms. These assessed

Opposite: **The scene in Hales Lane on 10th April 1941 with smoke still in evidence.**

Between 1947 and 1948 the two houses were rebuilt from scratch. This picture was taken in 1982, by which time they had been given the new address 23 and 25 St Mark's Road. Delwyn Griffith

Luftwaffe prisoners. Sqn Ldr E.S. Rickards was sent to collect Müller and escort him to 5 Balloon Centre HQ also. Later, both prisoners would be formally interrogated before being taken to prisoner of war cages. RAF intelligence officers had very little to report following the interviews with the two Germans, though it was commented that their morale was not as high as other interviewees of that time.

A SOURED OUTCOME

The Heinkel must have been very low when Müller got out and even lower when Strecke took his leave. What was the nature of the aircraft's descent in the moments prior to it hitting the ground? Was it a near vertical dive, a wide or tight spiral earthwards, or had the pilot managed to trim the aircraft before baling out, so that its attitude was one of a fairly straight descent? The last seems the most likely. Personal testimonies suggest that during its final moments the aircraft passed in a line over Selly Oak, Harborne, Warley Woods and the residential area beyond, literally skimming rooftops at the top of The Oval. It finally hit the ground in Hales Lane. There was a dull crumph as the aircraft hit the rear of numbers 281 and 283. The time was 01:40.

The machine had already been on fire when airborne and now the ruptured fuel tanks caused

A souvenir from the Heinkel wreckage in the form of a manufacturer's plate. The *Werke Nr* (w/n) 1555 is visible towards the bottom right of the plate.
via Philippa Hodgkiss

the extent of war damage and classified properties according to whether payment could be made for rebuilding or repair, which was known as a cost-of-work payment, or whether compensation should be paid for a total loss, which was known as a value payment. In due course the technical staff dealt with the specifications which were put in for repair work and assessed the proper cost of making-good war damage.

The Commission paid over four million claims in respect of 3½ million separate properties, and the total paid by 1964 approached £1,300 million. Against this, £200 million was collected by the Inland Revenue Department for 1941-46 in the form of war damage contributions from property owners.

There were two principal sections to the War Damage Act. Part I dealt with properties and fixed plant in two ways, either value payments or cost-of-works payments. Part II of the Act dealt with goods and chattels, which were covered under two insurance schemes administered by the Board of Trade, one for business chattels and one for private chattels. The former was to cover movable assets and a yearly payment of 1.5% of the insured items

was demanded. A similar premium was required for the Private Chattels Scheme, but this scheme was entirely voluntary. On these two elements covered by Part II of the Act, large sums were paid out; about £117 million in claims on private chattels alone.

By 1961, the Government reckoned that £40 million in claims were still to be made and, in December 1961, published a White Paper in respect of winding up the War Damage Commission. The Act would involve fixing a time limit for the making of war damage claims. This spurred many claimants into action and by 1964 the Government estimated the liability had been reduced to £20 million. In round figures this amount comprised about £1 million for dwelling houses, £2 million for churches, £5½ million for local authority and public buildings – libraries, public baths, etc, of which £1½ million represented the claims in respect of County Hall and the Guild Hall and about £9 million for commercial property – such as public houses, hotels, offices and shops.

In addition to this £17½ million, an estimate of £2½ million was made for contingencies and for the remaining few claims that might come forward on the Board of Trade side, (the Part II claims on

chattels), hence the total probable liability of about £20 million.

In view of the need to wind up the scheme and disband the War Damage Commission, staff were transferred to the Inland Revenue. It was this department which oversaw the remaining work.

No doubt, the mechanics of the scheme broke down on occasions and individual claimants had some cause for complaint. Nevertheless, it was to the nation's credit as a whole that, when backs were against the wall, the Government under the strong leadership of Winston Churchill could implement a plan which was founded on the faith in ultimate victory and a restoration to peacetime conditions.

As the scheme was being brought to a close, a Scottish MP, Cyril Bence, summed things up well: 'We have, with reasonable equity and justice, repaired the material losses suffered by a large section of the community, and it is a wonderful achievement.

'Unfortunately, there are some losses that we can never repair, but it is a great compliment to the nation that we can now rest assured that, in the main, we have replaced for individuals the material things lost as a result of enemy action.'

The aftermath at the crash site on the following day with the fin of the wrecked Heinkel on the left.

Some of number 281 Hales Lane survived the impact but 283 was utterly wrecked.

a huge explosion, which was accompanied by a blinding flash. Burning fuel, bits of aircraft and chunks of masonry were flung in all directions. A pillar of flame reached skywards and was seen at Thimblemill, about a mile away, where there was an ARP/ambulance/first aid station based in the flats adjacent to the public baths in Thimblemill Road. On duty was 19-year-old Ron Carr, who took to his heels and ran for all he was worth up the steep incline to the source of the fire. He lived at number 279 Hales Lane. His arrival revealed a nightmarish scene. His father, pregnant mother

and four siblings had been in the air raid shelter as the aircraft hit and exploded, literally a few yards away. They were all safe. The semi-detached house belonging to the Carrs was paired with number 281, while 283 was paired with 285. The bomber had finished up with the fuselage between 281 and 283, with the wings and engines demolishing the two homes.

An eyewitness who was fire-watching told of how he saw a member of the Home Guard run to the blazing aircraft and pull an airman clear. It would be easy to doubt this story of heroism as there was no medal awarded in relation to this incident, although many commendations were made in the light of acts of valour carried out in the city during this and the following night. In fact, a message from ARP Control, Smethwick, to the Midland Region and Group Control, informed them that the pilot's body had been found in the aircraft. This message was timed at 02:00 and was a compilation of messages received from ARP posts during the preceding 20 minutes, so lending credence to the eyewitness account. There seems little reason to doubt that this was the corpse of Grolig, which would have been in the nose of the aircraft. The story is told that the call went up for something to cover the body with. A Mrs Mynott provided a newly-washed bedcover for the purpose. When a neighbour queried her spoiling it in this way, she responded by remarking quietly that, 'He is some poor mother's son, after all.'

A policeman ran to the police box located in Hurst Road to send a message, timed at 01:59. He reported, 'Six houses on fire, Hales Lane near Two Brewers.' People were using stirrup pumps to douse flames where burning fuel had spewed on to the terraced houses opposite. Smethwick Fire Brigade arrived, putting a number of pumps into action. Furniture was taken out of the Carrs' house and piled in the front garden, so that hosepipes could be run through number 279 to tackle the fire at the rear. The scene of devastation was far from safe. Ammunition, which fed the bomber's defensive machine guns, was spontaneously firing in the heat, pock-marking the shops on the other side of the road. Very lights and incendiaries were also igniting, adding to the conflagration; there was the possibility of bombs still being onboard. Lastly, the substantially-demolished houses were unstable.

For the many hundreds of people who heard the Heinkel in its final seconds of flight, and the dozens who witnessed the explosion, the event created an indelible memory. The noise was tremendous.

Les Bannister's family had not gone down the shelter that night. 'The noise of the plane was so loud I thought it was just above our roof. We all dived under the table,' said his 13-year-old daughter Doris. Indeed, with number 38 The Oval being near the summit of the hill, the Heinkel would have been at rooftop height.

Rosa White of 114 Hales Lane was 11 years old, '…and all of a sudden, we heard a noise like a train coming up the garden … I remember going into the garden; everyone cheering and shouting and the flames sky-high.'

It soon became apparent that the two destroyed houses had been occupied and that the Anderson air raid shelters in the gardens were empty. In number 281, Amy Hanson (48 years old) and her daughter Doreen Hanson (24 years old) had died. Evidently, neighbours had seen them bailing water out of the air raid shelter earlier in the day but they must have considered remaining in the house a better option. Mother and daughter had left their London home some time before, having been casualties of the Blitz. Amy had relatives living in Handsworth, Birmingham. Doreen's marriage was planned for two weeks time, the banns having been read for the first time the previous Sunday.

Next door at 283, two related families were victims. Widower, 37-year-old Alfred Smart, with his young son, 2-year-old Malcolm, was killed. Alfred's brother, Albert, was out on fire-watching duty, but his wife, 34-year-old Doris, and their sons Albert (aged 13) and Brian (aged 8) also perished.

By 03:00 the rescue party had Häcke's body out with that of Grolig lying in the street, the police having requested that the Controller send a conveyance to remove them. By 04:30 the

Incident Officer had instructed the rescue parties to return to their depot, as the RAF had taken charge of the demolition work prior to the removal of the aircraft. Air Intelligence was keen to examine equipment on board the Heinkel; any fragments of documentation which might be found would be scrutinised very carefully. The resulting evaluation report, however, revealed nothing of special interest. So damaged by the impact and fire was the wreck, that not even evidence of Jonas' machine gun bullet strikes was found.

At 05:40 the police requested that the Public Health Department send a van to collect further human remains found at the demolition site. At 07:30 it was the turn of the fire brigade to make a similar request requiring that two bodies be removed.

By the afternoon, orders had been issued to the effect that, of those who had been up all night working at the scene, as many as could be spared were to take a rest. The Chief Constable of Staffordshire arrived mid-afternoon to inspect the various incidents of damage which had occurred within his area of responsibility, notably that at Hales Lane.

AFTERMATH

In connection with the Hales Lane tragedy, four separate funerals took place in the following week. The first of these was on Easter Monday 14th April when Grolig and Häcke were buried at Lodge Hill Cemetery, Weoley Castle. They were allocated a single plot in which both bodies were buried. Doubtless, a brief graveside committal would have taken place. On 16th May 1962, they were exhumed and transferred to the German Military Cemetery, then under development at Cannock Chase. The work on this war cemetery had begun in 1960, but it was not until 1967 that the formal opening took place. Grolig and Häcke were given separate graves adjacent to one another in Block 3. The former has grave number 74 and the latter 75.

The first of the Smart family funerals took place at the Methodist Church in Waterloo Road, Smethwick on Wednesday 16th of April. This was for Doris Evelyn Smart and her children, Albert Frederick Smart and Brian Roy Smart. The Minister conducting the service was Rev. J. Clifford Mitchell who had the unenviable task of expressing the sympathy, felt by many, for the grievous loss which had been sustained by husband and father Albert Smart. The internment was at Uplands Cemetery, Smethwick, where mother and two sons shared the same grave (plot 22, grave number A13448).

On the same day was the funeral of Alfred Leslie Smart, and his son Malcolm Leslie Smart. This time the funeral service was conducted

Note (see next page)

6 An excerpt from the speech delivered to an audience at Bristol University, Saturday, 12th April 1941. The Prime Minister was officiating at a presentation ceremony. He had spent the previous night in a special train parked in a railway siding outside Bristol. From there he observed the attack on the city. Next morning he inspected the damage whilst people were still being rescued from the smouldering ruins.

Part of the German War Cemetery at Cannock Chase. In the foreground is the grave of Fw Helmut Häcke, and to the left, that of Fw Egon Grolig. Author

Doris Smart and her two sons share the same grave at Uplands Cemetery. Carole Richards

Along with the other civilian victims of the Heinkel crash, Amy and Doreen Hanson are buried at Uplands Cemetery, Smethwick. Carole Richards

by Rev. S. Bernard Coley at St Mark's Church, which is near to Hales Lane and Uplands Cemetery, where father and son joined wife and daughter in their family grave. It is close to the other Smart family grave (being plot 22, grave number A13443). It is hard to imagine the ordeal of the day as experienced by Albert Smart who had left the five members of his family in 283 Hales Lane, in order to fulfil his fire-watching duties.

The last of the four funerals was conducted the next day, Thursday 17th April. Again it was at St Mark's Church with the same Minister leading the service. Amy Hanson and her daughter Doreen Joan Hanson were also buried in Uplands Cemetery (plot 20, grave number A9155). As with the previous two funerals, the Mayor of Smethwick, Edmund H. Charnock, was present.

On Easter Saturday, 12th April 1941, following the two consecutive nights of heavy bombing on Birmingham and then one on Bristol, Prime Minister Winston Churchill said in a speech:

'I see the damage done by the enemy attacks; but I also see, side by side with the devastation and amid the ruins, quiet, confident, bright and smiling eyes, beaming with a consciousness of being associated with a cause far higher and wider than any human or personal issue. I see the spirit of an unconquerable people.' [6]

One wonders what degree of comfort William Hanson (husband of Amy and father of Doreen) and Albert Smart found in these words.

Once the remains of the Heinkel bomber had been removed and the ruins made relatively safe, Hales Lane functioned as normally as wartime conditions permitted. With the war over, preparations were made to rebuild the houses in their original style, so as to match the semi-detached houses of 279 and 285. The reconstruction took place between June 1947 and June 1948. The south-western end of Hales Lane was renamed St Marks Road in 1953 and 281 and 283 became 23 and 25 respectively.

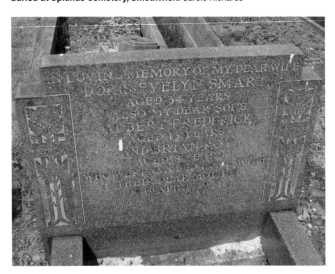

PART TWO

THE CITY
UNDER ATTACK

Damage in Queen Street, Highgate following the
raid of 20th/21st November 1940. The overturned
Birmingham City Transport bus is a Daimler
COG5 (BOP 814). Mirrorpix/Birmingham Mail

EARLY DAYS

Note

7 L19 was lost later on the sortie. It was experiencing difficulties with the engines and did not cross the British coast on its homeward journey until 05.25 hours. It continued to have difficulties over the North Sea and matters got worse when the Zeppelin was subjected to Dutch rifle fire over the Friesian Islands. Later, three of the four engines gave up and the aircraft came down in the sea. All on board were lost.

The first air attack on Birmingham took place on 31st January 1916 when two P Class Zeppelins attacked the suburbs and other towns to the immediate north-west. Illustrated here is a P Class Zeppelin. Nigel Parker

One of the two naval Zeppelins which carried out the attack on 31st January 1916 was L21 (the other was L19) commanded by Kapitänleutnant Dietrich. He believed that he was over Birkenhead/Liverpool! Nigel Parker Collection

Ships in the night

The first air raid on Birmingham occurred on the night of 31st January 1916. German Naval Zeppelin airships L19 and L21 dropped bombs on the city's suburbs and in the Black Country (Tipton, Wednesbury and Walsall). The area was not deliberately targeted. The commander of Zeppelin L19, Kapitänleutnant Odo Löwe, believed that he was over Sheffield, whilst his comrade in L21, Kapitänleutnant Max Dietrich, thought he was over Birkenhead and Liverpool! Nine Zeppelins were assigned the target of Liverpool, each of them operating independently. L19 spent about 10 hours over England, crossing the Norfolk coast passing over Stamford and Downham Market before penetrating to the West Midlands.[7] L21 made landfall at Cromer and proceeded across The Fens to the Birmingham area.

The only defensive fighter which might have caught L19 and L21 was an R.E.7 of 5 Reserve Aeroplane Squadron (RAS) based at Castle Bromwich. This aircraft (serial number 2363) was crewed by Major A.B. Burdett (Squadron Commanding Officer) and 2nd Lt R.A. Cresswell. They took off at 20:20 hours. The purpose for the flight was to check the blackout over Birmingham which was found to be adequate over the city centre, though the suburbs and link roads were illuminated. The crew were unaware of the bombing in progress to the north-west, though the timings did overlap. The R.E.7 made for home, only to find the airfield at Castle Bromwich under mist. Here a crash-landing was made at 21:50. The aircraft did not survive but the crew were unhurt.

No doubt mindful of the fact that elsewhere 61 people had died that night as a result of Zeppelin attacks, the Mayor of Birmingham, Neville Chamberlain, was disturbed by the lack of warning regarding the enemy infiltration. He made his concerns known at government level. Indeed, earlier in the day radio interceptions had warned British defences that raids were planned for that night. The assumption was that the target would be London and so Royal Flying Corps defensive patrols were put in place to cover the approaches to London. In the event, most of the Zeppelins roved around over the East Midlands confused as to their whereabouts.

Doubtless Mr Chamberlain's fears subsided as many months passed before the next Zeppelin incursion. On 19th October 1917, L41 arrived over the Austin works at Longbridge, which was building complete aircraft as well as aero engines. The commander of L41, Hauptmann Kuno Manger, was something of a well-known airman amongst his contemporaries. He reported finding the factory 'brilliantly lighted' and dropped a bomb, damaging a building and injuring two people. Further bombs fell in suburbs and it has been said that this raid caused the only First World War fatality in the Birmingham area that resulted from a German air raid. The victim was Dame Elizabeth Cadbury's pet monkey, Jacko, which died of fright.[8]

Manger returned again on the night of 12/13th April 1918. With Zeppelin L62, he was part of a force of five 'V Class' Zeppelins which had crossed the coast between 21:20 and 22:00 hours and were at large over the North and the Midlands. Manger dropped bombs on Coventry, then found himself over Hockley Heath and proceeded north to Hall Green, on Birmingham's southern boundary. The Zeppelin circled and then a bomb was released which fell on to Robin Hood golf course and another on to Manor Farm in Shirley. Further bombs may have dropped in Olton Reservoir before L62 retreated eastwards towards the coast, descending several thousand feet to escape the headwinds.

At this stage in the war, Air Defence units were in place to combat German bombing raids, be they day or night attacks.[9] Protection over the night skies of Birmingham and Coventry fell to 38 Squadron (Sqn), which dispersed its F.E.2b aircraft across three locations to offer better coverage.

Kapitänleutnant Dietrich.

Lt Cecil Henry Noble-Campbell of 'B' Flight, 38 Sqn, took off from his home airfield of Buckminster, on the Leicestershire/Lincolnshire border at 23:25. He was patrolling at 16,000 feet, when at 01:15 he saw Zeppelin L62 north-east of Birmingham. He manoeuvred his F.E.2b (A5707) fighter to make an attack.

However, Noble-Campbell was not the only fighter pilot giving his attention to the Zeppelin. Lt William Alfred Brown of 38 Sqn's 'C' Flight, had taken off from RAF Wittering at 23:18, and also made an attack on the Zeppelin.

Suddenly, Noble-Campbell's propeller was smashed and he sustained a head injury. He broke off the attack and nursed his crippled fighter down on to the ground at Coventry where he got out before the machine caught fire.

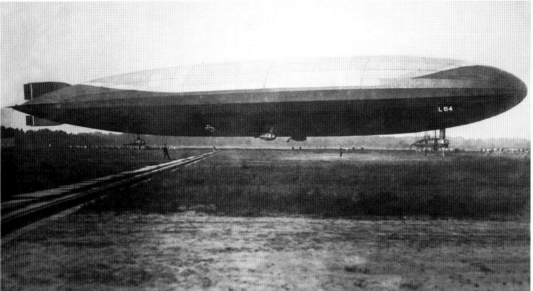

Zeppelin L41, an R Class airship, made an attack on Longbridge on 19th October 1917. It is seen here with L44, a T Class airship.

On the night of 12/13th April 1918, a force of five Zeppelins crossed the east coast. One of these, L62, penetrated the Birmingham boundary at Hall Green where it did negligible damage. This photo shows a similar airship, part of the V Class.
Nigel Parker Collection

An F.E.2b as built by Boulton Paul in 1915. Night fighter versions were later produced as flown by Lt Cecil Henry Noble-Campbell and Lt William Alfred Brown on the night of 12/13th April 1918 when attempting to intercept Zeppelin L62.
via Les Whitehouse

Notes

8 Some have expressed scepticism about this, but it is true. See *Portrait of Birmingham* by Vivian Bird, page 159.

9 At the time of Birmingham's third Zeppelin raid, the RAF was not yet a fortnight old. The Royal Flying Corps and the Royal Naval Air Service had merged on 1st April to form the new service.

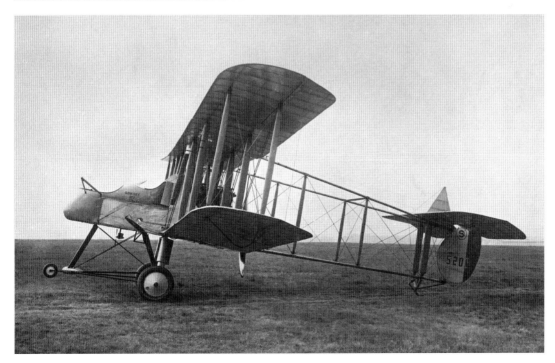

10 Radford airfield was the home of No.1 Aircraft Acceptance Pool.

11 As the international crisis grew, so did the AFS. By the end of 1939, the organisation in Birmingham had nearly 12,000 personnel, 178 stations and 535 trailer-pumps which were to be towed by a variety of vehicle types.

The east side of the Bull Ring looking down towards Digbeth as it was in the mid-1930s.
Ray Greyo collection

His forced landing had finished up at the boundary wall of White and Poppe (an artillery shell-filling factory). Brown's F.E.2b (A5578) was also in trouble and he forced-landed 200 yards short of Radford airfield near Coventry.[10] Brown was seriously injured. Both fighters are recorded as having forced-landed at 01:30.

Squadron records document that each pilot assumed that he had been the victim of defensive gunfire from the Zeppelin. As Manger never made any report of an attack upon his airship, we are left with something of a mystery. It is possible that the two fighters had collided in the dark, or even shot one another down.

This was the last occasion that German bombers appeared over Birmingham prior to August 1940. The city had come through the Great War virtually unscathed. Aside from fighter aircraft, the city's only other defences were searchlights and 75mm guns (14 of each in June 1918).

The City Prepares For War

During the mid 1930s, as the months turned into years, the British government was taking the increasing threat of a revived Germany ever more seriously. In response, some government-led preparations began while, at the same time, politicians worked hard to avoid tension between the two nations. At this period the Royal Air Force (RAF) Expansion Scheme was being rolled out. As a consequence this brought to Birmingham government-sponsored shadow aircraft factories, including the largest at Castle Bromwich, which would provide 12,000-15,000 welcome jobs. Yet, while government money was forthcoming in large amounts for this expansion programme, next to no money was being made available to protect the workers' homes and cities by way of civilian defence.

It was not as though the government did not appreciate the plight of civilians in the face of air attack, but at this stage, at least, it was to local councils they looked – urging them to make moves to protect their own citizens.

In July 1935, the British government formally distributed literature to local authorities and private employers, inviting them to co-operate with the government in the setting up of the Air Raid Precaution (ARP) Service. The public was encouraged to volunteer to man this organisation.

Birmingham City Council, feeling obliged to respond, did put in place an ARP Committee, but amongst councillors there was little appetite for war preparation. In preceding years the coffers had been most carefully managed and now there was much reluctance to spend money on protection against a war which they hoped would not materialise. Furthermore, even if a war commenced and the doomsday predictions of thousands of bombs dropping soon after the announcement of hostilities did occur, it was claimed by some that German bombers could

not reach Birmingham from their home bases in the Fatherland. This was actually an irresponsible optimism. In July 1934, Air Marshal Edgar Ludlow-Hewitt, Deputy Chief of the Air Staff, advised that aircraft operating from North Sea coast bases in Germany were capable of attacking industrial centres in Birmingham.

Prior to the summer of 1938, a minimal amount of ARP work was done. In July of that year, it became clear just what generous amounts of money the Air Raids Precautions Act 1937 would make available to Birmingham City Council. The Munich Crisis in September provided the impetus for many volunteers to come forward. Even so, the council was still reluctant to spend any ratepayers' money on ARP without a thorough scrutiny. By January 1940, however, the city was having to spend £5,000 a day on matters relating to civil defence, 80% of which was financed by the Government, the balance coming from the city rates.

Things became more pressing in March 1939 when Hitler completed his invasion of Czechoslovakia, but preparations were still not complete at the outbreak of war on 3rd September 1939. Fortunately, fire precautions were well in hand, as might be expected with the gloomy prophecies that the city might see 1,000 fires start in a matter of minutes. The city's own fire brigade was efficient and possessed modern equipment. It was not, however, likely to be able to handle the number of fires that would occur during a serious air attack. The Auxiliary Fire Service (AFS) was established in the city on 15th August 1937.[11]

Arrangements to supplement the vulnerable water supply were made. The facility to interconnect the water supply with that of Coventry would subsequently prove valuable and the canals and River Rea were to be prepared as an alternative source of supply. Five miles of additional water pipes were laid in the city to facilitate rerouting of water and a 24-inch main laid between Dudley Road and Newhall Street. Hundreds of water tanks were strategically placed as back-ups for fractured water pipes.

A strong Air Raid Warden body of men and women existed at the commencement of war. As almost a year elapsed before the city experienced air raids, they were gainfully employed in various associated duties. Being considered responsible citizens, they functioned as leaders in matters of civil defence within their local communities. From April 1939, in order to oversee and provide proper leadership, the wardens were placed under the control of the Chief Constable.

Contingency plans to cope with high numbers of casualties that could result from air attacks were drawn up. To avoid less seriously injured cases overwhelming the hospitals, 32 first aid stations were strategically positioned and 12

mobile units gave added flexibility. This arrangement was to prove quite sufficient. Later on, casualty annexes in the basement of Lewis's department store (in the city centre) and Ansells Brewery (at Aston Cross) were set up. Their purpose was, should the need arise, to help handle large numbers of emergency cases, especially if hospitals themselves were bombed, as in the raids which were to afflict the city in April 1941. Lastly, a fleet of 500 improvised ambulances (and also cars for less serious casualties) was gradually established.

A system of air raid warning sirens was in place at the outbreak of war. Many of these were factory sirens and hooters, while others were electrically activated by remote control. Tests, and indeed some of the early air raids, revealed that the sound of the warning did not penetrate to some areas and this needed to be corrected. Further independently operated sirens were added to the system.

During 1938-1939, good work was done in providing the city with a system of report and control. The Council House in Colmore Row was the location for the main Control Centre, where a section of basement was specially strengthened. From here a reporting and control system

At the outbreak of war, Birmingham's fire brigade possessed modern equipment as represented by this Leyland Tigress turntable escape fire engine. It was new in 1935. The turntable and ladder (which could be extended to 103 feet) was manufactured by Metz of Germany. This vehicle (BOF 389) is now preserved at the Transport Museum, Wythall. The British Commercial Vehicle Museum

Communal pavement shelters tended to give people a false sense of security as they were not capable of withstanding blast. This shelter was in Norman Road, Smethwick. via Peter Kennedy

Most famous of the domestic air raid shelters was that known as the Anderson shelter.
via Mike Kemble

A German map of Birmingham's north-east districts showing factories, utilities and transport infrastructure. Such maps were based upon pre-war British publications. (Note the out-dated reference to Midland Railway Carriage & Wagon Works which, by the time of the Blitz, had become Metropolitan-Cammell Carriage & Wagon.) via Nigel Parker

was managed. With Home Office approval, this system comprised ten Reporting Centres, five of which were Report and Control and five were just Report; all of which were built underground.

The need to provide air raid shelters was a sizeable headache for the authorities. For civilians who lived in homes with gardens, Anderson-type shelters, which were arched steel huts partially buried in the ground and then covered over with soil or sandbags, were made available. In 1939 large numbers of these were distributed and, by October, the number totalled 82,000, providing shelter for 410,000 of Birmingham's citizens. Inner-city residents, many of whom did not have gardens, were given assistance in the strengthening of cellars. Basements were also the obvious refuge for many commercial properties, especially in the city centre. Of course, these provisions did not meet every contingency and there was a pressing need for public shelters.

The Munich Crisis in September 1938 had brought about basement strengthening, potentially providing shelter for 10,000 people. Also, at that time, there was the digging of three miles of trench shelters in public parks, supposedly capable of catering for 20,000 people. By the

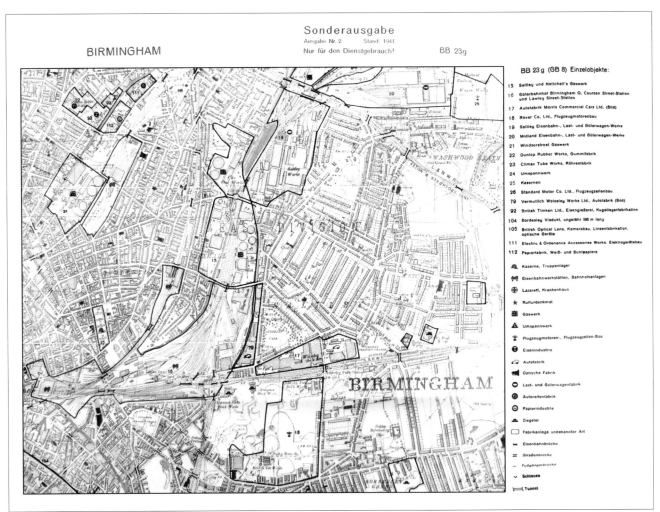

following February a further seven miles of trenches was in the process of being excavated.

Upon the outbreak of war, the ARP Committee claimed that about half of the city's population had access to air raid shelters. Even this state of affairs was only marginally down to the Council's own effort, as 80% of shelter provision was in the form of Andersons, the cost of which was underwritten by the Government. The majority of the council's supply of shelters was, in fact, trenches. In the first months of the war the programme of strengthening basements continued. Where streets had dwellings with cellars or floors below ground level, one in five was reinforced to act as a local community shelter. In properties where an Anderson was impractical, Morrison-type shelters were often installed. The Morrison was a steel-topped table-like cage, to be erected in a downstairs room, under which occupants could take cover. The design was such that it could withstand the collapse of a building on top of it.[12]

Although the local authority had provided some basic protection, it was substantial brick-built, public shelters which were being called for by many citizens, in particular (especially after the bombing started) deep, bomb-proof shelters. These latter were expensive to construct and there was no Government subsidy available for such shelters. A programme of building communal pavement shelters did get under way, but these were above ground. Government and local authorities did not like the idea of communal shelters, and saw them as a potential breeding ground for disease and feared the high death rate if such a structure received a direct hit, as happened in Hockley on the night of 24th October 1940. The authorities preferred to see people dispersed rather than gathered during a raid, but some residents of the inner-city had little or no alternative. Initially, many people held a misplaced belief that the communal shelter would offer better protection than their Anderson. These structures were of brick with a concrete roof, but were jerry-built affairs and would not survive a direct hit, or even a near miss.

A contemporary observation, made by the artist Frank Lockwood of Acocks Green, in his diary entry dated 24th August 1941, states: 'The most striking feature....was the number of surface shelters marked "closed". Unfit for use because of poor mortar. We counted well over a hundred such shelters. Such workmanship is a scandal – but all over the country there are thousands of such shelters still to make fit for use. Birmingham city centre has a considerable number – many of these have been rebuilt – many more need rebuilding – and in the suburbs there is the same wilful waste of public money on erections that instead of protecting life merely gave the occupants a false sense of security.'

Civil Defence

The Home Office established the Air Raid Precaution Service (later to become the Civil Defence) in 1935, a force which was to consist of civilians – mainly volunteers. During the war, over 1.9 million people served within the Civil Defence and nearly 2,400 lost their lives to enemy action. In the main Blitz period (September 1940-May 1941) Britain's military ability to respond to the night bomber was woefully inadequate. It was the civilian defenders, in particular the fire-watchers and all who doused the hundreds of thousands of incendiaries, who utterly frustrated the enemy's purpose.

The Government delegated the organisation of civil defence to local authorities. Volunteers were directed to different elements of the service, dependent upon experience or training. Each local civil defence service was divided into several elements, namely:

Wardens were responsible for local reconnaissance and reporting; leadership, organisation, guidance and control of the general public. They would also advise victims of air raids about the locations of rest and food centres and other welfare facilities.

Rescue Parties were required to assess and then access bomb-damaged buildings to retrieve the injured and those who had been killed. They were also responsible for turning off gas, electricity and water supplies, and to make safe buildings which were damaged.

Medical Services included **First Aid Parties** which provided on-the-spot medical assistance. More serious injuries were passed to First Aid Posts by **Stretcher Parties** and to local hospitals by **Ambulance Personnel**. If necessary, bodies could be removed to emergency mortuaries.

Gas Decontamination Teams were kitted out with gas-tight and waterproof protective clothing and were to deal with any gas attacks. They were trained to decontaminate buildings, roads, rail and other material that had been contaminated by liquid or jelly gases.

Report and Control dealt with the stream of information that was generated during an attack. A local headquarters had an ARP controller who directed rescue, first aid and decontamination teams to the scenes of reported bombing. If local services were deemed insufficient to deal with the incident then the controller could request assistance from surrounding local authorities.

Fire-watchers (Fire Guard from 1941) were responsible for a designated area/building. They reported the outbreak of fires to the fire services and were expected to douse incendiary fires if possible with sand or stirrup pump, or by smothering.

Welfare supported the injured and those bombed out of their homes. This involved finding suitable accommodation, issuing new documentation (ration books, identity cards) and the provision of some money to buy food.

Messengers conveyed information from the site of bombing incidents back to the ARP HQ. Many were teenagers.

Supporting the Civil Defence was the Women's Volunteer Service (WVS) which provided and operated the mobile canteens, street kitchens and rest centres. They also offered comfort and support to the victims of air attacks. Other voluntary organisations included: St John's Ambulance Brigade, Friends Ambulance Unit, Red Cross, YMCA and Church Army.

The Police, many of them Special Constables, assisted with aspects of ARP. Military personnel, including those from local RAF barrage balloon sites and Home Guard personnel, also supplied manpower when civilian resources were stretched.

Note

12 Anderson and Morrison shelters were named after successive Home Secretaries John Anderson and Herbert Morrison.

Birmingham: A Beckoning Target

Birmingham and its suburbs were home to numerous factories, both large and small, which were to be crucial to the war effort. The fact was not lost on Germany and it is almost certain that aerial photographs of factory sites were taken from civilian aircraft for the German intelligence services prior to the outbreak of war. These intelligence services were well-informed, possessing street maps of Birmingham and smaller scale ones which showed: factories (by name), hospitals (marked with a red cross), all major roads, railway lines and goods yards, waterways, the electricity grid and telegraph grid.

The Ministry of Home Security identified thousands of locations in the country which it deemed to be key points important to the war effort. These included infrastructure such as the railways, utilities such as gasworks and power stations, and factories. Key points were graded as to their importance e.g. the Windsor Street gasworks was Category 1 as was the Castle Bromwich aircraft factory and the Bakelite factory Category 2. A contemporary British report stated:

'Birmingham has more key points than any other town outside London. It dominates the country's production of non-ferrous metal and machine tools and is very important in the finishing of steel goods and the manufacture of guns. There are three fairly noticeable concentrations of key points in the City and area:

1. In the south-east, the Acocks Green-Sparkbrook-Tyseley district.
2. In the north-east, the Wilton [sic]-Nechells-Castle Bromwich district.
3. In the north-west, the Smethwick-West Bromwich district.'[13]

In addition, silversmiths and jewellers were well suited to use their specialist skills to produce component parts for rifles, aircraft and radar equipment.

It was the ever-increasing involvement with the production of military aircraft which guaranteed that the Luftwaffe's attention would be directed towards Birmingham, and accounts for the city being bombed as early as it was, in August 1940. It was at this time that the RAF was the force which could (and did) frustrate Germany's military intentions and so the Germans considered it necessary to impede the production of new aircraft.

During the much-needed expansion of the RAF in the late 1930s, the Government sponsored the shadow factory scheme to help the aircraft industry cope with the large numbers of aircraft being ordered. Motor car manufacturers, with experience of volume production, were recognised as ideal for organising and running such operations. Austin was to take on a new factory located at Cofton Hackett near to the company's Longbridge plant. Morris Motors, under the headship of Lord Nuffield, was tasked with the crucial production of Spitfires at a new factory at Castle Bromwich. Rover, firstly at Tyseley and then from late 1940 also at Solihull,

A German map highlighting much of Birmingham's infrastructure.
via Nigel Parker

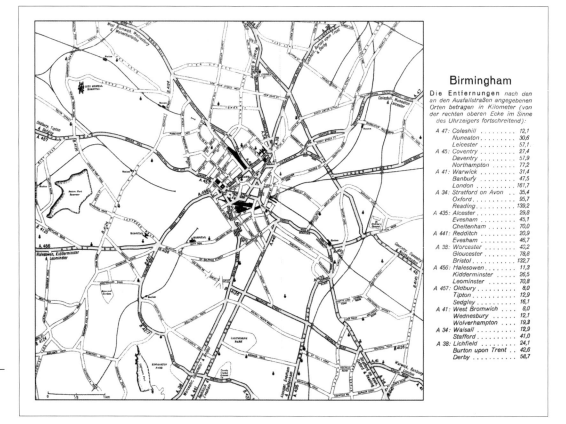

Note

13 Ministry of Home Security Appreciation, November 1940.

was to be involved in both the building and development of aero engines.

Construction of the new Austin aero factory got under way in mid-1936 and by the following year Fairey Battle aircraft and components for Bristol Mercury engines (which powered the Gloster Gladiator and Bristol Blenheim) were being made. In 1938 the first complete Mercury engine built at the factory had been successfully tested and the first of many hundreds of Fairey Battles to be built at the site had flown. The aeronautic output from the Austin factory was considerable and included: in excess of 1,200 Fairey Battles, 300 Hawker Hurricanes, 620 Short Stirlings and 330 Avro Lancasters. Also built were: 1,100 Miles Master wing and centre sections, 3,000 Bristol Beaufighter wing and centre sections, component and wing

assemblies equivalent to a further 200 Hurricanes and the fuselages for 360 Airspeed Horsa gliders. Added to this should be: 14,300 Bristol Mercury and Pegasus engines, 42,185 engine sets, landing gears, components for Rolls-Royce engines, gears for Rotol propellers, gun turrets, 15,000 fuel and oil tanks and 122,000 exhaust rings for Bristol engines. A small proportion of the work was dispersed to other factory units. From 1941 final assembly of all aircraft was done at Marston Green, where a new factory had been constructed the previous year in anticipation of receiving Austin-built Short Stirling sub-assem-

blies. Test flying of completed aircraft from the Marston Green factory was conducted from Birmingham's Elmdon aerodrome, necessitating the aircraft being towed from the factory, across the LMS (London Midland & Scottish) railway line to the airfield.

In October 1936, the Air Ministry proceeded to build a factory at Acocks Green. It was completed within a year and put into the hands of Rover, who were to build components for Bristol Hercules engines, which would power the forthcoming Short Stirling and Bristol Beaufighter. The facility was known as the No.1 Factory, as

Rover would be put in charge of a second larger factory at Solihull. In October 1940, the first Hercules engine to be built completely by Rover was tested. The No.1 factory also built half a dozen gas turbine jet engines at this time. Following Luftwaffe air attacks on Birmingham however, it was considered safer to move this secret work to Lancashire in April 1941.

The largest of the new factories was to be built at Castle Bromwich and building commenced in July 1938. The Air Ministry had struggled in securing a suitable partner to share this sizeable venture. The choice seemed to hover between the Nuffield Corporation and aircraft manufacturer Vickers. Nuffield won the day with 1,000 Spitfires as an initial order. Repeated changes of policy together with personality clashes frustrated the start of Spitfire production. As a result, the whole scheme was taken out of the hands of the Nuffield Corporation and given to Vickers. The first Castle Bromwich-built Spitfire was delivered to the RAF on 27th June 1940. The 500th machine had been completed by the following February. When Spitfire production at Castle Bromwich was concluded in late 1945, more than 11,500 had been turned out

Spitfires and Lancasters awaiting delivery from the Castle Bromwich factory in May 1944.
Peter Arnold Collection

(including work done at dispersed sites). This figure accounted for more than half of the total Spitfire production. From 1943, 299 Lancasters were also built, with a further 12 being assembled from sections built elsewhere. By this stage in the war, serious interference from the Luftwaffe was only a small risk and the need for dispersed production reduced. Finally, Vickers Wellingtons were also repaired on site.

Morris Commercial Cars (using the ex-Wolseley factory) at Adderley Park was involved in the construction of Horsa glider wings, while its main effort was in military vehicles including armoured types such as the Crusader tank.

Wolseley Motors (another member of the Nuffield empire) at Drews Lane, Ward End shared in the work of Morris Commercial Cars. In addition to producing military trucks and cars, components for the aircraft industry were made as well as munitions for the Admiralty. Bombing in April 1941 and July 1942 caused £500,000 of damage to the factory.

Tyseley-based Serck Radiators provided coolant radiators and oil coolers for all early marks of Spitfires and Hurricanes. SU Carburettors at Adderley Park provided all carburettors for Merlin engines up to 1943. When the factory was bombed in November 1940, it was decided to move its plant and the 700 strong workforce to Shirley's industrial estate, then on the edge of the green belt. Here the workforce increased to 1,500. Carburettors were also made for the Rolls-Royce Vulture and Peregrine engines, along with the Napier Sabre and Dagger powerplants.

In July 1938, Lucas opened a new factory at Great King Street, Hockley. This was to handle sub-contract orders for Austin's Fairey Battle work. Initially sub-assemblies for Spitfire wing sections were provided to the Castle Bromwich factory, but in November 1940, because of the bombing in the area, this work was moved to the Cadbury factory. Lucas managed the machine shops at Castle Bromwich after the factory was taken out of the hands of the Nuffield Corporation. The Great King Street site also made Boulton and Paul gun turrets, but this work too was evacuated, this time to South Wales. Thousands of gun turrets

were also produced at the Lucas Formans Road, Sparkhill site. Together with the nearby Rover factory at Acocks Green, Lucas' Shaftmoor Lane site in Hall Green was involved in the top-secret development work of the gas-turbine jet engine. As with Rover's share in this project, it was decided that the factory was too vulnerable to air attack and the work was moved to Lancashire.

Besides the Spitfire wing sub-assemblies, of which there were 12,500 in total, Cadbury's Bournville factory also made aircraft hydraulic pressure bodies, radiator flap jacks, dive brake assemblies and vertical milling machines. Some manufacturing of chocolate did continue!

Other factories worthy of note include:

The famous **Fort** (Fortified) **Dunlop** at Erdington where tyres and wheels were made;

Moss Gears at Tyburn made transmission units for tanks and other military vehicles;

Metropolitan-Cammell Carriage and Wagon Company (MCCW) produced armoured fighting vehicles (tanks: the Cruiser, Valentine, Comet and Tetrarch) and specialised rolling stock at Washwood Heath, and more than 3,000 radar vehicles and spares for tanks at their Saltley works;

Fisher & Ludlow (metal pressings) at Bradford Street, Deritend/Rea Street, Digbeth was engaged on munitions work and, later, wings for Lancasters;

James Booth at Nechells and Kitts Green produced aluminium components for Spitfires;

ICI Ltd (Metals) (Kynoch Works) at Witton, along with its sub-contractors, turned out a vast amount of munitions. The Witton site, at its peak, employed 20,000 people;

GEC at Witton was involved in both electrical and chemical (notably plastic) products;

Witton Kramer Ltd at Witton manufactured mine detectors and other specialist military components;

William Newman & Sons Ltd of Aston was concerned with the production of Bofors guns;

BSA (Birmingham Small Arms) **Guns** at Small Heath was the sole manufacturer of rifles until 1941 and produced Browning .303 machine guns for RAF aircraft. Large numbers of other precision weapons and associated equipment, as well as pedal cycles and motorcycles, were also produced at this factory and dispersed sites e.g. Redditch, Tyseley and Shirley;

Bakelite at Tyseley made (plastic) components for communications equipment, ordnance and aircraft;

Reynolds Tube at Tyseley made light alloy tubing and was involved in the production of Spitfire wings;

Above: **A wartime advert for Tyseley-based Serck. Radiators built here were fitted to all Hurricanes and Spitfires which flew in the Battle of Britain.**

Left: **Crucial to Birmingham's war materiel production was the ability to transport workers to and from the factories. Here a row of Birmingham City Transport double-deckers is headed by Daimler COG5 COX 973 with Leyland TD6C EOG 291 behind. Note the khaki (camouflage) roof, white blackout markings and shielded headlamps. Of interest is the advert between the decks; at the end of the war it was declared that 'no other town or city in England reached Birmingham's per capita figure in savings.'**
David Harvey Collection

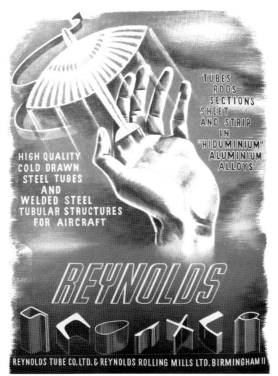

Another wartime advert again for a Tyseley-based company. Reynolds provided tubing used in airframe construction.

In conclusion, a review such as this explains why the Luftwaffe was to give the north-eastern and southern districts the degree of attention that it did. Despite the 2,000+ tonnes of high explosive bombs and countless incendiaries which would rain down on the city, particularly between October 1940 and April 1941, the air attacks were never to seriously interfere with the city's manufacturing output.

Eye on the Sky – the Observer Corps

By the late 1930s, a network of coastal radar stations ensured that the country was well placed to benefit from the advanced warning of the approach of enemy aircraft from the direction of the sea. However, the plotting of aircraft flying over land, be they friend or foe, could only be done by the human eye aided by binoculars and instruments for gauging the course, height and speed of an aircraft.

An observation and reporting system had developed during the First World War, though this was restricted to the south and south-east of England. Through the inter-war years a national organisation, known as the Observer Corps, was established and progressively built up.

Parkinson Cowan at Stechford manufactured ammunition boxes, hand grenades and bomb cases;

Guest Keen & Nettlefolds (GKN) was a manufacturer of nuts, bolts and screws, together with various steel products and components for the military.

W & T Avery at Smethwick, produced artillery pieces;

Chance Brothers, also at Smethwick, manufactured glass products, lenses in particular.

The scope of the Observer Corps was extended to cover the West Midlands in 1938. Following the Munich crisis in September of that year, the Corps was mobilised for a week and the following months were used to address problems highlighted by that exercise. On 24th August 1939, notices of mobilisation

This 1938 aerial view shows the W & T Avery factory (Soho Foundry site) in Smethwick.
Avery Historical Museum

were issued by regional Chief Constables to the volunteers who manned observation posts and control centres. At this stage, the Chief Constables acted under the authority of the Air Ministry.

It was upon the work of the Observer Corps that the air raid warning system, which utilised factory sirens and hooters, depended. In the later stages of the war, the general warnings were initiated by officers of the Ministry of Home Security from Observer Corps centres. The value of the work done in plotting all aircraft movements by both day and night was recognised when, in April 1941, the prefix 'Royal' was added to the organisation's name.

Birmingham came within the area of No.5 Group of the Royal Observer Corps (ROC) and there were observer posts at Shirley (site E4), Erdington (site F1) and Selly Oak (site F4), with many others further out from the city. In common with other sites, the personnel of the Birmingham posts were, in the first instance, supplied with the striped armband of the Special Constabulary overprinted 'Observer Corps' while the beret was adopted as sensible headwear for use with the field telephone headsets. Later they would be issued with one-piece boiler suits before receiving their own uniforms in 1942.

The area of No.5 Group, with Coventry as its control centre, covered about 4,000 square miles. Within this region were 35 posts linked on 10 circuits (known as clusters) and these were able to give a complete 'sky picture' of all aircraft movements. The personnel of the Group

consisted of part-time and full-time members.

There was a sophisticated link-up with adjacent centres at Derby, Shrewsbury, Gloucester, Lincoln, Cambridge, Bedford and Oxford. In this way, constant tracks could be maintained as aircraft moved from one Group's area to another.

When the Blitz got under way, German raiders, flying at about 15,000 feet, flew towards Birmingham over the Cotswolds. So regular was this course that the ROC site at Broadway dubbed it 'Heinkel Alley'.

Observation posts and control centres were not relieved of their 24-hour watch until five days after the formal announcement of the end of the war in Europe. This deferred stand-down was in fear of possible renegade Luftwaffe outfits mounting final raids of defiance.

There were three Observer Corps posts located within the Birmingham area: Selly Oak, Erdington and Shirley. ROC Trust

At the heart of each Observer Corps Region was the Control Centre. In the case of 5 Region (Midlands) this was located at Coventry. ROC Trust

The Balloon Goes Up

Following the establishment of a balloon barrage over London during 1936-1938, the Air Staff became convinced of the value of such barrages as a means of keeping enemy aircraft at reasonably high altitudes. Balloons were tethered by steel cables, which if hit by an aircraft would almost certainly cause it to crash. It was therefore decided that key provincial towns and cities would have their own barrages and so was born RAF Balloon Command.

The structure of Balloon Command consisted of Groups under which were Balloon Centres. These centres governed the squadrons in the field, providing supply, maintenance and administration (including sick quarters). The new units were initially established on a skeleton basis with a small force of regular personnel which was supplemented by local part-time auxiliaries.

Recruiting for the Auxiliary Air Force barrage balloon squadrons, which were to defend Birmingham and Coventry, began in the first weeks of 1939. Typically, the Territorial Association (TA) volunteers were aged between 25 and 50. They trained during the evenings and at weekends throughout the summer months, receiving instruction from regular serving RAF instructors.

Birmingham was divided into two distinct barrage balloon regions, the northern barrage and the southern barrage. The former initially comprised three squadrons (911-913), which came under the control of 5 Balloon Centre at RAF Sutton Coldfield (opened 16th June 1939). The southern barrage had two squadrons (914-915) and was under 6 Balloon Centre based at RAF Wythall (opened 8th June 1939).[14] All of these squadrons were given the title 'County of Warwick'. Both of the balloon centres reported to 31 Barrage Balloon (BB) Group, which had its headquarters in Birmingham.

5 Balloon Centre covered an area from Oldbury to Elmdon, encompassing the Castle Bromwich airfield and factory. 6 Balloon Centre covered Solihull up to Longbridge and onwards towards

Opposite page:

An essential part of Birmingham's air defence was the balloon barrage. This photograph was obviously taken at a balloon station, rather than a site, possibly RAF Cardington.
RAF Museum

A rare wartime colour shot of a barrage balloon with winch. Generally a balloon crew consisted of 10 men. IWM

the Hagley Road, encompassing the Austin factories. Within this perimeter the areas of responsibility varied from time to time as the needs changed, such as in May 1940 when the new factories at Rover in Solihull and James Booth & Co in Kitts Green were allocated balloon protection.

Suitable balloon sites were identified and occupied; billeting for personnel was secured. The squadrons and their flights were also provided with headquarters, normally in requisitioned rooms or buildings.

912 Sqn left Birmingham on 15th February 1940 and was relocated to the port of Boulogne in France. When the Germans were within 2 miles of Boulogne, the Squadron evacuated to Calais and from there sailed, on board *City of Christchurch,* to arrive at Southampton on 24th May.

In April 1940, 911, 913, 914 and 915 Sqns were obliged to provide mobile units for service with the British forces in France. Upon receiving the code word 'Aston Villa' on 26th April these units were sent to RAF Cardington, Bedfordshire. They were then dispatched to a port of embarkation. Just weeks later their equipment was abandoned in the face of the German onslaught but personnel were evacuated safely in late May. As with 912 Sqn, after disembarkation leave, they re-mustered at RAF Cardington for training and re-equipment.

On 10th May 1940, the day when German forces swept into France and the Low Countries, the Birmingham balloon squadrons were ordered to fly a large number of balloons. At least 88 are known to have been inflated and flown by the four squadrons. By the summer of 1940, with the exception of London, Birmingham had more barrage balloons than any other defended area in the country. According to the official history this was a total of 168 balloons (with Coventry having 48). At this time Birmingham was host to four balloon squadrons:[15] 911 with its HQ at West Bromwich (48 balloons), 913 with its HQ at Sutton Coldfield (40 balloons), 914 with its HQ at

Northfield (40 balloons) and 915 with its HQ at Rowheath (40 balloons). Each of the squadrons had five or six flights with a usual establishment of eight balloons per flight.

As the threat of invasion grew, Birmingham was divided up into various defensive sectors and in some of these it was the balloon squadrons which took on command and control. Personnel were given regular weapons training and, together with the Home Guard, were given specific responsibilities for defence in the face of enemy infiltrations on the ground. By way of example, the Garrison Commander gave 913 Sqn the responsibility for the defence of Birmingham

This page:

A crew at work on a deflated balloon.
A.B. Burr

A local recruitment poster encouraging applicants to join 911 and 912 Squadrons, part of 5 Balloon Centre, Sutton Coldfield.

An APPEAL
To YOU *and* YOUR FRIENDS

From :— Nos. 911 and 912 (County of Warwick)
BALLOON SQUADRONS.
ROYAL AIR FORCE.

Town Headquarters :
885, TYBURN ROAD,
ERDINGTON, BIRMINGHAM, 24.
Telephone : ERDington 2704

Flying Field :
WHITEHOUSE COMMON,
SUTTON COLDFIELD.

Notes

14 6 Balloon Centre was also responsible for 916-917 (County of Warwick) Sqns which were allocated to the defence of Coventry.

15 Prior to deployment to France, most of 912 Sqn had been part of Birmingham's northern barrage. Following its return from France and after its time at Cardington, it transferred on 26th June 1940 to 11 Balloon Centre Brockworth, Gloucester.

from the Lichfield Road to the Coventry Road. This meant close liaison not only with the Garrison Commander, but also commanders of the Home Guard, both Field Force and Factory Units.

RAF personnel often shared in the civil defence role during and immediately after air raids. Another role given to the RAF balloon squadrons was that of organising and operating decoy fires. Carefully laid out trench systems containing petrol, could be ignited to simulate a town on fire when viewed from the air. These Special Fires were first tried in late 1940. Subsequently they became known by the codename 'Starfish' sites. In January 1941, all Starfish sites became the responsibility of Balloon Command. Around Birmingham, there were Starfish sites at Balsall Common (between Solihull and Coventry), Holt End (north-east of Redditch), Maxstoke (south-east of Coleshill), Fairfield (north of Bromsgrove), Bickenhill (south-east of Elmdon airport), Peopleton (north of Pershore), Halford (south-east of Stratford-upon-Avon) and Silvington (north-west of Cleobury Mortimer).

5 Balloon Centre transferred to 33 BB Group HQ (Sheffield) on 20th September 1941 and 6 Balloon Centre to 32 BB Group (administered from Romsey/Bath) on 13th November of the same year, whereupon Birmingham's 31 BB Group disbanded. Once it became clear that Birmingham was no longer in danger of serious air attacks, the administration of balloons was further reorganised. In June 1942, 5 Balloon Centre disbanded and its squadrons transferred to 6 Balloon Centre. In August 914 Sqn amalgamated with 915 Sqn to become 914/15 Sqn. In the following May, 911 Sqn amalgamated with 913 Sqn, to become 911/13 Sqn. These two squadrons disbanded in 1944 and therefore no balloon squadrons were represented at the city's VE/VJ marches in 1945.

The balloons were a passive mode of defence, with the sole intention of deterring enemy aircraft from flying below predetermined heights, thereby reducing accurate bombing. A few enemy pilots did brave the balloon cables which rose up 8,000 feet into the sky, but such low level penetrations were rare.

In the Birmingham area only one enemy raider is known to have caught a cable and this aircraft was already as good as destroyed anyway. Generally the Birmingham balloon barrage was given a wide berth by friendly aircraft, but sadly the cables were to bring down no fewer than 12 RAF aircraft, most of their crews perishing. Balloon Site 61 at Longbridge had the misfortune to account for two of these.

Right: **Balloon squadrons were formed in the Birmingham area at the start of 1939. Here a barrage balloon is demonstrated at Aston Park in March of that year.**

Opposite, top: **A German reconnaissance photograph showing 5 Balloon Centre at Sutton Coldfield.**

Opposite, bottom: **This view of RAF Wythall was taken from the tower of the parish church in September 1948.** S.E. Ellerman

THE LUFTWAFFE OVER BRUM

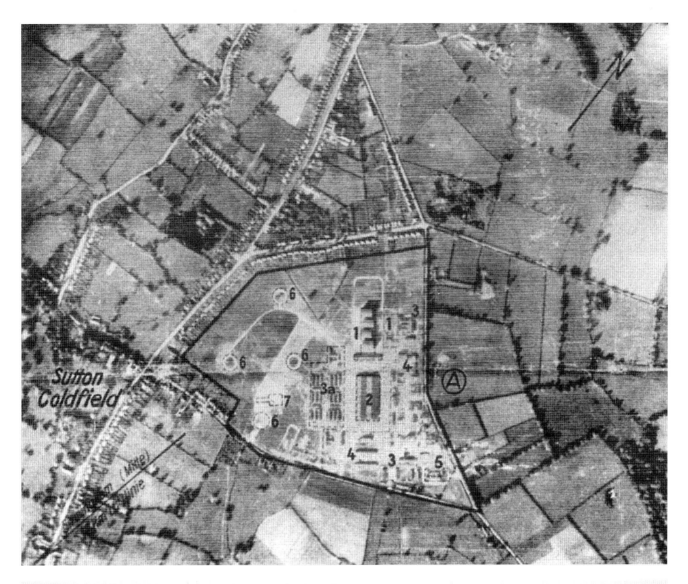

Balloons were susceptible to shrapnel damage and adverse weather conditions especially lightning, ice and wind. When balloons broke loose from their moorings the trailing steel cable, which was 0.31 inches thick, could leave a path of damage on the ground below as the rogue 'blimp' floated across the city.

The Guns

From the mid-1930s on, considerable thought was given to the nation's requirements for an adequate anti-aircraft artillery defence, a part of the Air Defence of Great Britain (ADGB). A plan for the distribution of guns was formulated which in brief was as follows:

There was to be an Outer Artillery Zone (OAZ). This was a 6-mile deep belt of guns, which was to extend down the east side of the country, from the Tees to the south coast, skirting London to the east and then west, as far as the Solent. Behind the OAZ would be a 20-mile belt of searchlights.

The London area was covered by the Inner Artillery Zone (IAZ). Ports and prime industrial centres were designated Gun Defended Areas (GDA). Of the latter were Birmingham, Leeds, Manchester and Sheffield. By 1940 other towns and cities were allocated guns e.g. Coventry, Derby, Nottingham, Crewe and Brooklands (the Vickers aircraft factory).

The guns were the responsibility of the Army, in particular 1 AA Corps. In April 1939, Anti-Aircraft Command was formed and then placed under the direct control of RAF Fighter Command. In July, General Sir Frederick Pile took over from Lieutenant-General Alan Brooke.

By the start of the war, Anti-Aircraft Command had been divided into seven divisions. Responsible for the Midlands and East Anglia was the 4th Anti-Aircraft Division, which was formed in July 1938.

Birmingham had an authorised establishment of 24 3.7 inch and 16 4.5 inch calibre heavy anti-aircraft guns (HAA). In reality, barely a couple of dozen heavy 'ack-ack' guns could be mustered at the start of hostilities. Thankfully, there was almost a year of grace before the Luftwaffe appeared over the city in August 1940. By then 71 guns were available. These comprised: 16 4.5 inch and 55 3.7 inch, of the latter 31 were mobile. These guns fell under the command of 34 Brigade, which provided six batteries from two different regiments (the 69th and 95th, some elements of which were at Coventry).[16]

As the months rolled on and gave way to years, successive policy and organisational changes to anti-aircraft defences were made. By November 1940, the seven divisions had been increased to twelve and these were divided between three separate AA Corps. The way in which the new boundaries fell out saw the 11th Division form at Birmingham (covering the West

Midlands, Welsh Marches and North Wales). This Division was a part of 2 AA Corps. It was 34 Brigade with its six regiments that provided anti-aircraft gun defence for Birmingham and Coventry.[17]

By the time of the air raids on Birmingham in 1942, the disposition of guns was far less concentrated in favour of a carpet-cover, which meant that areas like Birmingham and Coventry tended to merge. With guns being spread more thinly, there was a considerable increase in the number of sites. For example, whereas Birmingham and Coventry had 31 sites between them in 1940, by 1942 these had increased to 61.

Of the guns themselves the 4.5 inch weapons were static affairs on formally acquired sites. The 3.7 inch types were a mixture of static and mobile. The latter were adaptable; not only could they be moved around the country at short notice, but also placed temporarily on a street corner if required. The 4.5 gun could hurl a 50 pound shell as high as 40,000 feet. The 3.7 gun, which had almost as high a ceiling, used a smaller shell but had a quicker rate of fire. For a brief period (January 1941), Birmingham also had four 3 inch guns, reconditioned weapons from the First World War. Light Anti-Aircraft guns (LAA) such as the Swedish designed 40mm Bofors, were for use against low-flying aircraft. Low-level attacks were not considered a major threat in a city with a large balloon barrage, but were important for potential targets such as airfields.

The most realistic use of the guns was to keep the enemy flying high and to dissuade him from keeping a straight and level course when on the bomb run. The fact that the night bombers did not come over in formations but in crocodile fashion and well spaced, meant that it was extremely difficult to place a shell anywhere near the targeted aircraft. In order to seriously cripple a bomber, it was necessary for the shell to burst closer than 75 feet. Predictors were employed to compute the necessary settings in order to place the exploding shell in the same bit of sky as the target, but this only happened rarely. Things improved slightly from October 1940, when gun-laying (GL) radar began to reach the AA batteries. Until this time both guns and searchlights used sound locators in an attempt to obtain a fix on an unseen aircraft. In an effort to frustrate these sound locators, which were not very accurate anyway, German twin-engine bombers flew with desynchronised engines. Desynchronisation produced a pulsating drone. This distinctive sound of the German bomber was a source of apprehension for many on the ground below.

There remained a serious shortfall of anti-aircraft guns and some hope was placed in filling the gap by using UP (unrotated projectile or, unofficially, Uncle Percy) rocket projectors. These were relatively simple to manufacture

and so they could be turned out quickly in good numbers. However, tardiness in the production of the 3 inch projectiles and the training and organising of units to fire them resulted in delay after delay. Initial deliveries of these weapons reached operational units towards the end of the main Blitz period in spring 1941. Known as Z AA Batteries, such units were made up of four Troops, each operating 16 projectors.

One of the early recipients of this unsophisticated weapon was the Austin works, where a double-Troop (32 projectors) was deployed. Because a Z unit did not demand much in the way of site infrastructure (the projectors could use mobile mountings), these weapons could be quickly positioned in any open space. Such units operated from Billesley Common in Kings Heath, Cockshut Hill on the Yardley/Stechford border, Harborne and elsewhere in the Birmingham area.

From the late summer of 1941, women of the Auxiliary Territorial Service (ATS) played an active role in the operation of the gun batteries. Such mixed batteries released men for other duties, though the women did not go into the gun pit itself. In the following year, when the intensity of air attacks had diminished, partial Home Guard manning was introduced. Such part-time soldiers were well-suited for the simpler Z batteries.

By the time air raids on Birmingham began in August 1940, searchlight sites were in position around the city. These were under the command of the 45th and 59th (Royal Warwickshire) Searchlight Regiments, Royal Artillery (Territorial Army) which, in turn, was part of the 54th Brigade. The 45th had four searchlight batteries, the 378th-381st; the 59th had three, the 399th, 427th and 428th.[18] As with the gun batteries, searchlight batteries were responsible for a number of sites and so were divided into Troops which operated each of them.

From November 1940, as improved models of searchlights and more sophisticated direction-finding instruments became available, a process began of 'clustering' lights. Each Troop manned two three-light sites. The revised site-manning was completed by February 1941, at which point there were 31 sites in the regimental area. Besides illuminating enemy aircraft for the gun defences, both lights and guns acted as pointers for the RAF night fighters, beckoning them to investigate the area indicated.

Gun and searchlight sites were officially considered a defended island, from which firepower could be directed towards enemy ground forces should the need arise. Searchlight sites often had a pair of Lewis machine guns for defence, while personnel were equipped with rifles. Such meagre weaponry succeeded in bringing down one German aircraft at Earlswood in May 1941 (see page 101).

(see page 101).

Opposite page:

A 4.5 inch heavy anti-aircraft gun with its crew. During the Blitz period of 1940-1941, 16 of these guns were included in the Birmingham defences.
IWM

According to General Pile, head of Anti-Aircraft Command, the 3.7 inch heavy anti-aircraft gun was '…the finest all purposes gun produced by any country during the war'. Here a mobile example is hooked to an AEC Matador gun tractor.
Warehouse Collection

Seen here is a Z battery with its multiple static rocket launchers in action.

Notes

16 See Appendix C.

17 Two years later, on 30th September 1942, the organisation would be simplified with each of the three corps, along with their 12 divisions, being dissolved so that all brigades were divided across six newly-formed groups. These mirrored the six groups of RAF Fighter Command.

18 The 59th SL was transferred to the Orkney Isles in November 1940 as part of the defence for the Royal Navy's Home Fleet at Scapa Flow.

THE BLITZ PHASE ONE
AUGUST 1940

As will become clear shortly, German air raids on Britain carried out up to mid-September 1940 were part of the build-up for a sea-invasion of England. Targets included ports and some centres of the war manufacturing industry. It was the latter which brought German bombers to Birmingham so early on in what was to become known as the Blitz.

Things started in a small way when, on the night of 25/26th June at 23:35 hours, the air raid sirens sounded for the first time. It was a false alarm and the single note of the all-clear was heard at about 01:10. Then, in the early hours of 9th August, a lone German bomber, perhaps on a probing mission, dropped bombs in the Erdington area. History records 18-year-old Jimmy Fry as being the first person to die in a Birmingham air raid. He was home on leave from the Army. Seven other people were injured. There can be little doubt that the bomber crew were looking for the aircraft factory at Castle Bromwich with, perhaps, Fort Dunlop as an alternative. Whatever the reasons for dropping their load of eight or nine high explosive (HE) bombs where they did, to deliberately hit a residential area would not have been their mission plan. The Air Raid Precaution (ARP) service was found to be wanting; the sirens did not sound a warning until one hour after the attack. Long overdue warnings were a feature of the early air raids on the city.

The Luftwaffe returned five nights later (night of 13/14th August) and this time was successful. The assigned targets were the factories at Fort Dunlop and Castle Bromwich (which was already turning out modest numbers of Spitfires). The German unit involved was the, soon to be considered elite, *Kampfgruppe* 100 (KGr100) which had just transferred from its German base to the French airfield at Vannes. The sun would have been setting on their port beam as the first of 21 Heinkel He 111s crossed the French coast bound for Birmingham. The bombers were split into sections of three aircraft each, and spaced at half-hourly intervals. KGr100 crews were using a very accurate form of radio navigation aid known as *X-Verfahren*. Three different routings were used in the attack so that waves of aircraft arrived in the target area from differing directions. By way of an example, one Heinkel assigned to bomb the Dunlop factory, flying at a height of 19,500 feet, routed Taunton-Swindon-Birmingham and for the return trip, Carmarthen-Brest.

The first bombs fell at 23:10 hours. From a German perspective bomb aiming over Castle Bromwich was to a satisfactory standard, with a good proportion of bombs finding their mark. General offices, F and Q Blocks were damaged as was machinery in D Block. As a consequence, it would soon be decided to disperse some of the

The first serious attack on Birmingham by the Luftwaffe was directed against the Castle Bromwich aircraft factory. This German reconnaissance photo was obviously taken pre-war before the construction of the main factory buildings. The Germans allocated the site the target number 7461.
via Chris Goss

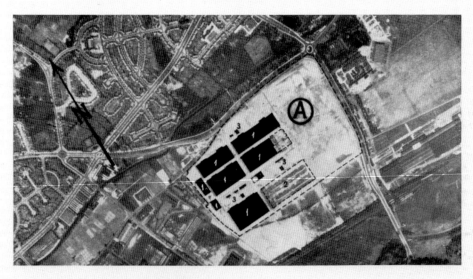

Anlage 5   Nr. 23

Wichtige Herstellerwerke von Jagdflugzeugen

„Spitfire"

Morris, Birmingham-Castle Bromwich (7461)
A. 1) 8 Hallen, 1 Halle z. T. im Bau, 2) 1 Halle im Bau, 3) 10 Nebengebäude

factory's work to other airfield sites, namely Cosford near Albrighton and Desford, Leicestershire. There were casualties; figures quoted vary, but they were in the order of 5 workers dead, 40 seriously injured and 100 less so. As a result of the air raid there were two other deaths in the area. In addition, shortly before midnight, a soldier at a searchlight site was injured by a bomb splinter and he died the following day.

The Dunlop factory was unscathed, with bombs falling wide onto Sutton Park (Sutton Coldfield) and Bromford damaging the Rollaston Wire Company factory between midnight and 01:15. Other stray bombs hit Wolverhampton, Pensnett, Redditch, Wootton Wawen (no less than 20 HE) and even an area 10 miles southwest of Hereford.

A crew member on board one of the Heinkels (coded 6N+FK), detailed to attack the Dunlop factory, was Hilmar Schmidt, the navigator/bomb-aimer/observer. He was the *X-Gerät* operator.[19] His personal diary entry written on the 14th includes the following portion, relating to the previous night's operation:

'...down there on the ground a ghostly brightness had sprung up – like the fingers of a corpse a great number of powerful searchlights were groping for us, trying to seize us but only touching us and slipping off our soot-black coat of paint. Then there were lights and red flashes on the ground along the direction of our flight. Was this to indicate our track to night fighters? We were on the alert and Kurt [flight mechanic] thought he saw a fighter on one occasion.

'Bomb release was due soon so I carried out all the necessary settings, went through the procedures and the bombs fell as programmed. However, "big fires and explosions" were not observed.'

One of the returning Heinkels went out of control in the Cheltenham area. The pilot ordered the crew to bale out. The aircraft stabilised and the order was cancelled, but not before the wireless operator had vacated the machine. He was captured and made a prisoner of war. Another Heinkel (6N+CH) failed to reach its home airfield and forced-landed on a French beach near Bordeaux, all of the crew alighting safely.

On 15th August, the head of the Luftwaffe, Reichsmarschall Hermann Göring, stated: 'Our night attacks are essentially dislocation raids, made so that the enemy defences and population shall be allowed no respite.'

That night Luftwaffe aircraft returned to Birmingham. Once again, in accordance with Göring's dislocation policy, they spread their arrival times over the city so that the raid lasted into the early hours of the 16th. Factories and, inevitably, houses were hit. Bombs fell in: Stechford and Yardley at 00:45 hours, Hay Mills and Small Heath (including the Singer Motors factory) at 01:40, Bordesley Green, Acocks Green, Erdington, Saltley and Sutton Coldfield. Casualties included eleven deaths of which seven were

Note

19 *X-Gerät* was the onboard apparatus, part of the *X-Verfahren* radio navigational aid system.

By the late summer of 1940, Spitfire production was well under way at Castle Bromwich.
Peter Arnold Collection

20 From 1942 Erdington House Hospital was called Highcroft Hall.

21 See page 48.

in a shelter in Bordesley Green East, when it received a direct hit. Some damage was done to the Yardley Green Sanatorium and the Erdington House Hospital.[20]

Two nights later the bombers were wide of the mark when they dropped HE bombs and around 1,500 incendiaries. These were scattered across the Black Country, Stoke-on-Trent, Market Drayton, Lichfield and Minworth areas, the vast majority falling harmlessly in fields. Birmingham did not escape entirely when, just before midnight, some HE bombs were dropped, notably in the Castle Bromwich area, but they did little harm.

Another scattered raid took place on the 19/20th when bombs fell across western counties of the Midlands. It was reported by the ARP services that Shirley and Sutton Coldfield were bombed but no casualties were sustained.

Then there was a brief respite until the early morning of 24th August. Proceedings got under way when, at 02:00, between 200-300 incendiaries rained down on fields near Sutton Coldfield. Shortly after 04:00 incendiaries dropped near Fort Dunlop. Houses and shops in the Erdington area were destroyed. High explosives fell on the east side of the city, including Castle Bromwich (04:30), namely on the railway, aerodrome and factory site. At the last mentioned, a negligible amount of damage was done to the Repairable Equipment Depot No.1 facility which was housed in the British Industries Fair building. The bombers would have had to beat a hasty retreat in order to clear the coast before they lost the cover of darkness.

The next night (24/25th) the alert was in force for six hours commencing 21:50 hours. The raiders included 12 He 111s of KGr100, which set out to attack Castle Bromwich aircraft factory, taking off between 22:00 and 01:00 hours. One of the last Heinkels (6N+OK) to get airborne was piloted by Fw Adalbert Knier. The crew of this

An Explanation of Luftwaffe Unit Designations and Markings

What follows is an explanation of Luftwaffe unit designations and markings, as applicable to this current work. German bomber units, which flew their missions against Birmingham, belonged to *Luftflotte* 2 and *Luftflotte* 3. The first of these two air fleets was located in an area of France north of the River Seine and the other occupied the area to the south and west.

Each of the *Luftflotten* had a number of *Kampfgeschwadern* (large bomber formations). A *Kampfgeschwader* (KG) had a number of *Gruppen*, each of which was equipped with up to 40 aircraft. A *Gruppe* was identified with Roman numerals (I, II, III, IV etc). So the accepted way to refer to an aircraft from the second *Gruppe* of *Kampfgeschwader* 51 was II/KG51.

The *Gruppe* was then subdivided into three *Staffeln*. Each *Staffel* was numbered consecutively (using Arabic numerals), so I *Gruppe* had 1, 2 and 3 *Staffeln*, II *Gruppe* had 4, 5 and 6 *Staffeln*, and so on. An aircraft noted as belonging to 4/KG27, therefore, is known to be from the fourth *Staffel*, second *Gruppe*, *Kampfgeschwader* 27.

A further formation was the *Gruppenstab* which consisted of three aircraft. These were flown not by regular flying crew but by members of the *Gruppe's* staff (*stab*). Such units were identified, for example, as: *Stab* II/KG53. Finally, the *Kampfgeschwader* staff was also allocated its own aircraft, e.g. *Stab*/KG55.

In a small number of instances a single *Gruppe* operated independently of a *Kampfgeschwader*. In such cases the unit was referred to as a *Kampfgruppe*. A typical example was *Kampfgruppe* 100, abbreviated as KGr100.

With regard to aircraft identity markings, these were painted either side of the national insignia, located on the rear fuselage. To the left of the German cross was a combination of a single numeral and a single letter, which identified the *Geschwader*. There were two letters to the right of the cross. The first was the individual aircraft's identity letter, which was painted, or at least outlined, in the *Staffel* colour. Three colours were used in a repeating cycle, white, red and yellow across the *Gruppen*. The second letter

Dornier Do 17 F1+FM of 4/KG76. ww2.com

identified the *Staffel*. The latter utilised letters commencing H but omitted I, J, O and Q. A typical example was a Heinkel He 111 belonging to 5/KG53, which was marked A1+LN. Here 'A1' was the *Geschwader* code; 'L' (coloured red) was the individual aircraft identity letter; 'N' signified the fifth *Staffel*.

Stab aircraft used the colour green on the individual aircraft letter. Identifiers for the fourth letter on *Stab* aircraft were: those belonging to the *Geschwader* 'A'; for the first *Gruppe* 'B'; for the second *Gruppe* 'C'; for the third *Gruppe* 'D' and so on.

STAB AIRCRAFT IDENTIFICATION

Geschwader Stab = A	I Gruppe = B	II Gruppe = C	III Gruppe = D	IV Gruppe = E	V Gruppe = F

STAFFEL COLOURS AND CODE LETTERS

Staffel Colour	I Gruppe	II Gruppe	III Gruppe	IV Gruppe	V Gruppe
White	1st Staffel = H	4th Staffel = M	7th Staffel = R	10th Staffel = U	13th Staffel = X
Red	2nd Staffel = K	5th Staffel = N	8th Staffel = S	11th Staffel = V	14th Staffel = Y
Yellow	3rd Staffel = L	6th Staffel = P	9th Staffel = T	12th Staffel = W	15th Staffel = Z

aircraft failed to find the radio beam with their *X-Gerät* and finally dropped their 16 x 50kg bombs at 03:55. The target, however, was obscured by cloud. The 18 HE bombs which other crews of KGr100 dropped were not concentrated upon a given area. Between 24:00 and 01:30 some bombs fell on Castle Bromwich (including the aerodrome and factory) and on nearby Moss Gears Ltd at Chester Road, Tyburn, but the effect was of little consequence. Once more others fell in the vicinity of Erdington and Fort Dunlop, and also Acocks Green/Olton. Around Sutton Coldfield some HE bombs fell between 02:00 and 02:30. From the German point of view the raid was not successful.

That same night, like Fw Adalbert Knier, other Luftwaffe bomber crews were having trouble identifying their target and, inadvertently, dropped bombs on London – a target which, at that time, was off limits. This latter action can be said to have changed the course of history.[21]

The following night while the RAF was making its first raid on Berlin, 50 German bombers targeted Birmingham again. The raid was led by 15 Heinkels of KGr100 which were detailed to mark with incendiaries the large ammunition factory of ICI Ltd (Metals) known as the Kynoch Works at Witton. Thus, in the Witton and Aston areas, several factories were damaged; the Kynoch Works, Hughes Stubb Metal Company, Veritys Ltd, Perfecta Steel Tube Company and British Timken Ltd. At Perry Barr two other key factories, Ellison Insulations and Perry Barr Metal Co were damaged. At Erdington Birmingham Electric Furnaces Ltd was set alight by incendiaries.

Bombing was also highly concentrated causing much damage to the city centre. This would be for many 'Brummies' the start of 'The *Blitz*', although this term was not in use at that early

A Heinkel He 111H of KGr100 which came down on the beach at Hourtin near Bordeaux in mid-August 1940.
via Chris Goss

stage. The Market Hall was wrecked and there was much damage to the Bull Ring, Corporation Street and Newtown Row. Bombs also fell onto the LMS Railway at Marston Green, Shirley where houses were hit, Sutton Coldfield and Walsall. The ARP services reported 180 HE bombs, of which more than half were either of the delayed-action type or duds. This large raid started some 60 fires, of which 15 were serious; 25 people were killed, a figure which would have been higher save for the fact that it was a Sunday night and the city centre was relatively quiet.

On the night 26/27th there was no relief when, once more, bombs fell in the city centre and on the inner-city suburbs, in particular fire did considerable damage to railway infrastructure around Bordesley, the James Cycle factory in Greet and the foundry of George Jones Ltd in Lionel Street which was entirely gutted. The BSA Tools factory in Montgomery Street, Small Heath, sustained considerable damage with 750 machines being either destroyed or damaged

Heinkel He 111H 6N+EK belonging to 2 *Staffel* KGr100. Clearly visible are the three radio masts, part of the *X-Gerät* navigational equipment.
via Ken Wakefield

causing disruption to the production of Browning machine guns. Other affected areas included: Sparkbrook, Sparkhill, Balsall Heath, Moseley, Kings Heath, Solihull, Erdington, Fort Dunlop and Castle Bromwich. The raid was spread over a six-hour period and is known to have included 10 Heinkels of KGr100 which was again seeking out the Castle Bromwich aircraft factory. At least 270 HE bombs were recorded as being dropped in this attack, 60 of which did not explode.

The next night brought a minor attack just before midnight. Bombs fell principally in the Erdington/Castle Bromwich area, although one of the unexploded bombs was recorded at Kings Heath. Again, the proportion of unexploded bombs was high, being 18 of the 55 HE bombs logged by the city's defences. In addition to the five civilians killed, four soldiers died and a further nine were injured when a searchlight site was hit by a bomb.

On the 28/29th what was likely a single raider dropped bombs to the south of the city, inflicting minimal casualties and some residential damage in Kings Norton. The final raid of the month was on the night of the 31st when a bomb fell harmlessly in a field at Shirley and an unexploded bomb landed at Streetly.

By this point, Birmingham had been attacked on 12 nights with the north-east districts in particular receiving the attention of the Luftwaffe. These raids were painful for the people of Birmingham. Lives had been lost, casualties suffered and properties destroyed or damaged. The sirens had sounded on most nights; a number of these warnings turned out to be false alarms. First the warning, then the all-clear, followed by another warning – in a succession of alerts, as enemy aircraft approached the city at differing times, either singly or in small waves, bringing stress, confusion and disruption.

Other towns and cities were also receiving similar attention to that meted out to Birmingham. The Luftwaffe was building up experience in night bombing using the pathfinder (fire-raiser) unit KGr100 and quite likely KGr606. With the target suitably marked, other units would drop their loads of incendiaries and high explosive bombs. KG27, KG51 and KG55 were beginning to specialise in night attacks. Defence against the night bomber was largely ineffective. During August, RAF fighters managed 828 night sorties resulting in just three confirmed 'kills'. There were six Bristol Blenheim Mk.1F squadrons serving as night fighters at this time, plus a couple of experimental flights.[22] The anti-aircraft guns made optimistic claims for a further 16 enemy aircraft brought down during August.

Nevertheless, all of this was but a small part of what the enemy was about at that time. From early August through to mid-September, the emphasis was tactical rather than strategic. The Luftwaffe's objective was to cripple the RAF's ability to interfere with the proposed sea-invasion of England. This necessitated the destruction of RAF Fighter Command and also, but to a lesser extent, the aircraft-manufacturing industry. This plan was re-emphasised by Göring in a conference held on 19th August 1940:

'Regarding the continuation of the attacks on the enemy Air Force and aircraft industry, the following points will require more attention than hitherto, if our losses are to be kept down to the minimum, and the enemy Air Force swiftly and irrevocably destroyed.

'Until further notice, the main task of *Luftflotten* 2 and 3 will be to inflict the utmost damage possible on the enemy fighter forces. …We must succeed in seriously disrupting the material supplies of the enemy Air Force, by the destruction of the relatively small number of aircraft engine and aluminium plants.

'These attacks on the enemy aircraft industry are of particular importance, and should also be carried out by night. Should it, however, not be possible to locate an industrial target because of poor visibility or bad weather conditions, some other worthwhile target must be attacked… There can no longer be any restriction on the choice of targets. To myself I reserve only the right to order attacks on London and Liverpool…

'…To sum up: we have reached the decisive period of the air war against England. The vital task is to turn all means at our disposal to the defeat of the enemy Air Force. Our first aim is the destruction of the enemy's fighters. If they no longer take the air, we shall attack them on the ground, or force them into battle by directing bomber attacks against targets within the range of our fighters. At the same time, and on a growing scale, we must continue our activities against the ground organisation of the enemy bomber units. Surprise attacks on the enemy aircraft industry must be made by day and by night. Once the enemy Air Force has been annihilated, our attacks will be directed as ordered against other vital targets.'

REICHSMARSCHALL HERMANN GÖRING
Karinhall, August 19, 1940

For three and a half weeks the Luftwaffe went about this task by attacking airfields and radar stations and enticing the defending Hurricanes and Spitfires into the air, where they might be destroyed in combat.

Opposite page:

A *Kette* (three aircraft element) of Heinkel He 111Hs belonging to KGr100 over the North Sea. EN-Archive

The raid of 25/26th August 1940 saw substantial damage to the Bull Ring's Market Hall. Ray Greyo collection

This page:

Reichsmarschall Hermann Göring was head of the Luftwaffe, having himself been a fighter pilot during the First World War.

Note

22 These were: 23, 25, 29, 219, 600 and 604 Squadrons. A few aircraft had experimental Airborne Interception (AI) radar equipment (these were allocated to 25 and 604 Squadrons). The Fighter Interception Unit (FIU) and the Special Duties Flight (SDF) were also tasked with airborne radar development at this time.

THE BLITZ PHASE TWO
SEPTEMBER 1940-FEBRUARY 1941

The Rationale behind the Blitz

On 7th September the Germans switched tactics. No longer were airfields the target. Instead, a massive day and night offensive against London commenced. Why this shift in policy?

Reichsmarschall Hermann Göring, fed by faulty intelligence (which confirmed what he wanted to hear), believed that RAF Fighter Command was on its knees. All that was needed were a few hammer blows against London – the city was as yet unmolested. These attacks, so went the theory, would force the RAF to expend its last reserves of fighters in order to protect the capital of the British Empire. Once in the air, the Hurricanes and Spitfires could be overwhelmed by superior numbers of Messerschmitts.

The fact was that the switch from attacking airfields brought relief to the hard pressed squadrons of Fighter Command's 11 Group which had, so far, borne the brunt of the air war over England. There was no such relief for the Luftwaffe. With London as the target, the single-engine Messerschmitt Bf 109 was at the limit of its endurance, restricting the time it could spend in actual combat. Furthermore, the proximity of Fighter Command's 12 Group, with its squadrons based in the Eastern Counties, meant that they could easily be brought into the battle; a battle which the Luftwaffe had to win if an invasion was to proceed. For the RAF's part, it was a battle for which a draw was as good as a win.

Fighter Command held its own and 10 days after the first dreadful day and night assault on London, Hitler postponed indefinitely *Operation Sea Lion*, the invasion of England.[23]

Once again, there was a shift in German policy. Heavy daylight bombing raids reduced noticeably, while night attacks on London continued and were extended to include other towns and cities throughout the country.

The reasons for the continued bombing campaign against Britain, and the switch from daytime to night operations, may be summed up as follows:

1. The Luftwaffe did not have the resources to continue heavy daylight attacks. Night operations would bring some relief to the Luftwaffe while continuing to bring pressure to bear on Britain.
2. The waging of economic war, defined as the bombing of industrial centres, infrastructure and political buildings, would adversely affect Britain's military capability and also drain the people's will to fight. Indiscriminate bombing of residential areas was not on the target schedule. The latter is academic, as it was surely known that workers' dwellings would suffer, being located, as they were, adjacent to factories.[24]
3. There was a spirit of vengeance. Nazi anger and frustration surfaced when the RAF, despite Göring's boast that no enemy aircraft would fly over the Reich, had, under the cover of darkness, bombed Berlin on the night of 25/26th August 1940. This significant, though largely ineffectual, raid by more than 80 Hampdens, Wellingtons and Whitleys of Bomber Command,[25] was by way of retaliation for bombs dropped on London the previous night, by a small number of Heinkel He 111s from KG1.[26] These German bombers were actually seeking to attack the Short's aircraft factory at Rochester and the oil refineries at Thames Haven, but had lost their way. They jettisoned their bombs as they made for home. Until this time, both the British and German governments had deliberately targeted only military, industrial and port facilities.[27] Prime Minister Churchill was keen to get the gloves off but did not wish to be the first to do so and thus incur the displeasure of the United States. The small raid on London gave him the excuse for bombing Berlin and other German cities, without being overly concerned if other than industrial targets were hit.[28] The fact of the matter was that the RAF had a hard job navigating its way to specific targets in Germany. The Luftwaffe had an easier time finding their British targets, flying as they did from northern France and using the sophisticated navigational aids at their disposal.

Following the raid on Berlin, Hitler delivered a belligerent speech at a rally held in the city's *Sportspalast* on 4th September. He shouted, 'When they declare that they will attack our cities then we will wipe out their cities.'[29] The consequence of Hitler's declaration was the campaign dubbed by the British as 'The *Blitz*'. It commenced on 7th September, when the Luftwaffe turned its attention away from striking at the RAF's fighter airfields and began its campaign against London in particular, but also other towns and cities throughout Britain.

Another RAF raid which would stoke the fires of Nazi wrath occurred on the evening of 8th November. An attack by Bomber Command on railway yards at Munich was so timed as to disrupt the Nazis' 17th anniversary rally of the Munich *Putsch*. The event was delayed; an acute embarrassment for the Nazi party which left Hitler furious. It is widely believed that the severity of the raid on Coventry six nights later was, in part, retaliation for the Nazis' felt humiliation.

Before leaving this aspect of vengeance, it should be said that, over the summer of 1940, the German civilian population was increasingly wanting to hear of attacks on

Notes

23 On 12th October, Hitler postponed the invasion until the following spring and then, in January 1941, ruled that all preparation be stopped.

24 The practice of indiscriminate 'area-bombing' was introduced by the RAF in 1942. The United States 8th Air Force did not adopt such a policy when attacking targets in Germany. Later, the German V1 and V2 weapons used against England were, by their very nature, indiscriminate.

25 Squadrons involved included 5, 58, 64, 78, 99, 144 and 149. Targets allocated included two Siemens aircraft factories, Berlin-Tempelhof aerodrome and an electricity power station, none of which sustained any notable damage.

26 As to the number of aircraft involved, sources differ. Basil Liddell Hart quotes as many as 10.

27 Hitler had prohibited air attacks on London. Following this incident, Göring was angry, demanding: 'It is to be reported forthwith which crews dropped bombs in the London prohibited zone. The Supreme Commander reserves to himself the personal punishment of the commanders concerned by remustering them to the infantry.'

British towns and cities. They wished for reprisals in response to RAF raids which, since May 1940, had been flown against the North Sea ports and the Ruhr. The Germans perceived these bombing attacks to be indiscriminate or 'terror' raids. This is understandable because, due to poor aiming, the RAF bombing was so scattered and widespread that it appeared to have no obvious strategic value other than creating fear and tension.

4. It was hoped that intense and prolonged attacks on England's capital and lesser raids on other towns and cities, might break civilian morale, forcing the British Government to seek a peace settlement rather than face anarchy. This was not implausible; the disastrous raid on Coventry 14/15th November 1940 brought the population and local authorities near to collapse. The British Government and its advisers were both surprised and relieved that the enemy did not capitalise on its success by returning to Coventry in force the following night and, perhaps, even a third.[30] If they had, and the treatment was replicated on other industrial cities, then to what extent could the resilience of people belonging to a democratic nation be stretched? At this stage in the war, no one knew.

The Pressure Builds: September-October
While London would receive unprecedented air raids by both day and night, September was relatively quiet for the people of Birmingham. Around midnight on the night of 2/3rd September, what was by now considered a minor raid occurred. Bombs fell at Acocks Green, Bordesley Green, Yardley, Erdington, Walmley and Pype Hayes. At Pype Hayes a shelter received a direct hit killing two people and injuring five. Damage

was done to factories and residential areas. While 15 HE bombs exploded, a further 28 did not. One of the latter fell near the Dunlop factory, later exploding and destroying the company's telephone communications. Another delayed-action bomb incident, which illustrates the disruptive nature of these weapons, occurred when a bomb exploded five days later, during which time it had been necessary to evacuate residents in a 200-yards radius and provide alternative accommodation.

On the evening of the 12th, a nuisance raid saw bombs fall near the LMS railway in Sutton Coldfield and elsewhere on houses, including some in Hall Green. Two nights later, the alert sounded at 19:10 and a few HE bombs fell in Solihull and Tanworth-in-Arden, with the all-clear at 23:55. A similar raid took place on the evening of the 16th, this time affecting Shirley, Yardley Wood, Kings Heath and Edgbaston. On this occasion, the gusty conditions meant that some barrage balloons cut loose, the balloons and trailing cables causing damage to properties.

The afternoon of 27th September was overcast and the clouds hung low. It was Friday teatime and the last thing the people around the city were expecting was a German air attack. At 17:36 an aircraft – identified locally as a Junkers Ju 88 – dropped out of the cloud and deposited an HE bomb, apparently meant for either the Castle Bromwich aero factory or Fort Dunlop. The aircraft returned to the safety of the cloud and was gone. The local sirens sounded a couple of minutes later. In the event the bomb missed its target. The manner in which the aircraft had descended out of the low cloud base in the immediate vicinity of the target (whether that be the Castle Bromwich aero factory or Fort Dunlop) would suggest that the crew were using *Knickebein* for navigation. The all-clear went at 18:00 and the brief attack was over.[31]

Notes

28 In the First World War, Germany had made numerous air attacks upon the British mainland. In the final year of the conflict, Major General Hugh Trenchard, who was in command of the newly-formed RAF, planned to use his new bomber force to attack industrial and transport targets in Germany. In September 1918, Sir William Weir, President of the Air Council, wrote to Trenchard: 'If I were you, I would not be too exacting as regards accuracy in bombing railway stations in the middle of towns. The German is susceptible to bloodiness and I would not mind a few accidents due to inaccuracy.'

29 In 1942, using more measured tones, AOC-in-C Bomber Command, Arthur (Bomber) Harris said something similar, 'They have sown the wind, now they will reap the whirlwind.' Following German air attacks over Britain, there was a general call for retaliation.

30 It is true that a smaller raid was made on Coventry the following night, involving 16 He 111s of KG53 (only 8 are believed to have found the city). One of these aircraft broke up in mid-air due to icing and crashed near Much Wenlock, Shropshire. Two of the four crew survived.

31 It is likely that this is the incident which is related in Alex Henshaw's book *Sigh for a Merlin* (Hamlyn Paperbacks, London, 1980) pp 68-69.

A Dornier Do 17Z of KG76 flying over Guernsey in September 1940. ww2.com

32 KGr100 operated this variant for just two weeks. Height and speed had to be sacrificed to carry the larger bombs and as the unit's primary role was fire marking, the H-5s were not retained.

Some time after 20:00 another low-flying raider dropped half a dozen HE bombs on Kings Heath and Edgbaston. In Kings Heath residential properties were destroyed or damaged and seven people killed and six others severely injured.

These had been audacious penetrations for, as it would seem, solitary Luftwaffe aircraft. These 'hit and run' raids, known by the Germans as *'Piratenfluge'* (pirate operation), were encouraged by Göring as noted here in a further extract from his 19th August conference: '…attacks on aircraft factories must be carried out under cover of weather conditions permitting surprise raids made by solitary aircraft. Such operations demand the most meticulous preparation, but can achieve very satisfactory results.'

During September, 16 people had been killed as a result of air raids on Birmingham as compared to 87 in the previous month. With many raids now directed against London, eight of Birmingham's mobile 3.7 inch heavy anti-aircraft guns were transferred to the capital, the loss being offset by a single static 3.7 inch gun.

From mid-October, raids on Birmingham increased in their intensity.

On the night of the 15/16th the Luftwaffe's main effort was a devastating raid on London, although 20 Heinkels of KGr100 attacked Birmingham. Four of these aircraft were examples of a new variant, the He 111H-5, which had external bomb racks to allow 500kg bombs to be carried.[32] On this night four such bombs were

A War of Attrition

During August and early September 1940, for the first time, the Luftwaffe met its match when faced with the RAF over southern England. The latter had the advantage of playing at home. British fighter pilots did not have to keep an anxious eye on their fuel gauge, as did the Messerschmitt Bf 109 pilots, who also had to face a sea crossing before they could feel safe. If an RAF pilot baled out and wasn't too badly injured, he could fight another day but, for a German baling out…? 'For you the war is over' and

he would find himself in a prisoner of war camp. German bomber crews, in particular, felt vulnerable in their lightly armed and relatively slow machines.

Just as tiredness and stress affected the 'few' (as Churchill dubbed the young RAF fighter pilots), so Luftwaffe aircrew and fighter pilots were similarly affected. A case of *kanalkrankheit* afflicted many a bomber crew member. Later, when roles were reversed, RAF Bomber Command would label its own sufferers as LMF (Lack of Moral Fibre).

In the war of attrition, the RAF was being provided with an ample number of Hurricanes and Spitfires; the main concern was keeping up a supply of pilots to fly them. On the other side, Luftwaffe statistics show that its own losses of aircraft and flying personnel, together with the casualties, which it had suffered since the invasion of France in May 1940, were not sustainable.

Quoting from the biography of Adolf Galland: 'Luftwaffe fighter losses in September had been a disaster. They started the month with a base of 735 pilots available for the 740 operational Bf 109s on strength; by the end of the month they had lost 229 men, a staggering 31%. The monthly attrition rate had now reached 23.1%, up from 15% during August and 11% in July. More aircraft were being lost than could be immediately replaced from reserve, and too few pilots coming through the training schools.

'The wear and tear on aircraft and equipment had been equally bad. Losses during the months of July, August and September for the Luftwaffe as a whole totalled 1,636 aircraft, or 37% of the initial strength three months earlier. Of those, 518 were Bf 109s, a staggering 47%; when the 185 Bf 109s damaged in the same period were included the total reached 64% of initial strength. The total number of aircraft lost since Germany attacked in the West on 10 May had reached 3,064, or 57% of initial strength; the total for Bf 109s had reached 775, also 57%. As telling was the availability figure, which by the end of September had dropped to 68% for the fighters and 52% for the bombers.'[33]

In respect of bomber losses the following is in accordance with German Air Ministry figures: Between mid-July and the end of September Luftwaffe bombers had suffered a 69% casualty rate during daylight raids. This total comprised 621 aircraft destroyed and 334 damaged. When this number is added to the 724 bombers destroyed or damaged during May and June, the rate of attrition suffered by aircrews is obvious.

A Dornier Do 17 of KG2 following its forced landing in November 1940.

This Heinkel He 111H-3 1G+BL of 3/KG27 came to grief in a French field in 1940. EN-Archive

Note 33 Quoted from *Adolf Galland: The Authorised Biography* by David Baker.

dropped on Birmingham. At 20:40 hours a low-flying aircraft, risking the balloons, dropped incendiaries. More incendiaries and HE followed over the next six hours or so. The bright moonlight aided the attackers; one German pilot operating over England that night commented, 'The night was so light that, from our altitude of only 3,500 metres, we could see every detail on the ground.'

The city centre was again hit as well as houses and factories. Of the factories, Fisher & Ludlow in Rea Street was hit by HE and incendiaries at 23:41 hours. Of the former, one was a delayed-action type which exploded at 18:00 the next day. Of less impact was the damage done to the Deritend Stamping Co, Chamberlain & Hookham Ltd (a GEC company) in New Bartholomew Street, and Diamond Screw and Cotter Ltd in Bordesley Green. The most serious fire was at the Curzon Street goods yard.

Casualties were high, with 59 killed and 43 seriously injured. It was after four o'clock in the morning before the all-clear was given. The last of the German crews to depart the target area later reported seeing two very large fires to the north of the city and a medium one to the south.

Further enemy attacks occurred for the next three nights, maintaining the pressure upon the civilian population and civil defences. On the night of the 16th, although no significant damage was recorded, about two dozen HE bombs plus additional incendiaries were dropped on the city centre, notably New Street station where No.5 signal box was destroyed. In the Witton district the factories of Hardy Spicer and GEC were slightly damaged. Utilities and residential properties were also hit. Casualties included eight fatalities and fourteen seriously injured.

Between 20:00 and 23:00 on the 17th the scale of the attack increased, with raiders dropping around 100 HE bombs as well as the usual incendiaries. As a result there was an increase in casualties, with 17 people killed and 14 seriously injured. Sixty houses were destroyed. Many key points were affected but escaped with only slight damage. These included: BSA Guns in Armoury Road, Small Heath, BSA Tools and Bakelite in Tyseley, MCCW in Saltley and Birmetals in Woodgate. The enemy aircraft had tracked from approximately the south-west to the north-east of the city.

On the 18th it was districts to the north and east of the city which were affected, when 14 Heinkels of KGr100 visited between 20:00 and 21:00 hours, with Windsor Street Gas Works at Nechells being the principal target.[34] Returning aircrews reported three especially large fires to the north of the city remaining visible at a great distance away. On the LMS (London Midland & Scottish) Railway, the Curzon Street goods yard was the site of a big fire. The nearby GWR (Great

Western Railway) was bombed at Small Heath station and also the shed at Bordesley Junction. The Aston and Witton districts in particular suffered. Two timber yards at Aston were set ablaze and two nearby paper works and a bakery sustained damage. The roof of ICI (Kynoch Works) at Witton likewise was damaged. The Veritys factory in Aston was subjected to a serious fire which was under control by midnight and nearby Lucas Ltd (Powell & Hanmer) sustained roof damage. Delta Metal in Dartmouth

As well as Dornier Do 17s, KG76 also operated the superior Junkers Ju 88 as illustrated here by F1+JR. EN-Archive

Many factories were located in Witton, amongst them Hardy Spicer which suffered its first damage (albeit slight) due to bombing on the 16th October 1940. This wartime advert would have been drafted the following year.

Note

34 Birmingham Corporation operated five gas works: Adderley Street, Windsor Street, Nechells, Saltley and Swan Village. The last of these was actually in West Bromwich and the only one to remain unscathed during the Blitz.

35 These incendiaries were carried in groups of 36 which were contained in a canister known as a BSK 36. The canister was fitted with a mechanism designed to make it come apart shortly after release from the aircraft, allowing the individual 1kg incendiaries to spread as they fell.

36 These casualty figures are according to police records of the time. More recent accounts lower the total fatality figure to 25, which seems extremely doubtful.

A bomb crater in Bull Street, Birmingham gives cause for curiosity following one of the October 1940 raids. D Harvey collection

Street was seriously damaged and William McGeoch on the Coventry Road, which produced wireless and electrical equipment for both the Air Ministry and Admiralty, was hit by incendiary bombs. Altogether some 200 fires were reported, affecting industrial, commercial and residential properties.

There was respite on the 19th, but the 20th/21st saw a protracted alert lasting from 20:53 to 05:50 hours during which, at 22:25 hours, the Erdington House Hospital was hit by two HE bombs, killing three people, seriously injuring two and a further 32 were slightly injured. At the time the institution was accommodating evacuees from London, but it is not reported whether any of these were amongst the casualties. No notable damage was done elsewhere in the city, although a single HE bomb was reported at Yardley Wood.

The next night incendiaries and two HE bombs were dropped at Aston and at Cannon Hill, and there was a further pair of HE dropped elsewhere, one of which did not explode. Damage was negligible. The following night (the 22nd) Coventry was the main target, though a number of bombs and incendiaries were scattered across Birmingham, starting several fires. Areas affected were: Harborne, Winson Green, Yardley and Yardley Wood. The 23rd was another night of respite; it was the calm before the storm.

On the evening of the 24th the alert lasted from 19:46 to 23:13 hours, with most bombs dropping in an intensive 30-minute period, as 10 Heinkels of KGr100 went about their work. The 2,304 1kg incendiaries dropped[35] caused great damage to the city centre. Among the buildings affected by high explosive and/or incendiaries were: the Marshall and Snelgrove, C & A Modes and Grey's department stores, the Town Hall, Council House, University, Bank of England, Midland Hotel, New Street station, and the Hippodrome and Empire theatres. These last-mentioned theatres, together with Tony's Ballroom, were the site of the night's one 'major'

fire. The Empire was completely burnt down and the Hippodrome would not re-open until the following February. By the early hours there were scores of large fires, four of which were termed 'serious'. The local fire services employed 371 appliances and another 84 were drafted in from the East Midlands and Reading, before the fires were brought under control. The suburbs were also affected. A tragic incident occurred when a public shelter in Cox Street, Hockley received a direct hit. More than 20 residents of Cox Street and nearby Livery Street were killed in this incident.

As the Blitz on Britain developed and provincial towns and cities came under attack, an oft-repeated tactic was to hit the same target with a sizeable force on two consecutive nights. This happened to Birmingham in the last week of October 1940, when the Luftwaffe returned on the night of the 25th. Twelve Heinkels of KGr100 marked the target with incendiaries for the first hour, these devices dropping first in the Highgate district. The number of incendiaries deployed was 2,304, the same as the previous night.

The raid spanned 19:49-00:14, during which time 67 industrial premises located in and around the city centre were subject to fires, with some being burnt out entirely. Of the latter Brass Turned Parts Ltd's tool room in Highgate was destroyed, adversely affecting production at the company's nearby factory in Sherbourne Road, Balsall Heath. Deritend Stamping Company in Liverpool Street, Fisher & Ludlow in Rea Street, Digbeth, and Forward Radiator in Charles Henry Street, Balsall Heath, were each damaged by fire. Delta Metal in Dartmouth Street was hit by four HE bombs which did considerable damage. Factories which were slightly damaged included: Lucas in Shaftmoor Lane (while the nearby electricity sub-station was demolished); J. Lucas (Powell and Hanmer) in Aston; Britannia Tube Co in Glover Street and Ludlow Brothers in Fazeley Street. Once again Windsor Street gasworks was bombed. Much damage was caused to gas, electricity and water supplies. Commercial concerns and residential properties across the city were affected in the districts of: Highgate, Balsall Heath, Deritend, Duddeston, Nechells and Aston.

Police records of the time quote 75 fatalities and 50 others badly injured on this night.[36] A direct hit on the Carlton Cinema in Sparkbrook caused many casualties amongst the audience; 20 were killed and 20 were injured, 5 of them seriously. A further direct hit involved a fire tender and a corporation bus at the junction of Great Lister Street and Dartmouth Street, which killed five people including three Auxiliary Fire Service (AFS) men.

Oil bombs, which consisted of an explosive charge in a mixture of highly inflammable oil, were used on this night. A number of these large incendiary devices dropped harmlessly in Warley Woods, Smethwick.

On the evening of the 26th, the city suffered its worst attack to date, when 15 aircraft from KGr100 found the city centre once again. Between 20:03 and 23:31 hours they proceeded to unload HE bombs along with the same number of fire-marking incendiaries as they had on the previous two nights. The result was extensive fires, and extra pumps had to be sent from Nottingham and Manchester. Of the 300 fires, five were considered serious and one major; the last involved offices and commercial buildings. The city centre was again successfully pinpointed by German crews. A mixture of commercial establishments, churches, a college, hotels and Birmingham University were hit. New Street station was closed when an HE bomb exploded on number one platform. The Council House and nearby post office in Paradise Street were among a number of public buildings hit. At James Archdale Ltd, the foundry was destroyed and damage was sustained at Belliss and Morcom, both of Icknield Square, Ladywood. The factories of Stratton & Co in Bromsgrove Street and Bulpitt & Sons at Hockley were said to be gutted. Webley & Scott of Weaman Street, producers of the famous revolver but now also making oil sumps, suffered minor damage.

Besides the city centre, other districts affected included: Hockley, Ladywood, Perry Barr, Edgbaston, Bordesley, Highgate, Balsall Heath and Kingstanding. Devastation amongst houses, shops and small factories was widespread, many being burnt out or demolished. Casualties are believed to have been as bad, if not worse, than the night before. Others, about 400, suffered the trauma of being rendered homeless.

Dr R.V. Jones of Scientific Intelligence had, that afternoon, received decoded transcripts[37] from Bletchley Park.[38] These had enabled him to deduce that the target was Birmingham and what the precise line of attack would be, as the Heinkels flew along the X-beam. Following the raid an assessment of the bomb pattern was made to check the accuracy of KGr100's effort. Dr Jones found that the main line of bombs, which ran along a north to south axis, was about 150 yards to the east of the aiming point. If, as seems likely, the raid was carried out by just the 15 aircraft from KGr100, then the amount of destruction done to the target area was relatively high and, from the German point of view, must be considered a success.

The 27th saw a nuisance attack. The alert lasted between 20:03 and 02:18 during which time there was some damage to residential property in Handsworth. The next night the bombers were back in force, dropping mainly incendiaries over many areas from 20:00 to 23:00

hours. Around 300 incidents were reported. A number of factories were hit, that of Barker and Allen Ltd (engaged in non-ferrous metal work), Eyre Street, Hockley, sustained considerable damage. Much damage was done to shops and houses but most serious were the fires at New Street station. Here, and elsewhere in the city centre, a shortage of water hindered their extinguishing. The city centre appeared to be the principal target area, though other areas which suffered were: Handsworth, Perry Barr, Aston, Stechford, Sparkhill, Kings Heath, Moseley and Harborne.

The ordeal continued on the 29th when incendiaries, HE bombs and a number of delayed-action bombs fell on Kings Heath, Moseley, New Oscott and Sutton Coldfield but it was the city centre areas that suffered most. The raid commenced at 22:50 and lasted for about 75 minutes. Of the 50 fires kindled three were deemed serious; all had been brought under control by 02:00. Railway property at the Curzon Street goods yard was damaged. Once more KGr100 with its fire-raising speciality had been at large on these past two nights.

A solitary aircraft, taking advantage of the cloudy conditions, attacked during the mid-afternoon of the 31st. The raider machine-gunned some houses in Castle Bromwich and slight damage was done to the Repairable

On 25th October 1940 an HE bomb fell in front of the screen of the Carlton Cinema at Sparkbrook. The devastation resulted in the death of 20 people and injured a similar number.

Notes

37 Such transcripts were codenamed *Ultra*.

38 This highly secret establishment in Buckinghamshire was known by the codename *Station X*.

AA guns in action during the night Blitz.

Equipment Depot. Bombs caused damage when they were dropped on the LMS sidings at Washwood Heath. In the early hours of the following morning the raiders returned and a small attack developed from 03:15, when at least 20 HE bombs were dropped. Four boats, together with their cargo, were sunk on the canal at Fazeley Street. In Digbeth an HE bomb demolished a building which fell onto a public shelter, causing some casualties. Fires were started and houses wrecked in the central area and Aston. The most serious fire of the night was at the factory of Dobson & Crowther Ltd in Aston. The all-clear sounded at 05:25.

The second half of October had been a testing time for the life of the city, its residents, workers and civil defence being as they were on the receiving end of 217 tons of high explosive and around 20,000 incendiaries. Morale might have been worse had the general public known to what extent the German bombers were having a free hand. During August and September, RAF fighters had held their own against the Luftwaffe's daylight attacks in the south, but at this

stage there was virtually no defence against the night bomber. A German bomber pilot participating in these night attacks commented, 'The raids were all quite routine, like running a bus service.'

The anti-aircraft guns made a lot of noise and encouraged the civil population in their shelters. The guns around Birmingham had far more success at bringing down barrage balloons than they did enemy machines. What was urgently needed was night fighter aircraft to engage the bombers. The need had been discussed at high-level during the preceding March, when the Deputy Chief of the Air Staff, Air Marshal Richard Peirse, foretold, 'At some stage our good defences will force the enemy to adopt night bombing.' Nevertheless, other war priorities came thick and fast, and progress in establishing a useful force of night fighters was lamentably slow.

As it became clear that the main German effort was invested in night attacks, military, scientific and political leaders began to convene frequently to see what could be done to combat the nocturnal enemy; first under the auspices of

In 1940 the mainstay of the RAF's night fighter force was the ineffective Bristol Blenheim. This example carries the markings of Wg Cdr the Hon J.W. Max Aitken when Commanding Officer of 68 Sqn in spring 1941.
Author's collection

the Night Interception Committee and then, from mid-October, under the banner Night Air Defence Committee chaired by the Prime Minister, Winston Churchill.

Fighter Command's Air Officer Commanding-in-Chief (AOC-in-C), Hugh Dowding, was increasingly challenged by his superiors. 'Why', they asked, 'aren't the Spitfires and Hurricanes aloft in the night skies, bringing down German bombers?' During September, night fighters had only accounted for four destroyed with a similar number the following month. The truth was that the twin-engined Blenheim was under-gunned and underpowered, being slower than some of its quarry. Dowding appreciated how almost impossible was the task to spot an enemy bomber in the dark over a blacked-out country while flying a single-engine aircraft; impossible, that is, on all but a moonlit night. His fighter pilots had little or no experience of night flying, an activity which could be most hazardous.

In a similar manner to when he had refused to dispatch additional fighter squadrons into what he considered a lost cause during the Battle of France, he now resisted pressure to commit day fighter squadrons into the night arena. Nonetheless, some of his own pilots disagreed. Max Aitken (son of Lord Beaverbrook, the then head of the Ministry of Aircraft Production), was a successful fighter pilot; he reckoned that Hurricanes could operate in a night fighting role. No doubt his views were expressed and made known to those who had influence. On 21st October the Air Ministry ordered Dowding to release three squadrons of Hurricanes for night fighting duties.[39]

Dowding was becoming increasingly isolated. Those above him and some to the side of him pressed for action, even if it meant radical or ill-conceived and untried methods. This ran contrary to the AOC-in-C's methodical approach. He was convinced that the answer lay in twin-engine fighters (especially the Bristol Beaufighter which was just about entering service), equipped with Airborne Interception (AI) radar; so equipped, these aircraft would work together with Ground Control Interception (GCI) stations. This method of interception relied upon ground controllers directing a fighter to the vicinity of an enemy aircraft, whereupon the radar operator in the fighter picked up the contact on his cathode tubes and guided the pilot to within a few hundred yards of the hostile aircraft for a visual sighting. During the preceding months, trials had been conducted, with mixed results. Now, with the fast and heavily-armed Beaufighter and the improved AI MkIV apparatus on the way, Dowding had little time for half-baked schemes. The trouble was that the new aircraft and radar were not being delivered quickly enough. The German night offensive had come three or four months too soon …

Target 52 *Bild:* November-December [40]

A handful of Ju 88 and He 111 aircraft attacked the city on the first evening of November. The raid was considered minor, with some bombs dropping in Perry Barr, Kingstanding, Aston and Sutton Coldfield. About a dozen houses were destroyed, others damaged and one factory seriously damaged. Eight people were killed.

A rare victory was credited to the ground defences when a Ju 88A (w/n 4145) L1+MB was brought down on its return flight. It belonged to *Stab* I/LG1[41] and at 21:35 hours it crashed at Storrington, Sussex. The pilot attempted a forced landing but hit trees and the aircraft was wrecked. Two of the crew died immediately and one soon afterwards. There was one survivor.

Three days later Kings Norton had a lunchtime visitor. At 13:50 a single aircraft flew low through the balloon barrage at 1,000 feet, dropping three bombs in the area, damaging some houses and two factories. Minutes earlier the same aircraft had bombed and machine-gunned Henley-in-Arden. In the evening four Heinkels from KGr100, using their *X-Gerät,* dropped their loads on Birmingham between the hours of 19:48 and 20:36. Areas affected were Edgbaston, Moseley and Yardley Wood, while the factory of City Castings and Metal Co in Digbeth was set on fire. The X-beam transmitting stations were now so adept at setting and re-setting their beams that KGr100 could mount two such directed attacks in succession on the same night. On this occasion it seems the beams were set for Birmingham and then Coventry. The same feat was repeated the following night when Coventry was attacked first and then Birmingham,[42] in a minor Guy Fawke's Night raid, involving a pair of Heinkels which dropped HE and oil bombs on Small Heath at 22:41, causing damage to houses and injuring 17 people. Raiders returned shortly after midnight. Factories and houses in the Ladywood and Five Ways area were hit, and casualties included a single fatality.

On the evening of the 6th, Dornier Do 17s of KGr606 dropped bombs on the city, inflicting damage mainly on residential properties. At around 21:25 a pair of houses was damaged in Bearwood. An hour and a half later HE bombs and one delayed-action bomb fell on Sutton Coldfield, damage being restricted to a few homes. Also on that evening at least one KGr100 machine set out for Birmingham, taking off from Vannes in Brittany at 20:00 hours and heading first for the Bristol Channel; from here the Heinkel turned north-east in order to find the X-beam. This it failed to do and to compound the crew's problems the aircraft's two compasses were giving erroneous readings. The experienced crew decided to abandon any further thoughts of Birmingham but instead to descend below the cloud with a view to bombing the port of Bristol. Low cloud and poor visibility

Notes

39 These were 87 Sqn (10 Group), 85 Sqn along with 422 Flight, which would later form the basis of 96 Sqn (11 Group) and 151 Sqn (12 Group).

40 German planners allocated codenames for different British towns and cities. Birmingham was *Bild* (picture) and Coventry *Korn*. Likewise, target numbers were given to hundreds of potential targets e.g. Austin aircraft factory was 7448 and the Castle Bromwich aircraft factory 7461.

41 This was a training and operational development unit, comparable with an RAF Operational Training Unit.

42 See *Most Secret War* by R.V. Jones.

Shortly after midnight on 9th November 1940 an Avro Anson, like the one illustrated, crashed onto the LMS railway at Stechford having struck a balloon cable. The aircraft was engaged in gathering intelligence regarding German radio beam transmissions.
Author's collection

This aerial view of the Austin factory was taken by the Germans on 5th September 1940, as a precursor to the daylight attack which took place on 13th November.

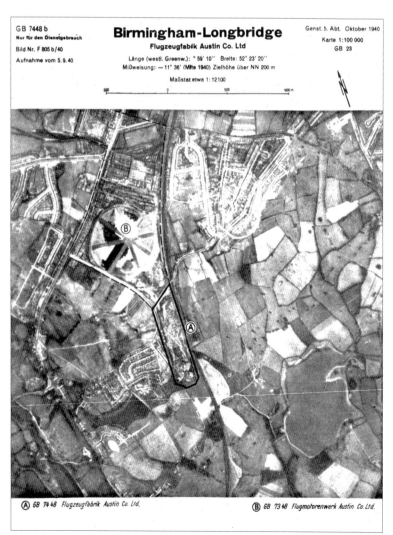

prevented this, and the crew, realising that they were lost, the pilot turned the aircraft south and headed for base. Not long afterwards, what the crew took to be a regular homing signal was picked up.

Disconcertingly, their home airfield was nowhere to be seen and spotting the sea below, they assumed that they had overshot and were over the Bay of Biscay. With fuel getting critically low they flew a reciprocal course. When a beach suitable for a forced landing was seen they elected to put down, believing it to be the French or Spanish coastline. They had been airborne for more than eight and a half hours.

The crew were thoroughly disorientated and had landed on the foreshore at Bridport, in Dorset. Three of the crew waded ashore but the fourth died in the landing. It is almost certain that RAF radio countermeasures, by operating a repeater transmitter in Somerset, had fooled the crew into believing they had heard their homing signal transmitted from St Malo. What they had taken to be the Bay of Biscay had, in fact, been the bay at Lyme Regis!

Having landed in shallow water, the Heinkel He 111 (w/n 6811) which bore the identity code 6N+BH, was salvaged in a rather ham-fisted fashion. This meant that the precious *X-Gerät* apparatus was all but ruined by sea water. However, some useful data was gathered and this confirmed previous assumptions held by the air intelligence staff.

Another minor raid took place on the 7th November which saw bombs exploding in Springfield and Greet. On the next night, a pair of KGr100 Heinkels attacked the city, using their *X-Gerät*. The beams had been reset following a single aircraft attack on Liverpool two hours earlier.[43] The first Heinkel dropped its bombs on Moseley and Balsall Heath at 21:47 and the second on Newtown Row, Aston and Perry Barr at 22:54. The Heinkels were not the only aircraft over the city that night. An Avro Anson with a five-man crew, which included a special wireless operator, was aloft also.[44] Their task was to gather information on German radio beam transmissions. Unfortunately, shortly after midnight, while flying over the Stechford area, the Anson struck a balloon cable and crashed onto the LMS railway track. All of the crew were killed.

On the following afternoon (9th), once again Kings Norton, together with nearby Cotteridge, was subjected to a daylight attack. A single Junkers Ju 88A from I/KG77 approached from the south-west. Shortly after 12:30 the raider dropped bombs and machine-gunned a number of streets in the area. It proceeded to its principal target, Elmdon aerodrome.[45] Here it dropped three or four bombs, inflicting minor damage on five aircraft, and then attacked two barrage balloons with machine-gun fire, damaging one.

Notes

43 The source regarding these double *X-Verfahren* attacks on 4/5th, 5/6th and 8/9th is R.V. Jones, in his autobiography *Most Secret War*.

44 The aircraft was from the Wireless Intelligence Development Unit. See page 137.

45 This grass airfield opened in May 1939 as Birmingham Airport. With the commencement of hostilities, all civilian flying was suspended and the airfield became the home of 14 Elementary Flying Training School which used dozens of de Havilland Tiger Moth training aircraft. The airfield would later increase in importance as aircraft built by Austin were test-flown from here.

46 Other German reconnaissance flights during 1940 are recorded as taking place on 14th July, 23rd September, 8th, 17th, 20th (shot down) and 27th November.

On the 9/10th Dornier Do 17s of KGr606 carried out a nuisance raid, most of the bombs falling outside the city boundary, namely at Solihull Lodge and Over Green (near Minworth). A small amount of enemy activity took place on the night of 10/11th, the usual mixture of incendiaries and HE causing damage to houses in West Bromwich. Some sources state that Birmingham was attacked by Heinkels of III/KG26 on the night of 12/13th, but this cannot be verified as no damage or casualties were reported locally.

Up until this point, unlike the aircraft factory at Castle Bromwich, the Austin aero works had escaped the attention of the Luftwaffe. German intelligence had the mistaken notion that the Austin factory was also producing Spitfires, and

a reconnaissance flight took place on 5th September and photographs were taken.[46] A plan of attack was drawn up on the 16th.

Shortly after 4 o'clock on the afternoon of 13th November, barrage balloon sites in the Longbridge area were alerted to the fact that enemy aircraft were approaching from the south. Orders were given for balloons to fly just below the cloud base. Within a couple of minutes the air raid warning sounded. Ten minutes later a solitary Heinkel He 111 of II/KG55 (w/n 2994 G1+GN?) was overhead with less than accurate anti-aircraft fire greeting it. The Heinkel turned to the west, circled and came in to attack. Over the next 10 minutes or so the Heinkel dropped at least 15 bombs, most of which fell in surrounding fields.

Above: **The daylight attack on the Austin factory was carried out by a single Heinkel He 111 of KG55. Shown here is He 111 (probably w/n 3354) G1+LT belonging to 9/KG55 which was to crash on take-off from its base at Villacoublay, near Paris, on 8th December 1940 killing its crew.** via Chris Goss

Left: **Nearing completion at Austin's Longbridge factory are these K2 ambulances which would give sterling service throughout many operational theatres.** British Motor Industry Heritage Trust

Hurricane V7118 UZ-V of 306 (Polish) Sqn seen at its Tern Hill base in March 1941. Three Hurricanes of 'A' Flight, yellow section, chased off the Heinkel He 111 which attacked the Austin factory in daylight.
via Wilhelm Ratuszynski

The electricians' shop at the Austin motor factory was hit, resulting in six fatalities and 25 injuries. The slight damage caused meant that the night-shift was cancelled for the following two nights. As for the important aero works at Cofton Hackett, only the water mains were damaged as three HE bombs missed their mark. A further three HE bombs fell in Northfield, completely blocking the main Birmingham-Bristol LMS railway track. 914 (barrage balloon) Sqn reported the Heinkel being chased off by three RAF fighters, which were in fact Hawker Hurricanes.

The Hurricanes belonged to the newly-operational 306 (Polish) Sqn, which had taken up residence the previous week at the Shropshire airfield of Tern Hill. Yellow Section had got airborne at 16:05 and was initially instructed to patrol the Coventry area. Within a few minutes the three pilots were given a series of new courses which led them to Birmingham. Anti-aircraft fire alerted them to the whereabouts of the Heinkel which was spotted about 1,000 feet below heading north-east. The Hurricanes prepared to make a head-on attack but the enemy aircraft, which had been flying at about 6,000 feet, executed a steep turn to the right and flew on a reciprocal course. With the fighters closing the gap, the bomber turned in a westerly direction making for the safety of the cloud below. The Section leader, Flt Lt Hugh Kennard, led his two Polish comrades into an astern attack, the Heinkel now down to about 4,500 feet. Closing in on the bomber at a distance of 250 yards, he let off a long burst from his eight Browning machine guns, and saw some of his bullets finding their mark. Next in was Plt Off Edward Jankowski, who also saw his bullets strike as he started firing from 350 yards. Last in was Plt Off Bohdan Bielkiewicz who commenced his attack by coming in on the Heinkel's starboard beam firing three short bursts from 300 yards, registering hits on the fuselage and port wing. Each pilot reported seeing the starboard propeller

slow down to tick-over speed and Bielkiewicz observed smoke issuing from that engine, while noting that the aircraft had decreased in speed. Bielkiewicz's own Hurricane V6950 coded UZ-T suffered some hits from the enemy's return fire. No further attacks were made as the Heinkel escaped into cloud. Kennard, aware of the proximity of the Malvern Hills, elected not to enter the cloud and broke off the engagement. The action had taken place at 16:40 over the Bromsgrove area and was witnessed by the residents below. Yellow Section arrived back at Tern Hill at 17:05. This had been 306 Sqn's first encounter with the enemy.

During the second week of November British Air Intelligence, using *Ultra* decrypts from the code-breakers at Bletchley Park, had become aware that the Germans were planning some major attacks on targets in the Midlands. These were to be carried out during the forthcoming full moon period. Birmingham, Coventry and Wolverhampton were considered the most likely targets, while London would invariably continue to receive the Luftwaffe's attention.

On 13th November all Luftwaffe bomber units of *Luftflotten* 2 and 3 received orders for two forthcoming operations. One was codenamed *Mondscheinsonate* (Moonlight Sonata), which was numbered Target 53 and referred to an attack on Coventry; the other, *Regenschirm* (Umbrella[47]) Target 52, an attack on Birmingham. As with the attacks on London, a strong force was to be used, requiring, as necessary, the cancellation of other previously-planned attacks.

The orders included the statement: 'In addition to destruction of industrial targets, it is important to hinder the carrying out of reconstruction works and the resumption of manufacturing, by wiping out the most densely populated workers' settlements.' The reference to 'workers settlements' is worthy of note. Whether the German planners made any distinction between the workers themselves and

Note

47 Apparently the umbrella was symbolic of Neville Chamberlain who, in turn, was associated with Birmingham.

German Navigational Radio Beam Systems

As early as June 1940, a young British scientist, Dr R.V. Jones of Air Ministry Scientific Intelligence, had confirmed his suspicions that the Germans were planning to employ a navigational aid utilising radio beams for Luftwaffe operations over Britain. The aid was to help aircrew flying in cloudy conditions when visual references were denied. Such poor conditions would often mean air operations had to be curtailed. However, if in poor visibility aircraft could manage to find their target, then this would offer protection from the enemy's defences. Of course, any system which could overcome cloudy days could also overcome dark nights, though the latter was a secondary consideration in the beginning.

The system, which had first come to the attention of Dr Jones, was known by the Germans as *Knickebein*. An aircraft simply flew along a directional radio beam (actually two slightly overlapping beams). When the aircraft was to the right of the beam, a series of audible dashes would be received in the aircraft and a series of dots if it was to the left. When flying in the centre of the beam (the desired heading), the dots and dashes merged to form an uninterrupted signal, known as the equi-signal. A second beam was transmitted from a different location to supply the cross-beam which, when the aircraft arrived at the intersection, informed the pilot that he was at a predetermined point. The big advantage of the system was that the equipment on board the aircraft, necessary to receive the radio beam signals, was the standard *Lorenz* blind-landing apparatus, simply upgraded to be more sensitive. Thus, any German bomber could potentially use *Knickebein*. The usefulness of the system progressively reduced as the British got to grips with it and introduced countermeasures. They gave *Knickebein* the codename *Headache*. Countermeasures, which interfered in various ways with the beams, were known as *Aspirin*.

Another system used concurrently with *Knickebein* was known as *X-Verfahren*. Once again there was a directional beam, this time using a much higher frequency. The width of the equi-signal was far narrower than that of *Knickebein* and, therefore, more accurate. With this system there were multiple cross-beams. The latter were fixed at known distances apart so that ground-speed could be accurately measured, as could the remaining distance to target. The calculation was made by the *X-Gerät*[48] apparatus carried in the bomber, which even released the bombs automatically at the proper moment. Use of this sophisticated apparatus was confined to the pathfinder, or target-marking, unit KGr100 whose crews were specially trained for their task. Once more the usefulness of *X-Verfahren* (known as *Ruffian* to the British) was susceptible to countermeasures (called *Bromide* in this instance). These countermeasures were delayed because the British were, until September 1940, under the

impression that *X-Gerät* and *Knickebein* was one and the same thing. In fact, KGr100 used their *X-Gerät* apparatus as early as mid-August 1940 when they attacked the Castle Bromwich aircraft factory. The first four *Bromide* transmitters were in place by 8th November; these were located at Hagley, Kidsgrove, Kenilworth and Birdlip. At first, the British believed that their countermeasures were effective because the Germans started to turn on their beams for limited periods of time only, and to switch frequencies while the bomber was on its way to the target. However, the true reason for this action was not to combat radio countermeasures but rather to throw off RAF night fighters which the Luftwaffe suspected were trailing bombers by flying along the X-beam themselves. In fact, the RAF had decided that there was little value in non-radar equipped night fighters using this approach. As it happened, the *Bromide* countermeasures were of no effect during most of 1940; the reason being that the modulation had been erroneously measured at 1,500 cps when, in fact, the *X-Verfahren* used 2,000 cps. Once this had been realised and corrected, countermeasures began to get the upper hand and the value of *X-Verfahren* progressively reduced, although this was not until the spring of 1941.

Lastly, there was *Y-Verfahren* (given the codename *Benito* by the British). This was a single radio beam which was transmitted by a ground station and picked up by the *Y-Gerät* apparatus in the bomber and automatically re-radiated back to the ground station. The time taken for re-radiated signals to return to the ground station enabled a German controller to gauge the exact range of the aircraft along a bearing determined by an auxiliary, direction-finding system. He was then able to direct the aircraft towards the target while making corrections for errors in navigation and/or due to meteorological conditions. The controller could then order the dropping of the bombs at the correct moment. Being reliant upon a ground controller meant that this system had the disadvantage that aircraft could only be directed singly. As a result, its use was confined to one unit, that of III/KG26, beginning in the late autumn of 1940. Air Intelligence was aware of the latest system when it was tested over England in October and November, but they lacked enough detail to put countermeasures (to be known as *Domino*) in place. Sufficient data was to hand by the following January. Unfortunately for the Germans, the radio frequency chosen for *Y-Verfahren* was the same as that for the redundant BBC Television transmitter at Alexandra Palace and so the ability to confuse Luftwaffe personnel was readily to hand. The use of countermeasures against *Y-Verfahren*, therefore, resulted in some heated exchanges between aircrews and their ground controllers! *Y-Verfahren* was advanced and very accurate. It was claimed that an aircraft flying at 20,000 feet could deliver bombs onto a target, such as a power station, at a range of 120 miles without the aircraft's crew ever seeing the ground. That said, *Y-Verfahren* was the easiest of the three systems to counter.

Perhaps, a little optimistically, Dr R.V. Jones reckoned that by February 1941 British countermeasures had the upper hand over all three systems. It was true that 'The Battle of the Beams' was as good as won, although final victory was still a few weeks away.

In November 1940 Heinkel He 111s of III/KG26 attacked Birmingham using a new radio beam navigational aid known as *Y-Verfahren*. Here, Major Viktor von Lossberg, Group Commander of III/KG26, is seen in his aircraft. Visible behind his head is the single *Y-Gerät* mast. via Chris Goss

Note 48 *Gerät* refers to the aircraft's onboard apparatus, while *Verfahren* refers to the radio direction system as a whole. The British were probably ignorant of the latter term in the early days and used the name *Gerät*, when *Verfahren* would have been more accurate.

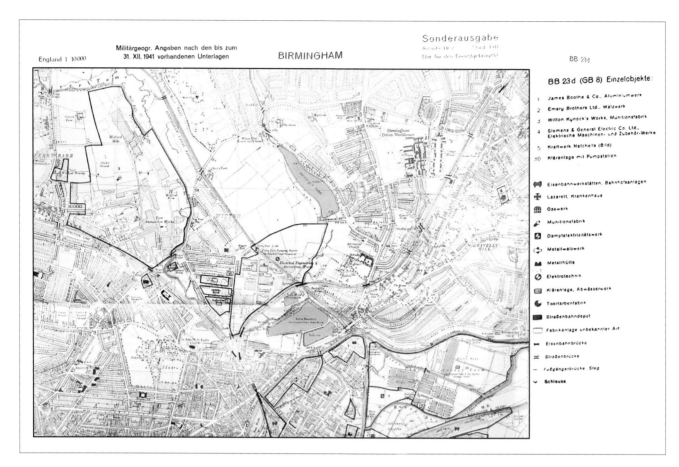

England 1 : 10 000

Militärgeogr. Angaben nach den bis zum
31. XII. 1941 vorhandenen Unterlagen

BIRMINGHAM

Sonderausgabe

BB 23d

BB 23d (GB 8) Einzelobjekte:

1   James Boothe & Co., Aluminiumwerk
2   Emery Brothers Ltd., Walzwerk
3   Witton Kynock's Works, Munitionsfabrik
4   Siemens & General Electric Co. Ltd., Elektrische Maschinen- und Zubehör-Werke
5   Kraftwerk Nefchells (Bild)
10   Kläranlage mit Pumpstation

  Eisenbahnwerkstätten, Bahnhofsanlagen
  Lazarett, Krankenhaus
  Gaswerk
  Munitionsfabrik
  Dampfelektrizitätswerk
  Metallwalzwerk
  Metallhütte
  Elektrotechnik
  Kläranlage, Abwässerwerk
  Teerfarbenfabrik
  Straßenbahndepot
  Fabrikanlage unbekannter Art
  Eisenbahnbrücke
  Straßenbrücke
  Fußgängerbrücke, Steg
  Schleuse

their dwellings is a moot point. However, the emphasis of the 1940-1941 Blitz as a whole was not 'terror' or indiscriminate bombing.

The devastating raid on Coventry, which was carried out on the night of 14/15th November, is a subject in its own right and falls outside the scope of this present volume. Doubtless many people in Birmingham would have seen the red glow in the sky to the east and heard bombs exploding and anti-aircraft gunfire. Firefighters were dispatched from Birmingham and other parts of the country to assist their harassed colleagues in Coventry. On this night Birmingham was also attacked and 12 people killed. The air raid warning was in force from around 19:10 through to 06:30 hours, during which time bombs fell on South Yardley, Stechford, Kings Heath, Castle Bromwich, West Bromwich and Walsall.

The following night both Coventry and Birmingham received a minor raid. The one on Birmingham saw a number of incendiaries dropped on Warley around 20:30 and others at Selly Oak and Edgbaston. Great Barr railway station was hit by HE.

Decrypts from Bletchley Park reported that a Ju 88 7A+LM of 4(F)/121 took off at 07:50 GMT on the 17th November to make a reconnaissance flight over Birmingham. Doubtless this was in preparation for the attacks which would be made during the following nights.

On the night of the 18/19th November, ten Heinkels set out to attack Birmingham, although one aborted en route. The attack was in two distinct phases. In the first, a number of incendiaries fell shortly before midnight. Districts affected by these were: Smethwick, Hockley, Aston, Lozells and Rotton Park. One incendiary ignited a gas-holder belonging to the Smethwick Corporation Gas Works in Rabone Lane. The holder had a capacity of 2.5 million cu ft and the resulting flame lit up the surrounding area. Two brave employees voluntarily climbed up and onto the top of the holder and, within the space of 40 minutes, were able to plug the hole, thus extinguishing the flame. A repair was completed within 12 hours and the holder was functioning normally a month later. The second phase commenced at 00:50 and lasted just under one hour. Another important factory damaged was the ICI (Kynoch Works) at Witton, while the GWR Birmingham-Paddington railway line was blocked at Bordesley by an HE bomb. The raid had left 15 dead and 9 seriously injured. Half of the Heinkels detailed for the operation belonged to III/KG26, while the others were from KG1. The appearance of III/KG26 over the city is of significance. This was the unit which had been selected to use the advanced radio beam navigational aid *Y-Verfahren*. The unit had used this new system the previous night when attempting to attack the gas works at Beckton, London.

III/KG26 would employ it again a few nights later against Birmingham. This mission of the 18/19th was something of a trial run.

The Germans considered an air attack to be a major one if more than 100 tonnes of high explosive were dropped on the target. So far, by the enemy's measure, Birmingham had escaped a major attack. This was about to change with the implementation of *Regenschirm* on the night of 19/20th November.

As with the Coventry attack five nights earlier, the Luftwaffe planned to bomb the whole of the city, although the north-east, north-west and southern districts were prioritised. Heinkel He 111, Junkers Ju 88 and Dornier Do 17 bombers made up the attack force, which was drawn from *Luftflotten* 2 and 3. During the course of the evening a total of 439 bombers took off from their bases on the continent, bound for Birmingham. Around a fifth of these failed to bomb their primary target of Birmingham; some aborted and others diverted to alternative targets. According to German statistics, this left a large force consisting of 357 aircraft to unload 403 tonnes of HE and nearly 30,000 incendiaries. Some German units, which were normally engaged in maritime mine-laying operations, were included in the raid, delivering 48 parachute 'land mines' (16 x 500kg and 32 x 1,000kg). These weapons had a fearsome reputation and rightly so. Descending by parachute meant that they were indiscriminate, as it was impossible to aim them with any degree of precision. As they did not bury themselves into the ground on impact, the blast effect could wipe out a small street. The attack also included the operational training unit LG1 with their Ju 88s.

The raid commenced with Heinkels of II/KG55 dropping flares to illuminate the target, following up with incendiaries. They kept this up for an

Opposite page:

A German map showing various factories in the Witton area.
via Nigel Parker

A formation of Heinkel He 111 bombers belonging to KG55.
EN-Archive

Below: **One KG55 crew which attacked Birmingham on a number of occasions was that of Oblt Johann Speck von Sternberg (back centre). Martin Reiser (back right), Fw Siegfried Rühle (front left) wearing his Luger holster and Ofw Rabenstein (front right) have been identified but not the airman to the left of Speck von Sternberg.**
via Martin Reiser

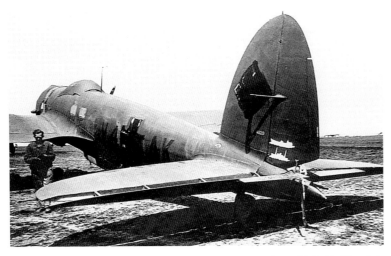

hour from 19:12 hours, using 13 bombers. Some of the first flares were released over Hockley.

A steady stream of enemy aircraft continued to arrive over the city. At this period in the campaign, German bomber crews flying against Birmingham had a round trip of about 3½-4 hours. By way of example, a Heinkel He 111P (G1+FT) of 9/KG55, commanded by Oblt Johann Speck von Sternberg,[49] took off from its base near Paris at 18:22 and landed at 22:00 (times BST).

With 425 fires being reported by the fire services, many German crews had a beacon visible from as far away as 45 miles, guiding them to their objective. The final all-clear did not sound until 04:30 next morning.

Casualties were very high, with about 420 killed and many seriously injured. Of the fatalities, 53 were workers sheltering behind a blast wall in the BSA factory in Small Heath. At West Bromwich the district hospital was hit and surrounded by fire, necessitating the evacuation of the patients. Jensen Motors saw its factory gutted by fire as was M B Wild & Co, while in neighbouring Wednesbury the buildings of Masters & Son were destroyed. With 54 people dead, this was the worst night of the war for West Bromwich/Wednesbury.

Incidents were widespread. For the first time, bombs falling on Shirley and Solihull resulted in deaths; nine civilians, two searchlight personnel and three members of a local barrage balloon crew. In Shirley a key point on the Cranmore Industrial Estate was affected, this being the factory of the Gear Grinding Co where blast

THE LUFTWAFFE OVER BRUM

damage occurred. The only Birmingham districts to escape bombs were: Northfield, Weoley Castle, Harborne, Selly Oak, Kings Norton, Kingstanding and the extreme east of Sheldon.

Thousands of houses, together with schools, churches, shops and other commercial premises, were either destroyed or badly damaged. The Windsor Street gasworks and the power station at Nechells, though hit, suffered lightly, unlike the railway installations in and around Birmingham, which were badly affected. The No.4 signal box at New Street station received a direct hit (at 22:34 hours) putting the station out of action. The LMS mainline was hit at five places within the local area and various suburban lines were blocked. The GWR faired little better, with the Paddington-Birkenhead mainline being affected at four points in the Birming-

ham area. At Snow Hill, the head offices, hotel and a ventilation shaft in the tunnel were all damaged.

Many factories were hit. Examples include: Ludlow Brothers in Great Barr Street, Chance Bros at Smethwick, Ham Baker & Co Ltd at Oldbury, Wilmot-Breeden at Hay Mills, GEC (Magnet Works) at Adderley Park, GEC and the ICI (Kynoch) factories at Witton, New Hudson Ltd at Hockley, Lucas (Formans Road) and Guest Keen & Nettlefolds (GKN) at Kings Norton were all hit with incendiary bombs. BSA Guns at Small Heath was hit at 20:25 and SU Carburettors of Adderley Park at 21:00 by HE. Also victim to HE bombs were Perry Barr Metal Co located in Handsworth where the damage was extensive, Motor Components (B'ham) Ltd at Bordesley Green, Rover's Tyseley factory, Dunlop at Erd-

Opposite page:
Luftwaffe bombers which regularly carried out night operations were roughly painted in night camouflage as seen on He 111H V4+AK of KG1. EN-Archive

A Ju 88 of KG51 departs from Orly, France bound for the Midlands in November 1940. ww2.com

Junkers Ju 88s of KG77. EN-Archive

This page, clockwise from top left: **John Bright Street and Hill Street showing the damage caused in one of the large November raids.** BirminghamLives

Tramcars and trolleybuses were vulnerable to air raids as wires and rails sustained damage. This trolleybus is a Leyland Titan, shown here at the Nechells terminus, Cuckoo Road in 1940. via Kidderminster Railway Museum

A pre-war picture of the GWR Snow Hill station. Ray Greyo collection

Note

49 Oblt Johann Speck von Sternberg was commander of 9 *Staffel* KG55. He flew on a number of Birmingham raids and died on 11th May 1941, when he was shot down at Earlswood.

The RAF's hopes for an efficient night fighter were vested in the Bristol Beaufighter but in the autumn of 1940 very few of this new type had reached operational squadrons.

John Cunningham was a successful night fighter pilot bringing down a Junkers Ju 88 on 19th November 1940, which was bound for Birmingham. Cunningham was to continue his flying career as a test pilot in the post-war period.

ington and nearby Bromford Tube Co. Morris Commercial Cars at Adderley Park received damage to buildings and plant.

One of the landmines floated down onto Colmore Row, blasting the Prudential buildings and damaging Boots, The Great Western Arcade, Greys in Bull Street and The Bank of England in Temple Street. A further landmine struck in St Georges Street and devastated the depot which housed the large fleet of vans and cars belonging to the Birmingham Mail. In Broad Street the BBC studios were hit, badly damaging the transmitter. Fractures to 150 gas and 58 water mains were reported.

Just as the German planners intended, the fires were widespread and many had to be left unattended. The city's fire services were overwhelmed. The way in which the firefighting was handled came in for criticism, from both within the service and without. The lack of integration in respect of the regular fire service and the Auxiliary Fire Service was highlighted and the night in question revealed a distinct lack of leadership. Two days later the Chief Fire Officer resigned and his replacement was appointed directly by the Home Office.

As ever German losses were negligible. One Heinkel He 111H (w/n 2768) 6N+JJ[50] of KGr100,

having left its base at Vannes, suffered an engine fire and crashed near Guernsey at 19:45, killing the four crew members. Birmingham's anti-aircraft guns inflicted damage on Heinkel He 111P (w/n 2877) G1+KL of I/KG55, which crashed near Nuneaton at 21:05. Two of the four crew were killed and the others taken prisoner. One would-be Birmingham raider was Heinkel He 111H (w/n 3539) 1H+AH of I/KG26.[51] The anti-aircraft guns in the London area hit the aircraft then it fell foul of balloon cables, tearing off the starboard wing. It crashed at 00:19 on the marshes at Barking in Essex. Of the five crew three were officers, one of whom was on an air experience flight.

One Birmingham-bound bomber that night is worthy of special attention, as its demise is something of a milestone in military aviation history. The Junkers Ju 88A-5 (w/n 2189) B3+YL of 3/KG54 was flying over the southern Cotswolds when it had the misfortune to show up as a 'blip' on the cathode ray tubes in one of the RAF's brand-new Bristol Beaufighters. The crew of the night fighter were future ace and later test pilot Flt Lt John Cunningham and his radar operator Sgt J.R. Phillipson. For the first time an operational squadron aircraft was to destroy its quarry as a direct consequence of locating it with the aid of Airborne Interception (AI) radar.[52]

The RAF crew had taken off from their 604 Sqn base at Middle Wallop in Hampshire at 22:21, using the call sign 'Blazer 24'. Patrolling their allocated area at 12,000 feet, Cunningham saw a smoke trail indicating an aircraft travelling south to north. While attempting to investigate, he spotted another aircraft with navigation lights on and turned to follow, but he lost it in cloud. Soon afterwards he saw a number of navigation lights which turned out to be three twin-engine aircraft. He gave his attention to the leader, but switched to the left-hand machine because visually it showed up better. Again the enemy escaped into cloud. Undaunted, the crew requested instructions from their ground controller (call sign 'Harlequin') and were told to return to their original patrol line. Shortly afterwards the controller advised that there was an aircraft 10 miles to the east. Four bombers had already eluded the RAF crew and continued on their way to bomb Birmingham. Heading eastwards and pointing the Beaufighter towards some searchlight activity, the pilot spotted more navigation lights and turned to investigate. They were now at 15,000-16,000 feet. At this point Phillipson reported a contact on his radar showing an aircraft travelling south to north.

Phillipson had a little difficulty directing his pilot onto the enemy, as his microphone was freezing up! He managed to sort out the problem and guide his pilot. Cunningham recounted, 'On instructions from the operator, I climbed and was told to increase speed and after various

THE LUFTWAFFE OVER BRUM

alterations I came through top of cloud and almost immediately sighted exhaust flames about 1,000 feet above me.'

However, the bomber was not following a straight course and Cunningham's Beaufighter, being at a lower level, could not keep track. Phillipson still had the blip on his radar and directed his pilot accordingly. Cunningham's report continues, '… on instructions from the operator, I was brought astern of the target again and I then came up very slowly behind… to very near the same level and into about 200 yards astern, and then was flying at about the same speed as enemy aircraft and opened fire.' Cunningham had fired his guns for six or seven seconds, at a distance of 200 yards, and expended 190 rounds of ammunition.

The deadly projectiles found their mark in what was later to be identified as a Ju 88, fatally wounding the bomb-aimer Unteroffizier (Uffz) Heinrich Liebermann. The gunner Flieger (Fl) Peter May responded by firing in the direction of the Beaufighter, but it was gone just as quickly as it had appeared. The starboard engine was starting to glow. Continuing to Birmingham was out of the question and so the pilot (Uffz Kaspar Sondermeier) ordered that the bomb load, which was carried both on external racks and within the bomb bay, be jettisoned. He feathered the propeller of the crippled engine and turned south for home. The aircraft was losing height and, when 6,000 feet had slipped off the altimeter, the pilot attempted to restart the starboard engine which caused it to burst into flames. With the English Channel looming up ahead, the pilot ordered his two uninjured crew to bale out. He did likewise, leaving the now dead bomb-aimer to go down with the aircraft. Along with the wireless operator Gefreiter (Gefr) George Suess the pilot descended safely and both were taken prisoner. The gunner dropped into the sea and was drowned, his body being washed ashore a few days later. As for the Ju 88, it buried itself into farmland at East Wittering near Chichester.

It was one minute to midnight when Cunningham put his Beaufighter (R2098) down onto the grass runway at Middle Wallop. He probably had mixed feelings about the night's patrol. He had caught sight of a number of enemy machines, but was returning to base with nothing more than a claim for one aircraft 'damaged'. So brief and indistinct had this encounter been that he reported attacking a four-engine aircraft, probably a Focke-Wulf Fw 200 Condor. It was only when intelligence officers had gathered reports of other claims, crashes and prisoners taken, that his initial combat report was amended to reflect what had happened: 'One Ju 88 confirmed as destroyed.'

The following morning, although there was low cloud and poor visibility, a Junkers Ju 88A-5 (w/n 0458), 7A+FL belonging to the reconnaissance unit 3(F)/121, took off from its base at Dinard. It flew to Coventry, Birmingham and Bristol, to obtain photographic evidence of the recent attacks. The film was never processed because the Ju 88 was shot down by a Hurricane of 79 Sqn, piloted by Flt Lt G.D.L. Haysom, as it made its homeward trip across the Welsh mountains heading for the Irish Sea. It crashed in the water off Fishguard at 13:00 hours. None of the crew was found.

That evening, with the visibility much improved, the sirens wailed again in Birmingham at 19:30. Within minutes, fire-marking incendiaries were being dropped over the northeast of the city by the first of KGr100's Heinkels. The Gruppe's contingent of 11 aircraft kept their fire-lighting activity going for an hour and a quarter, using 7,488 incendiaries. As they approached, crews could see three fires still burning from the previous night's attack.

Fires in the north-eastern districts (one being a rubber dump at Ward End) started to take hold and soon linked up. German crews with their bird's-eye view estimated a mass of fire nearly four miles square. They noted three other conflagrations to the south-west.

Around midnight, cloud moved in from the west and by 01:00 the bombers were releasing their ordnance without visual reference to the ground, relying upon dead-reckoning navigation or Knickebein radio beams. These adverse conditions may account for bombs falling on residential properties in Willenhall (to the north west of Birmingham) killing 11 people.

According to German sources a total of 116 Heinkels, Junkers and a few Dorniers delivered their destructive cargo which amounted to 132 tonnes of HE (including parachute mines and oil bombs) and 9,472 incendiaries. Factories known to have been affected include: the Castle Bromwich aircraft factory where a fire broke out, Perry & Co at Tyseley, the new factory of James Booth & Co at Kitts Green, Wilmot-Breeden at Hay Mills where production was interrupted because of delayed-action bombs, Joseph Lucas (Formans Road) where a fire developed and delayed-action bombs caused disruption, Joseph Lucas (Bendix), Kings Road, Tyseley and Clifford Aero & Auto of Sparkhill which incurred damage that would see production halved for a few days.

Again, the blasting effect of parachute mines was witnessed when the Bakelite factory at Tyseley was badly damaged. Nearby Reynolds Tube was another factory to fall victim to a landmine which caused production to temporarily grind to a halt. In similar fashion, Wolseley Works at Witton was damaged and in Queens Road, Aston, a mine caused devastation. Similarly-named Queen Street in Highgate was hit by HE damaging house property, overturning a

Notes

50 The second 'J' in this code is something of an anomaly as this letter was not used when identifying a *Staffel*, but this is definitely as recorded in the German Quartermaster returns.

51 On the same night, this unit lost two other Heinkels in crashes near their home base of Beauvais.

52 Cunningham's victory was certainly the first occasion that a regular crew, on a normal operational squadron, had downed an enemy aircraft using airborne radar. A Blenheim Mk IF of the Fighter Interception Unit, while testing airborne radar, had managed a similar feat on the night of 22nd July 1940. On this occasion a Dornier Do 17Z of 2/KG3 was destroyed. The German crew were rescued out of the sea south of Bognor Regis.

Birmingham City Transport's Highgate Road garage was hit on the night of 20th/21st November 1940 damaging 53 vehicles.
Mirrorpix/Birmingham Mail

Note

53 In 1962, the hospitals at Yardley Green and Little Bromwich amalgamated to form East Birmingham Hospital and grew exponentially to become the current Heartlands Hospital.

corporation bus which was parked in the street and hitting the adjacent bus garage, causing damage to 53 vehicles. The all-clear sounded at 05:45. The alert had lasted for more than 10 hours which, bearing in mind the previous night's ordeal, must have been gruelling for the city's residents.

Although the Germans saw this attack as a major effort, the results were on a much reduced scale compared to the previous night. Research suggests that this attack fell outside the category of 'major'.

The fact remains that, in Birmingham/West Bromwich/Smethwick/Solihull, raids on these two nights (19/20th and 20th/21st) exacted a terrible death toll, with at least 525 killed. Doubtless other seriously injured people died as a result of their wounds in the days which followed.

Five Heinkels set out for Birmingham the following night. They were from II/KG26 and III/KG26. Once again it is tempting to suggest that the latter *Gruppe* was testing its *Y-Verfahren* ready for the role it would play in the next night's attack. How many aircraft actually found their way to Birmingham is unclear, but one bomb dropped on farmland near Elmdon. Local

reports state that there was an alert between 19:29 and 21:41. Conditions that night were windy and required many barrage balloons to be hauled in.

Another major attack, the second in the space of four days, occurred on the night of 22nd/23rd November, a raid which would turn out to be the most difficult to cope with so far. For the people of Birmingham the alert sounded at 18:45 and the all-clear would not bring a sense of relief until 05:55 next morning.

The Luftwaffe was determined that the attack would yield the desired result. With meticulous timing, all three fire-raising *Gruppen* were to start dropping their incendiaries and flare markers virtually simultaneously. For one hour, commencing 19:10, some 11 Heinkels of II/KG55 dropped flares along with the usual mixture of incendiaries and HE. Using the navigational aid, *Y-Verfahren*, the crews of III/KG26 put in their appearance two minutes later with five Heinkels, the last leaving the area at 20:19. Hot on the heels of KG26, the first aircraft of KGr100's contingent of nine Heinkels arrived at 19:14. KGr100 was using its specialist navigational aid, *X-Verfahren*. The unit stayed on the scene for about 40 minutes. Arriving with the first fire-raisers at 19:12 was the vanguard of 25 Junkers Ju 88s of KG77. This particular unit maintained a crocodile-like procession to the city, which ended at 22:30.

In addition, nearly 160 bombers (a mixture of Heinkels, Junkers and Dorniers) dropped their cargos of destruction over a 10-hour period. The last aircraft to depart were eight Junkers Ju 88s of II/KG54, which attacked between the hours of 04:35 and 05:10.

Luftwaffe records claim that 227 tonnes of high explosive, parachute mines and oil bombs and no less than 16,452 incendiaries had been dropped during the attack. In a short space of time the fire-raisers had started 45 fires, 15 of which were very large. Two and a half hours into the raid the glow of the inferno could be seen by the incoming raiders as they crossed the south coast of England. By 22:30 the raid did appear to be abating, with 300 fires already reported up to this time. The raid, however, was not yet halfway through.

It was later reported that, as the raid developed, in excess of 600 fires were burning simultaneously. A massive problem encountered by the firefighters was a lack of water pressure. This was because two of the three large, gravitation water mains, which were essential to move water flowing into the city from the Elan Valley reservoirs, had been ruptured at the Bristol Road by high explosive bombs. The adjacent main filled up with mud. It was a Herculean task for men to shift the debris from the 42-inch pipe. By working round-the-clock, partial restoration of the mains supply would be re-

Hockley Garage
Damage night of 22nd/23rd November, 1940
19 buses burnt out, 4 partly burnt out.

established on 27th November. Local water mains were invariably damaged, adding to the disruption already caused in the raids of 19/20th and 20th/21st. The use of canals was made, but these began to drop to a dangerously low level. Some temporary connections were made with neighbouring water authorities. Despite strenuous efforts by the fire services, some fires had to be left to burn themselves out.

The city centre was badly hit. Here, as in the suburbs, dealing with fires amidst the chaos was very difficult. Next day 250 firemen, with their equipment, were brought in from elsewhere to give relief to the local brigades who were exhausted by their efforts of the night. These reinforcements came from as far afield as Cardiff, Bristol, Manchester and London.

Other essential public services suffered: four wards at the City Hospital Little Bromwich (the fever hospital) were damaged;[53] telephone communications were seriously affected; considerable damage had been caused to gas supplies (a 38-inch main erupted in flames in Lancaster Street) and the Birmingham City Transport garage at Hockley was hit, with 19 vehicles being written off immediately and more than 90 damaged. Worthy of note is the fact that the Birmingham Municipal Bank in Moseley was demolished; no doubt all customer ledgers and cash would have been protected in a strong room. The railway network was also disrupted, including the closure of New Street station, due to delayed-action bombs. As ever, in such raids, houses and shops were destroyed or damaged to varying degrees. The gas offices in Edmund Street, the Midland Institute, Birmingham Law Courts and the gasworks at Adderley Street and Windsor Street were also damaged.

A number of factories were hit including: Fisher & Ludlow in Rea Street was hit early on at 19:30 hours when HE badly damaged the aero assembly works together with the company's nearby site where extensive fire damage to the tool room works occurred, W W Greener Ltd in St Marys Row, Mulliners Ltd at Bordesley Green, Joseph Lucas in Great Hampton Street had some buildings demolished by HE, Best & Lloyd at Handsworth, ICI (Metals) in Selly Oak, Newey Brothers in Summer Lane was badly damaged, Klaxon together with Wright Binley and Gell at Greet were both hit by incendiary and HE bombs, Singer Motors and BSA at Small Heath and its nearby dispersal site at Tyseley. Bakelite, also at Tyseley, was initially said to be gutted but later reports stated that production would cease for just one week. Also at Tyseley, Abingdon

The Abingdon Works Ltd factory, Tyseley, which manufactured the famous 'King Dick' tools, was severely damaged on 22/23rd November 1940.

Works Ltd was reported as burnt-out. Less serious were hits on nearby C H Parsons & Co, Reynolds Tube and Messenger & Sons, the last being in neighbouring Greet. Once again, bombs fell in the Olton/Solihull area (20:15) and an oil

bomb dropped in the engine factory of the newly-opened Rover works at Lode Lane, Solihull. One German unit, II/KG51, claimed specifically to have bombed Elmdon aerodrome in the early hours of the morning. This may well account for the seven HE bombs (four of which did not explode) that fell on Marston Green. Elsewhere, Wythall, Barnt Green, Oldbury and West Bromwich reported relatively minor incidents.

At BSA where, following the raid of 26th August, replacement machines for the factory had begun to arrive, the attacks of 19/20th and 22nd/23rd November resulted in a further 1,600 being put out of action. As a consequence, BSA urgently sought dispersal sites in order to maintain some production of Browning machine guns. Examples of such requisitioned sites were at Bromsgrove, Kidderminster, Mansfield and Stoke on Trent.

A secret signal was sent to the Ministry of Home Security on the morning of 23rd November. It read: 'Water for firefighting does not exist in four fifths of the city. In case Birmingham is attacked tonight it is hoped to muster the Home Guard at full strength to be dispersed over the city to undertake incendiary bomb fighting. Work on the restoration of the water supply will start immediately, but large mains have been damaged in several places and this will take many days.

'Arrangements are being made for men to work during the blackout. A regional call is being made for all available water carts to be placed at the disposal of Birmingham Water Department. It is hoped to make use of railway water tank wagons to bring water to strategic points where it can be collected.'

In view of the water situation, the prospect of yet another raid the following night was cause for great concern. In fact, the city would be almost defenceless. Royal Engineers were brought in so that, with the use of explosives, they could make fire-breaks if further fires were uncontainable.

In response to the fear that Birmingham and Coventry would again be targeted the next night, large trenches were dug at strategic sites outside the cities and filled with petrol. When lit, the intention was to give the impression of a large built up area ablaze, in the hope of diverting the enemy bombers away from their real targets. Amazingly, German bombers left Birmingham alone on that night of the 23rd, making Southampton their principal objective. Not for the first time, the Luftwaffe had failed to deliver the *coup de grace.*

It has not proved possible to ascertain exact casualty figures for each of these three large November raids, but the author's research yields a total of 767 killed and nearly 1,200 seriously injured.[54]

Concerning these three raids, the official assessment was that 79 of the hundreds of factories hit were considered to have been lost. Of these, 24 had actually been destroyed and 55 were in need of demolition. Probably the most serious was the damage to BSA Guns, where production dropped for a number of months; a fact which caused the Prime Minister himself some concern.

Late in the day of the 27th, a German reconnaissance aircraft photographed the new Austin assembly factory located to the east side of the Birmingham-Coventry railway line, adjacent to the airfield at Elmdon. Then, on the evening of the 28th, four bombers set out to attack the city. In the light of recent raids this one, which occurred shortly after midnight, was but a pin-prick, with just ten 50kg HE bombs being dropped on the city, causing minimal damage.

Three members of staff, however, at Monyhull Hall Hospital in Kings Norton, were killed.

Two months earlier, Birmingham had lost some of its heavy anti-aircraft guns to the London defences, leaving 64 in place. Now, in response to the attention the Germans were giving to the industrial concerns of Birmingham, the process was reversed. By bringing in 31 mobile 3.7 inch artillery pieces, the city's tally of guns was increased to 95. This made Birmingham the second strongest Gun Defended Area in the country.

Aside from the odd loss caused by the British defences, the German bomber crews continued to operate with little interference. The majority of their losses occurred due to accidents. Fighter Command, in accordance with the expressed wishes of the Night Air Defence Committee, was launching many more fighters into the night sky. Two examples will serve to illustrate this effort.

On the night of the large Coventry raid (14/15th November), some 35 sorties were flown by Blenheims, 12 by Beaufighters, 30 by Defiants, 43 by Hurricanes and 5 by Gladiator biplanes. The last, by now obsolescent, were from 247 Sqn based at Roborough near Plymouth, which was part of 10 Group guarding the south-west approaches. These figures include dusk and dawn sorties. Pilots or other aircrew reported seeing seven enemy machines between them. Two Blenheims opened fire, but without result. Anti-aircraft fire brought down a German Dornier Do 17Z on its way to Coventry. It hit the ground near Loughborough; at Birmingham gunners claimed to have seen an aircraft break up in mid-air.

On the night of 22nd/23rd November, when Birmingham was the principal target, Fighter Command put up 103 fighters. On this occasion

Note

54 Birmingham 661, Smethwick 33, Solihull 19 and West Bromwich 54.

In November 1940, as German bombers headed towards the Midlands, 247 Sqn was using the obsolete Gladiator biplane on night defence duties in an attempt to guard the skies over south-west England. No successful contacts were made.
Author's collection

the breakdown was: 36 Blenheims, 11 Beaufighters, 33 Hurricanes, 12 Defiants and 11 Gladiators. Only two fighters caught sight of enemy aircraft and neither of them got into a position to open fire. Although the anti-aircraft guns fired off nearly 11,000 shells, the best they could claim was that they had acted as a deterrent to the enemy and a comfort to those on the ground.

During the Battle of Britain, German bombers had favoured massed formations, which offered better protection in daylight. The Luftwaffe's general night tactic of arriving over the target crocodile-style and spreading the attack over

By the autumn of 1940 Defiants of 264 Sqn had been relieved of day operations and were used instead to bolster the night defences.

The Merlin-powered Defiant used a two-man crew, with the gunner located in a rotating turret immediately behind the pilot.
Both Simon Parry

many hours made things very difficult for the defences.[55] On occasion RAF fighter pilots did report seeing bombers in formations of three aircraft (such a formation of three was called a *Kette* by the Luftwaffe). When formation flying at night the German crews were happy to risk the use of navigation lights, so confident were they of the poor state of the RAF's night fighting ability.

On 25th November, Fighter Command's AOC-in-C, Hugh Dowding, was replaced, as was his subordinate Keith Park, head of 11 Group, three weeks later. Dowding's arch-critic, Air Marshal W. Sholto Douglas, Deputy Chief of the Air Staff, became the new AOC-in-C, while Trafford Leigh-Mallory was to take over 11 Group. Douglas believed that desperate times required desperate measures and immediately set about getting some in place. One such innovation, known as the 'Hampden Patrol', does form part of the Birmingham Blitz story, as will be seen shortly. Along with making many important organisational changes, he continued to press for the use of single-engine fighters to be used at night, together with the training of airmen to fly them in this role. The two-man-crewed Boulton Paul Defiant had shown itself to be vulnerable as a day fighter, but was now being given a second lease of life as a night fighter.

By the start of December, and following the major attacks of less than a fortnight earlier, the city's infrastructure was being returned to normal. Tram systems and railways were functioning well and water and gas supplies were almost fully reinstated. There were 107 roads which remained closed due to the filling-in of bomb craters being delayed while utility services were repaired.

On 3rd/4th December there was a big attack on the city, this being the Luftwaffe's main effort of the night. The number of bombers detailed for the mission was 69, of which 11 flew to alternative targets and 7 aborted. The remaining 51 Heinkels and Junkers dropped nearly 60 tonnes of HE and around 16,000 incendiaries.

The raid started early, shortly before 18:30 hours, with two Heinkel He 111s of III/KG26 using their *Y-Gerät* equipment to locate and drop their fire-marking bombs. At the same time Heinkels from I/KG1 arrived, and the regular early appearance of KGr100 commenced their precision attack at 18:48. The raid concluded at about 22:00. Casualties were, by contemporary standards, considered light: 36 killed and 60 seriously injured.

As with the raid of 27th October, there was a distinct bomb pattern running south to north for three miles in length and half a mile wide,

evidence of the X-beam being used by the pathfinding unit KGr100.

The large number of incendiaries caused many fires and, according to German aircrew, they were spread across the city centre. Water supply for firefighting was still a cause for concern, as many secondary mains were still not functioning following the raids of a fortnight earlier. Houses and shops appeared to have borne most of the destruction. Factories which were damaged to varying degrees included: Perry Barr Metal Co in Wellhead Lane at Perry Barr, Delta Metal in Dartmouth Street, J Lucas (Powell & Hanmer), Fisher & Ludlow in Rea Street (South Works) together with other company sites within the locality, Serck Radiators at Greet, MCCW at Washwood Heath and the industrial area of Kings Norton. A large timber yard at Cotteridge caught fire and the gas works at Adderley Street, Bordesley, was again hit. Railway services were disrupted and the Birmingham-

Hugh Dowding had successfully led Fighter Command through the difficult weeks of the Battle of Britain. The ineffectiveness of the RAF in dealing with the German night raiders played a significant part in his being forced to hand over the reins to William Sholto Douglas at the end of November 1940.

William Sholto Douglas immediately brought in some desperate measures to combat German night raiders. However, these made little or no impact. As his predecessor, Hugh Dowding, had predicted, things only improved when the radar-equipped Beaufighters appeared in larger numbers.

An He 111H-6 of III/KG26 prepares to take-off for a night mission in late 1940. The unit badge is visible beneath the cockpit; the undersides are painted black as is the externally-carried SC-1200 bomb.
EN-Archive

Note

55 Just how difficult it was for a pilot to place his aircraft, or for a gun crew to get a shell burst close to a bomber in the dark without the aid of radar, may be seen from the following official calculations. The average speed of aircraft – 180 mph; Influx strength – one aircraft crossing the coast every five minutes. Average linear distribution – one aircraft every twelve miles. Average superficial density – one aircraft per 180 square miles. Average volume distribution – since the aircraft flew between 10,000 and 20,000 feet, there was an average of one aircraft per 345 cubic miles.

An atmospheric picture of a Heinkel He 111 of KG55 as it heads for the British Isles.
via Ken Wakefield

Members of KG55 pose for the camera. Centre is Oblt Johann Speck von Sternberg. To his right is Fw Martin Reiser and, to his left, a war correspondent by the name of Kirchoff.
Martin Reiser

Worcester canal was put out of action for a number of weeks when the aqueduct at Bournville was struck by a bomb, so causing a 600-yards stretch of the waterway to empty, flooding local homes and parts of the Cadbury site.

As mentioned earlier, by now the Luftwaffe was regularly using a double-blow tactic by following up a raid with another of similar strength the next night. So, it was no surprise when the bombers returned on the evening of the 4th. According to German sources, this was a bigger effort than the previous night. They state that, of the 89 aircraft which set out to bomb Birmingham, 62 accomplished the mission. The proportion of incendiaries to HE was reduced from that of the night before with 6,624 incendiaries and 77 tonnes of HE reckoned to have been dropped. Among the latter were many big bombs, including five *Satan* 1,800kg and sixteen *Hermann* 1,000kg. Seventeen oil bombs complemented the incendiaries, but no parachute mines were dropped on this night.

The attack started even earlier, commencing at 18:15, when Heinkels of III/KG26, again using their *Y-Gerät*, began to light targets with incendiaries. Due to the fact that their ground controllers could only handle one aircraft at a time, the unit was present over the city until 21:00. The attack was carried out by a mixture of Heinkel He 111s and Junkers Ju 88s with the last aircraft, a Heinkel of II/KG27, departing the area at 23:00.

This was a sizeable attack and yet contemporary and more recent accounts do not give it much attention. Had the German airmen known the result of their effort, perhaps they would have been disappointed. The reports they took back to their debriefing officers spoke of seeing explosions, one large fire and a number of smaller ones.

Birmingham's anti-aircraft guns fired 260 shells over a three hour period, which does not seem high. Fatalities, if they occurred at all, numbered no more than three. Probably the most reported incident of the night occurred at 20:45, when the Corporation tram depot at Witton received a direct hit. Here 14 people were injured and a similar number of tram cars was so damaged that they would never be put into service again. The depot was out of commission until the following year and the roof was not rebuilt until 1947. Birmingham City FC's stadium (St Andrews) was hit and one of the stands wrecked. Residential properties bore the brunt of the destruction.

A tactic which appears to have been used at this period was that city centres were set alight by incendiaries prior to the dropping of HE. At night time there were far fewer fire-watchers available to cover city centre properties.[56] Success in this type of attack could result in disruption to local government, public services and commerce, and might, so it was hoped, deliver a blow to public morale.

If the raid on the 4th was considered light, one week later it was a very different story. The night of 11/12th would witness Birmingham's longest raid of the war, lasting 13 hours.

The assault was carried out in two phases separated by almost two hours. As ever, for large night attacks, *Luftflotte* 3 supplied the majority of bombers, while the more northerly *Luftflotte* 2 supplemented the numbers. The Heinkels, Junkers and Dorniers left the continent from four distinct areas. After having to contend with cloud, rain and even some snow, all converged on Birmingham, which was found by the German crews to be clear and, later in the evening, was mostly bathed in moonlight. Waterways and railways were visible making the location of the city centre straightforward. Only in a few instances were crews forced to drop their bombs 'blind'.

Air raid warning 'red' sounded at 18:20 hours. The first phase commenced ten minutes later on that Wednesday evening and lasted for nearly seven hours. The first bombs fell on Stechford, Witton, the city centre, Knowle and Solihull. The people who were huddled in their shelters, or on fire-watching duties, fighting fires, digging people out of rubble or tending to casualties in first-aid stations, must have been mystified (assuming that they had time to notice) by the absence of anti-aircraft gunfire and searchlight activity.

Both guns and searchlights in the Birmingham area had been ordered not to take any action before midnight, in order to give the 'Hampden Patrol' full freedom of operation. This patrol was an experimental measure to provide the city with an air defence of around 20 aircraft. They were to fly in layers of 500 feet intervals, in order to catch the German aircraft illuminated by the moonlight or silhouetted against the fires on the ground. Revealing a degree of desperation, the aircraft chosen for this mission were Handley Page Hampdens of Bomber Command. These were hurriedly fitted with a machine gun in the beam position which was to augment the weapons already fitted to the machine. It was presumably hoped that, as these aircraft would not be carrying their normal bomb load, their performance would be adequate for the task. Such aircraft had the advantage that they could remain in the air for many hours (designed as they were for longer-distance flights) and that their crews were used to flying at night.

Indeed, there were a number of sightings of enemy aircraft, but the Hampdens simply had not got the speed to follow up on such sightings and no interceptions were made. By midnight

the Hampdens were clear of the area and the guns and searchlights were released from their inactivity.

A young wireless operator, W.E. Clayfield in one of the Hampdens of 44 Sqn, subsequently told of his bird's-eye view of Birmingham's ordeal, 'Later, through cloud gaps, we saw the city ablaze. It was a dreadful sight. Every now and then we could see fires starting up, then bigger and darker flashes followed by great spirals of smoke.'

German crews also reported their assessment of the fires below, identifying them as being in the centre as well as the southern and northern districts. Reference was made to a particularly large explosion which resulted in a huge yellow-

Note

56 In a radio broadcast on 31st December 1940 the then Home Secretary, Herbert Morrison, made a national appeal for more volunteer fire-watchers. The appeal was successful and secured more cover for unoccupied buildings.

A number of Birmingham City Transport buses and trams were painted in a drab grey so that they were less obvious from the air – note the white blackout markings and shielded lamps. This particular bus is a Leyland TD6c, EOG 273, and is at the bus stops in Colmore Row near to Snow Hill station. via D Harvey

The low-visibility dark grey livery for the city's buses and trams was a requirement for those vehicles ferrying passengers to certain factories on war work. Here tramcar 603 is seen on route 70 at the Rednal turning circle. via Kidderminster Railway Museum

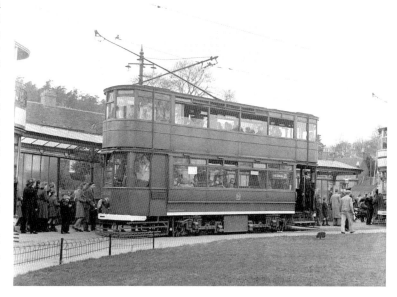

red sheet of flame which, it was assumed, emanated from a gas works. The German crews reported seeing a number of night fighters; these would have been the Hampdens. A single bomber was brought down by British defences when anti-aircraft fire dealt a fatal blow to a Heinkel He 111 from the Pathfinder unit 7/KG26. The pilot was *Staffel* Captain, Hptm Hans-Joachim Dittler.

The second phase of the attack got under way at 02:48 and was maintained until 07:15. A total of 278 crews claimed to have bombed the city. As with the raid of a week earlier, many large bombs and parachute mines were employed and included 19 *Satan* and 72 *Hermann*. Possibly in excess of 257 tonnes of high explosive was dropped, the effect being that many buildings were destroyed or badly damaged. Fortunately, large numbers of fire-watchers were on duty and, although more than 20,000 incendiaries fell all over the city, no disastrous conflagrations resulted from the 300 fires.

Nevertheless there were grievous losses and much destruction. The most widely reported casualty figures record 263 killed in Birmingham, 3 in Smethwick and 5 in Shirley, with a fur-

The Hampden Patrol

When W. Sholto Douglas became AOC-in-C of Fighter Command on 25th November 1940, his priority was to frustrate the German night raiders. Within 24 hours he had initiated what was codenamed the 'Hampden Patrol'. This initiative would make available Handley Page Hampden bombers to act as improvised night fighters, which were to criss-cross the targeted area. Nominated cities and towns for this close protection were: Birmingham, Bristol, Coventry, Derby, Liverpool, Manchester, Sheffield and Wolverhampton.

The Hampdens were to be provided by No.5 Group Bomber Command, with the burden falling upon five Lincolnshire squadrons: 44 based at Waddington, 49 at Scampton, 61 at Hemswell, 83 at Scampton and 144 at Hemswell. Each squadron would provide elements to make up the Patrol while still continuing with its normal bombing and mine-laying operations. For its newly improvised role it was necessary to equip each Hampden with an additional machine gun (this being mounted in the beam position) and another air-gunner to operate it. Extra ammunition was carried in lieu of bombs. The Patrol would consist of 20 aircraft and was to remain over the target area for four hours, operating inside a radius

of 10 miles. The 20 aircraft were to be vertically spaced at 500 feet intervals starting at 12,000 feet. Orders were issued so that the Hampdens were given a clear field, with no anti-aircraft artillery or searchlight activity within the patrol area. It was reckoned that the Patrol could be established over the target area within 90 minutes of 5 Group being told the most likely target. Predicting the target was a matter for Air Intelligence which relied heavily on the Germans setting their radio beams during the afternoon preceding a large night penetration.

On 28th November, the Hampden Patrol was put on stand-by but cancelled at 18:00 hours. A second attempt on the 3rd December to activate the Patrol was also cancelled due to poor weather. Nonetheless, a solitary Hampden (X3025) from 44 Sqn and piloted by Flt Lt Ogilvie, took off at 23:55. About 30 minutes later, a one hour patrol was commenced over Birmingham at 12,000 feet. The crew reported seeing large fires through the cloud but no enemy machines. They landed back at Waddington at 02:05.

The Operational Instruction as received by the squadrons themselves is typified by that which is recorded in the 49 Sqn operations record book (ORB) which is as follows:

```
No.49 Squadron to provide four aircraft to take part in an experiment to be carried out
as to the possibility of intercepting and destroying enemy bomber aircraft over their
target, by concentrating twenty Hampden aircraft in a stepped-up patrol over the area
being attacked. The patrol would operate if large-scale enemy formations attacked either
Coventry, Birmingham, Derby, Manchester, Sheffield, Bristol, Liverpool or Wolverhampton.
Timing.
The initial time at which aircraft are to be in the patrol area will be known as 'zero
hour', and will be signalled in the executive "GO" and patrol area will be given at the
same time, one and a half hours before zero hour. Period of patrol is to be four hours.
It is essential that aircraft do not arrive in the patrol area before zero hour or remain
there after zero hour + four hours, since guns and searchlights will be operating in the
area outside the period zero to zero + four hours. Each aircraft is to be allotted a sky
layer of 500 feet. Layers allotted to Scampton — 16,000'-20,000'.
Aircraft to carry maximum ammunition supplies, and an additional air-gunner
to man the midships guns.
```

Desperate times call for desperate measures. In late-November/December 1940 Handley Page Hampden bombers were pressed into service as night fighters. Hampden (AE436) PL-J is from 144 Sqn, one of five squadrons involved in the 'Hampden Patrol'. RAF Museum

ther 265 seriously injured.[57] For the second time, south of the city boundary, the town of Shirley suffered fatalities in one residential area.

As a result of the bombing, ten schools, two cinemas, one hospital and six churches, *viz*: Holy Trinity in Smethwick, the Congregational Church in Sparkhill, St Mary's in Acocks Green, St Peter's in Harborne, St Thomas' in Bath Row and St Anne's in Moseley, were all damaged to varying degrees. For a while, road and rail access in and out of the city was dislocated.

Of the dozens of factories hit, serious damage was done to the James Cycle factory at Greet (which was engaged upon government contracts), Fisher & Ludlow (Rea Street South Works) at Digbeth, and Carrs Paper at Small Heath. Elsewhere damage was sustained by Lucas (Shaftmoor Lane), Rover at Tyseley, The Mint (Birmingham), BSA Guns in Armoury Road and close-by BSA Tools in Montgomery Street, both of Small Heath, MCCW at Washwood Heath, London Aluminium Co at Witton, the Beehive Foundry of Samuel Smith & Sons at Smethwick and W & T Avery (gun-carriage department) also at Smethwick where production was halted for a number of days. Delayed-

Three nights later, the Patrol took up its post over Bristol, but was unable to interfere with the Luftwaffe's attack. Numbers of aircraft from participating squadrons were: six Hampdens from 44 Sqn one of which had to return before reaching the target area due to instrumentation problems, five aircraft from 49 Sqn, three aircraft from 61 Sqn and four aircraft from 83 Sqn. Only a few of the Hampdens managed to stay over Bristol for a duration approaching the planned four hours. A number of aircraft experienced technical issues and had to divert to other airfields instead of landing at their home base. Crews complained of inadequate heating in the aircraft and one of 61 Sqn's Hampdens recorded a temperature of -33°C. As a result, a number of crew members suffered frostbite. Severe icing on the external surfaces of the machines caused problems. A sighting, of what was probably an enemy aircraft, was claimed by one Hampden pilot from 83 Sqn as he approached Bristol. He was able to maintain visual contact for a period of four minutes, but could not close to make an interception. Another pilot this time from 61 Sqn, momentarily sighted a further aircraft but did not have a chance to identify it.

On 8th December most aircraft of the Patrol got airborne shortly before 19:00 and proceeded to Abingdon in Oxfordshire, where they orbited for two hours while awaiting directions to the target city. When directions were received it was a frustrating recall to base. Again 44 Sqn's contingent was six aircraft, 49 Sqn eight, with 61 and 144 Sqns each providing three, making the full complement of 20 Hampdens. In fact, 18 aircraft made the patrol, as one each of 61 and 144 Sqns' machines had to abort the mission.

On the evening of the 11th, Birmingham was subjected to a major attack. For the second (and as things turned out the last) time, the Hampdens established the Patrol over one of the nominated cities. From 19:15 until 23:15, the Hampdens were in position over Birmingham, using 20 aircraft. Squadron contributions were: six aircraft from 44 Sqn, three aircraft from 61 Sqn, eight aircraft from 83 Sqn and three aircraft from 144 Sqn. Several Hampden pilots saw enemy bombers, though none was able to make an interception.

Sgt Hazelden, one of the 44 Sqn pilots, in Hampden X2918, reported that his crew saw no less than six German machines. One of these was as

Hampdens belonging to 44 Sqn (including AE257 KM-X and AE202 KM-K) which in late 1940 was based at Waddington. RAF Museum

close as 50 yards. He turned to give chase, but could not catch it.

Pilot Officer (Plt Off) Skinner, also of 44 Sqn, flying Hampden X3026, saw five of the enemy, while patrolling at 18,000 feet. In an effort to bring guns to bear on one of these sightings, he dived his Hampden down to 14,000 feet, only to lose visual contact.

A number of aircrew from 61 Sqn reported hearing over the radio their opposite numbers in the German aircraft. This would have been galling as they witnessed the incendiaries and high explosive bombs igniting on the city below. The RAF crews were suffering badly from the low temperatures and they probably wondered whether Luftwaffe flying suits were any warmer.

A crew from 144 Sqn, in Hampden X3130, saw tracer fire coming in their direction from the starboard beam, emanating from a distance of about 300 yards, but could not identify its source. The same crew reported that towards the end of the patrol cloud started to move in across the city, causing them to drift out of the area.

That aircraft's pilot, Plt Off Haig, made the following observations: 'Beacons would be a great help in maintaining position. Controls of the W/T receiver froze and were very stiff. Temperature was -27°C.

'The range of vision of the beam gunner is so small, coupled with the fact that the gun may have to be changed from one side to the other on very short notice, that it is doubtful whether the beam gunner will have any chance of an effective shot. His position is uncomfortable and there is no heating provided for him.'

On 14th December, the experiment of using Hampdens as improvised night fighters was abandoned in favour of putting more single-engine fighters into the night skies over the designated target areas. On occasion these might include aircraft from day fighter squadrons, flown by hand-picked pilots. As with the Hampden Patrol, multiple fighters would fly at staggered heights and these defensive flights were known as 'Layer' operations. This term was subsequently changed to 'Fighter Nights'.

Note

58 *The Air Raids on Smethwick* by Peter Kennedy.

Right: **One of a number of churches hit on the night of 11/12th December 1940 was St Thomas', Lee Bank.** BirminghamLives

Below: **Considerable damage was done to the Avery factory at Smethwick by a parachute mine on 11/12th December 1940.** Avery Historical Museum

Opposite: **Two views of the damage sustained by the MCCW factory at Washwood Heath following the raid of 11/12th December 1940.** Avery Historical Museum

action bombs disrupted Steel Conduits Ltd's production at Witton, Wilder's Fireworks at Greet and Bakelite at Tyseley.

The Avery factory and Samuel Smith foundry were each hit by parachute mines. One source[58] quotes that during this raid 22 mines touched down but 12 failed to explode. One such device landed on the pavement outside the Smethwick Council House, with its parachute canopy snagged in the overhead telephone wires. As a consequence, the Smethwick Control Centre had to be evacuated.

At this stage in the Blitz, Fisher & Ludlow's factories, which were involved in important metal-pressing work, had lost, due to air attacks, 400,000 square feet of its 1,000,000 square feet of floor space.

When some of the large bombs dropped in residential areas they caused multiple fatalities. It seems that people were less inclined to take to their air raid shelters after a number of consecutive nights of enemy inactivity, being lulled into a false sense of security. As there had been no bombing for a week, this may be the reason for the high number of casualties for this night of the 11/12th. There is an additional explanation. With a protracted raid such as this one, German

THE LUFTWAFFE OVER BRUM

Dornier Do 17s of KG2.

aircraft approached different parts of the city in relatively small groups and at different times. Consequently the air raid warning and subsequent all-clear was heard with confusing regu-

larity and so the exhausted people elected to ignore the warnings and stay in their homes.

The final air raid warning 'white' (all-clear) sounded on the Thursday morning at 07:45. That

UXB – Men at Work

During the Blitz, large numbers of bombs failed to explode on impact. These were either deliberately fitted with delayed-action (DA) fuses or were simply 'duds'. The men who were detailed to make these unexploded bombs (UXB) safe were rightly held in high esteem by the general public, who witnessed first-hand their bravery.

An Australian, named Lieutenant Hugh Syme of the

Royal Naval Volunteer Reserve, was sent to diffuse the parachute mine which landed near the Smethwick Council House. It had wedged itself by penetrating the paving flagstones which turned inwards and kept the bomb upright: 'This was my first defusing assignment after my training. I was driven to a barricade near the Council House. It was extremely cold. On my way to the assignment people were

To the relief of civilians a notable proportion of parachute mines failed to explode upon touch down. This example appears to be a 1,000kg LMB (TYPE C). via Nigel Parker

calling out "Good luck!" As I got closer to the mine, there was not a soul to be seen. I arranged the tools on the ground and set up a pulley to the telegraph pole and the bomb. My hands were raw with the cold and they stuck to the metal. I attached a cord to the bomb fuse and stretched the cord for 35 yards to a dug-out shelter. I padded the pavement with layers of Hessian where the fuse would fall. The telegraph wires and parachute lines had to be moved. I turned the tap on the bomb fuse and the safety pin popped home. I slowly unscrewed the keeper ring. I tied a knot around the ring. I walked to the dug-out, pulled on the cord and the fuse fell out. I counted to 20. I walked back to the bomb and picked up the fuse. Now there was the hydrostatic clock which could have been booby-trapped. I tied a cord around this and repeated the same operation. As I approached the bomb I noticed two young boys playing with the clock. I was totally aghast. They asked me what I was doing. They had been hiding in the bushes for nearly two hours. I shouted at them and they ran away. Then it was all over; the mine was safe. Many people ran towards the site. I was dragged into a nearby pub. A hat was presented to me brimming with coins and notes. I told them they couldn't give me money so they gave me beer instead.'

same day a number of areas within the city were visited by King George VI. As he moved from one part of the city to another, he met many Brummies who were encouraged by seeing their monarch – a man, together with many Londoners, who knew what it was like to be bombed.

On the following night the Luftwaffe carried out another major attack, but instead of following up on Birmingham it was the turn of Sheffield.

However, a few Junkers Ju 88 and Dornier Do 17 aircraft are recorded in some sources as releasing bombs onto Birmingham, having abandoned their primary target. Indeed, an alert was in force between 19:04 and 04:21, during which time a few bombs dropped on Walmley (near Sutton Coldfield) and the Yardley/Sheldon area, causing no reportable damage.

On the night of 15th December, local anti-aircraft guns were in action as German bombers made their way to Sheffield. A typical 'friendly-fire' incident, which caused some disruption, occurred when, at 20:36 hours, a 914 Sqn barrage balloon (number SlZG2041) sustained shrapnel damage. It fell in Jacey Road, Shirley, where it was deflated by rip line. The cable fell across the main Birmingham-Stratford road and had to be cut to permit traffic to pass. One source claims that the German unit III/KG27 bombed Birmingham but this is not validated by local records.

On the 16/17th, weather conditions, especially over the German bomber bases in France, reduced Luftwaffe raids to 'harassing attacks only'. One respected source[59] gives details from German records which claim that the largest of these was against Birmingham, and states that 32 Heinkel He 111s, of III/KG27, managed to get airborne from their dual bases of Rennes and Saint-Jaques in Brittany. Using both *Knickebein* and dead-reckoning navigation, 20 succeeded in reaching the city. Orders were to concentrate the attack on the north-east districts. The raiders, it was claimed, dropped 10 tonnes of HE and 432 incendiaries. Wherever their navigation took them, it was not over Birmingham that the bombs were released. No damage or casualties were recorded locally for this night. The sirens did sound shortly after 20.00 hours, the alert lasting for about half an hour. One bomb was recorded as dropping on open land in Solihull Lodge, perhaps an accidental release as a few German aircraft passed overhead on their way to targets other than Birmingham.

The final raids of the month, and indeed the year, were the result of German crews diverting from their primary target and attacking Birmingham as an alternative. This happened on the night of the 21st/22nd, when Liverpool was the main target but a small number of Junkers Ju 88 and Heinkel He 111 bombers diverted to Birmingham. Bombs fell on Walmley and Minworth.

Around midnight, a parachute mine fell in a residential area of Erdington. Sqn Ldr Mawle was the Commanding Officer of 911 Sqn (barrage balloon), whose headquarters was in Erdington.[60] He arrived at the scene and such was the devastation that he ordered a mobile squad of 25 airmen to assist the three ARP wardens who were already at the bombed site. At least three dead bodies were retrieved from the rubble and a further 30 casualties were admitted to hospital.

Manchester was the main target on the next night, and again at least one Junkers Ju 88 of I/KG51 claimed to have bombed Birmingham as the alternative. Although local records indicate this was a quiet night, at 19:45 hours a delayed-action bomb fell on the A45 Birmingham-Coventry road at Bickenhill, causing it to be closed for a number of hours. Typical of the hazards during the Blitz period, on this night anti-aircraft shells were the cause of damage to a house in Sheldon, and another in Selly Oak resulting in one casualty.

The Germans claimed to have dropped 409 tonnes of HE and about 47,000 incendiaries on Birmingham during December, even though the second half of the month had brought only minor raids.

The Winter Lull: January-February 1941

The lull was set to continue during the months of January and February. The winter weather over north-west Europe was not conducive to air operations, particularly those at night. Rain, sleet, snow, ice and cloud ruled out bombing attacks on Britain for half of the nights in January. In that month the Luftwaffe only managed seven major raids and just three in February, none of these on Birmingham. In fact, the emphasis had switched from attacking aircraft factories and industrial centres to sea ports and shipping. Of the former, western ports such as Plymouth, Devonport, Avonmouth, Bristol, Cardiff, Swansea, Manchester, Birkenhead, Liverpool and Glasgow were targeted. As for shipping, some bomber units now concentrated on hitting ships at sea and mine-laying in coastal waters.

Although Britain's night defences had made little impact upon the Luftwaffe bomber force, availability of aircraft for bombing operations as at 4th January 1941 was down to 551 machines, a mere 41% of *Luftflotten* 2 and 3's heavy (by German standards) bomber strength. Accidents, overhauls and repairs were the reason for this low figure and reflected the pace of operations.

During the early hours of 2nd January 1941, two Dornier Do 17s, operating independently and separated by an hour or so, dropped parachute mines (one in Sparkbrook and another in Ward End) and HE bombs on the Sparkhill/Sparkbrook district. During this month of January, the government reckoned that of the 70,000

Notes

59 *The Blitz Then and Now Vol.2,* page 343.

60 Interestingly, 911 Sqn operations record book, from where this incident is taken, refers to Mawle as a Wing Commander, though this rank was not bestowed until he moved to Sheffield later, in 1941.

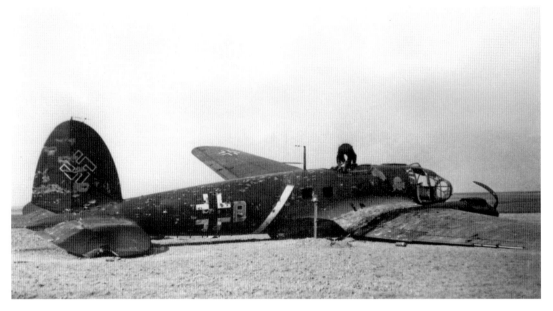

Birmingham homes damaged to date by air raids, 70% had been repaired.

At 19:53 hours on the evening of 4th February an oil bomb fell in Acocks Green, which fractured a gas main. Later in the evening minor incidents were reported in Highters Heath where a handful of HE bombs were dropped but there were no casualties and little or no damage. On the 15/16th there was another nuisance raid but, in fact, just a dozen incendiary bombs fell harmlessly near Bromsgrove and also near Walsall.

A daylight raid on the 17th February by II/KG76 was to specifically target Elmdon, no doubt due to the importance of the recently completed Austin aircraft assembly factory located there. This was to be followed during the night by III/KG77 attacking Birmingham. It has not proved possible to confirm from British sources that these attacks of the 17th actually took place.

It should be appreciated that many records of the time, especially German documentation, were lost to posterity. What contemporary sources are available, such as log books, unit diaries and Home Security reports etc, were written up by administrative staff. These clerks varied in their conscientiousness and accuracy. It probably never entered their minds that more than 70 years later researchers would be scrutinising their every pen-stroke or one-finger typing skills! With this in mind, of interest is an air combat which occurred on the last but one date mentioned, that of 15th February. The incident is plagued with ambiguity within both German and British records.

A Heinkel from KG27 was intercepted off the south coast by Flt Lt John Cunningham (who, it will be remembered, prevented a Junkers Ju 88 from reaching Birmingham on 19th November). On this occasion the luckless Heinkel was spotted off the Dorset coast around 19:00 hours.

Note

61 *Night Fighter* by
Robert Wright and C.F.
Rawnsley, published by
Corgi 1966.

British Summer Time (BST) had remained in force throughout the winter months and so the intruder was readily visible to the Beaufighter (R2101) crew, being set against the sky to the south-west. Cunningham turned to follow his quarry. The Germans did not see the Beaufighter, placed as it was, against the darker backdrop. The Heinkel proceeded to fly a series of 360 degree orbits, presumably killing time until the sky was sufficiently dark for a crossing of the coast. Sgt Jimmy Rawnsley was the radar operator in the Beaufighter and thanks to the account in his book *Night Fighter*[61] we can pick up the story:

'...the Heinkel sank slowly into our sights... when our own guns started their giant pounding. For the first few noisy seconds nothing at all seemed to happen. Then through the choking haze of smoke from the guns, I saw the flash of hits on the starboard engine as John shifted his aim.

'The ammunition ran out, and the enemy bomber slewed around into a gentle dive. I jumped on to the cat-walk and began feverishly clawing the empty drums from the guns, tossing them up on to the racks, and gingerly easing down the heavy refills on to the hot breech blocks. The last drum was still half full, and there was a live shell jammed in the breach. Time was running short so I left it and climbed back to my seat. Gasping for breath I reported to John: "Guns reloaded...set to fire."

'But the Heinkel had disappeared. John had lost sight of it as soon as it had dived below the

horizon, and the night had swallowed it up. I turned to the A.I., but the picture there was as empty as the sky. It was not until then that I realized that I should have stayed on the set and kept in contact before reloading.'

Rawnsley need not have berated himself as, shortly afterwards, the RAF crew spotted incendiaries bursting on the ground and then a large explosion. It seems that the Heinkel had jettisoned its load prior to crashing near Totnes in Devon. All four Luftwaffe crew were killed.

Had John Cunningham stopped another load of bombs falling on Birmingham and, unlike his interception the previous November, this time, without the use of the on-board radar set? Possibly, but the evidence is confusing.

German records referred to a Heinkel He 111 belonging to the second *Gruppe* KG27 taking off at 18:00 (BST) bound for Birmingham. The crew reported engine trouble at 20:04. Nothing more was heard and the aircraft and crew were posted as missing.

Cunningham stated that his interception took place at 19:16 and that there was a lapse of 20 minutes before they witnessed the explosions on the ground. The crash investigation report noted the aircraft as coming down at 20:15. The Heinkel, however, was identified as 1G+FR, which indicates that this particular aircraft was from the third *Gruppe* and not the second. The third *Gruppe* was given the target of Liverpool that night and dispatched 12 aircraft, but only one claimed to have bombed that city, this at 20:47.

**Bristol Beaufighter IF
T4638 is in the
markings of 604 Sqn
which began to use the
type in autumn 1940.
While flying
Beaufighters with 604
Sqn, Flt Lt John
Cunningham brought
down one, possibly two,
Birmingham-bound
Heinkel He 111s.**
Simon Parry

The Horrors of Bombing

In the autumn of 1940, Claudia Frances Renton was 57 years old, the mother of eight grown-up children (some of whom are referred to by name in the text). Her home in Mary Road, Stechford was named Clover Bank where she lived with her husband and youngest daughter Winifred (known as Peg). She also had a second home, renting the old gate lodges to Campden House, next to the church, in Chipping Camden, Gloucestershire. In October 1939, being a car-owner, Claudia Renton had offered her services as an ambulance-car driver. The following year she enlisted in the Mechanised Transport Corps (MTC) and continued to work in a similar role. What follows are extracts from her journal, as written in late-1940:

20th October 1940

About the middle of October I arrived on early morning shift at 7a.m. and Mr Cansell rushed me off at once to an incident and so relieve those who had been there all night. It was in Bishop Street/Gooch Street. Several had been buried in cellars there and gas and water pipes had burst too, so the poor beggars had no chance. I saw them bring about 15 out, one at a time, and I helped to tie them up in their shrouds. Oh the terrible sights! As we were fastening one up and examining her, thinking her dead, she turned her head and opened her poor, swollen black eyes and asked for a cup of tea. She was rushed off to hospital (after a sip or two of tea). But it was so sad to see the people standing about waiting for their children and mothers to be dug out. One poor man was only allowed to see his daughter's shoe – they wouldn't let him see her face to identify her. She was too terrible to look at. I followed him into his house, the rescue men had to nearly carry him, and his old wife was weeping in her apron. I patted them and took their hands and said, 'Let it comfort you to know she was killed outright, she would not suffer.'

'Oh do you think so, Ma'am?' the old lady said looking up from her apron. I said, 'Yes, most certainly'. She said, 'Those are the most comforting words I have heard.'

As I passed through the barriers where hundreds of people were, they called to me, 'God bless you for what you are doing'. I couldn't keep the tears back. One woman came clambering up from the back of ruins with her face all cut and coat torn. She had found her own way out somehow. It was just like someone rising from a grave for such it was. Five of the rescue-men went over the pile of ruins to get her and helped her over into the street where such a cheer went up from the crowd at sight of her and a man ran forward and kissed her and another boy too. One white-faced lad, about 17, had been standing around looking at each corpse as they were brought up. Then seeing one he cried, 'My Mam' and went away. I wanted to go after him but I was too busy, I couldn't leave. A lot of the dead could not be identified, even the neighbours could not identify them, they were so knocked about. We searched their pockets for any sign of identification but in some cases it was quite hopeless. I was there from 7a.m. until 1:30p.m. and still they had not dug them all out. Being the only one in khaki such a lot of people evidently thought I was in charge, for they came to me, ever so many parsons among them and I sent them into the homes of the bereaved. One gentleman gave me a very low bow and raised his hat, then came and talked and I was told after he was the Earl of Dudley, but I was too busy and worried to bother to talk to anyone. Some kind old workman came following me about with a jug of tea and a cup. I refused often, then in the end simply had

Claudia in her formal MTC uniform.

Claudia in the garden of her cottage at Chipping Camden.

to have it to please him. That was a ghastly grim business and made one realise what war is.

About the next night after that, there was a heavy raid around Stechford and Yardley. Two or three houses opposite Dorothy's old house in Vera Road were down. Dorothy had only left a week about. A bomb fell in Mary Road. I was in the hall at the time and it felt as though the lounge and dining room were falling together – the hall seemed to sink, I gripped the door of the dining room. Several of our windows were broken with it. Just round the corner from Richmond Road three or four houses were down. Seven children and a father were all killed in one house. Our night shift had to turn out and the seven children were all laid out under our shed. The garage where we get our ARP petrol was completely to the ground, and lots of houses in Bordesley.

End October 1940

During the last week or two there have been awful raids in Birmingham. Shops and factories down everywhere. Fires going all night. On Saturday night[62] I stood in the veranda watching the bombs dropping over Birmingham. You would see flashes like sheet lightning lighting up everywhere, then 'Bang', the bomb had dropped, and a *trrrrrrr* – the building falling, collapsing like a pack of cards or toy bricks.

I am not on night duty, but those who were went out. A bomb dropped close behind the escort car (which would have been mine had I been on) and it raised it high in the air, and down it came with a bump. The driver thought it was all-up. Our ambulances picked up a lot of dead from the Picture House, Stratford Road and had to take them to mortuary where floors were full of dead people,

A 1932 Morris Oxford after conversion for use as an ambulance. Claudia in her protective clothing for use in the event of a gas attack

A formal occasion with Mayor Wilfred Martineau outside Birmingham Council House in summer 1941. Claudia Renton is second from the right together with another MTC ambulance driver.

hundreds of them I was told, they just took them in and dumped them down – no one there to receive them, and a girl of 20 had to help carry them in!

18th December 1940

So much has been happening to poor old Birmingham the past month and more, and I have not had the least inclination to write it down, but I will recall just a few of the experiences, giving description of one week only.

About five weeks ago I went to Coventry – the Coventry that was – to give my off-duty day to help in any way I could. No traffic at all was allowed past Stonebridge, but being in uniform and having our sectional flag on car I was allowed to pass without even showing my identification cards. In fact, the policemen made way for me. When I got to Coventry I could not tell where I was, every street and building was down to the ground, all gutted, smoking and smouldering. It was a pitiful sight to see the Cathedral down, where Alec took us one Sunday afternoon about three years ago to a recital. I reported to Police Headquarters and there were hundreds of people waiting in queues to get a hearing – homeless people – a way was made for me by police and I walked straight through and offered my services. I was sent to Hospital Infirmary, and from there was given a list of people to look after and find homes for. The addresses of refuge homes were given to me but as all phones were down it meant actually going to these places to see how many they could take, and oh it was so difficult to find the places and all roads blocked.

I got hold of the first aid man from Courtaulds who was also on the same job and he was a great help in showing me the way. We found the slum district we went for, and the people there were just sheltering under bits of corrugated iron; their walls, ceilings, doors and windows were all out and if the beds were left they were drenched with water and bricks and rubbish. One old man in particular, he was nearly dead, he was sitting in a chair by a fire for his fire grate was left but no walls around it, and there he had sat since the place was bombed, no one had been near him, only neighbours to give him food. He was too weak to stand. The doctor had seen him and said he must be got away somewhere – but where – all hospitals were full. So that is why the hospital

sent me to him, but I had to climb over piles of bombed buildings to get to him, so I knew it would be a stretcher case to get him out of it at all. I went to the RP for an ambulance, but the whole place and ambulances had been bombed – in fact all of them had. There were ambulances from other towns working, but where? I went to the address of a refuge home given me and found it was just a chapel and filled with squealing children, no place for the poor, dying old man. Then I found this first aid man who helped quite a lot. We found the Sister of a First Aid Post who promised to send an ambulance for the old chap when one returned and the first aid man said he would go and see that it was done. In the meantime, I took several old people and children to refuge homes. It was most pitiful the things they wanted to take with them from their destroyed homes. There was no water, gas or food in the town. The people were being fed by mobile canteens and when a lorry arrived with loaves on, it was surrounded and soon sold out. The miles of people waiting for buses to get them away carrying their pet cats and canaries and pots and pans and all kinds of things, where they were going goodness knows, they didn't know themselves. They were all black from the bombing and no water to wash, yet you could see and hear rushing water at the bottom of all bombed premises. The Ministry of Information had a van there driven by one of our MTC ladies, and he was speaking through a loudspeaker telling the people all their children were to be at such a place at such a time to be taken away at once, they feared an epidemic, and he said no one must use their lavatories, they must do as their grandfathers did, dig a hole in the garden. There were craters everywhere and I saw a van had run down one and a car in another, so I had to leave Coventry before dark, leaving all the desolation behind me.

The next day I was on duty from 3 to 10 but sirens went and rain started and we are not off duty until the all clear goes, even though it is all night. So this Tuesday [19th November] night raid started early, bombs dropped all around this school (our post). Every house in the street at the side of school (Drummond Road) was struck and several on fire. The screams and shrieks of the people were only drowned by bombs falling all the time. Every morning

we expected this school to go too; for it is such a target. I am sure all the bombs dropped on Drummond Road were meant for this school for so many ARP posts have been struck. We were all sent down into those cellars, and the men called up as they were wanted to go out. Many of them returned soon on the verge of collapse and looking so black and sooty that you would hardly recognise them as the full-of-life fellows they were when they went out. Young Oakley from grocers Stechford was one, when he returned he could not speak, sweat was pouring down his black face. He had been fire fighting. There were fires, fires everywhere you could see – brighter than day and sunshine. Many of the rescued people were bandaged up and sent down into the cellars with us – poor things suffering from shock.

Then the call came down the trap door for Mrs Renton. So I had to climb up through this trap door and drive my own car and follow the ambulance to Cherry Wood Road. Fordrough Lane Post Office Stores had been bombed and was burning – in fact everywhere was burning. We had to drive on the footpath all the way up the road, and when we got to Cherry Wood Road where people were trapped under a house the men took the stretchers and clambered over the fallen house and I had to stand by ambulance and pass anything they called for. They had gone out of sight and hearing, over the wreckage to back of house and as I sat on back of ambulance gripping on, screaming bombs fell all around me, lights blazed from every window as the glass and blackout fell out and houses crashed all around me. I was spellbound and not afraid as I watched walls bulge, then collapse. I had a man with cut eye to take to first aid for treatment, and the way I had come was all blocked. I had to go another way then found a house right down across the road. Two men helped me to move some of the bricks to get over, I thought every minute the car would overbalance. Then I got through and another bomb in front of me blew down one of the big green standards and cables for trams, and a fire started. I had to drive between fire and craters and over these overheated cables. Whether they were dangerous or not I knew not, but thought the rubber tyres were non-conductors and I also had rubber boots on and so I got back to depot with my patient. Then I had to return to scene of incident. Still they had not got people out, they could hear cries and a baby crying. I said, 'Let me come, let me help', but they said 'No', it was a case for Rescue Squads who knew their work. We may have done more harm by trying to untrap them, more would fall on them. So I rushed away to report a rescue squad was needed. "Old Sugar" said, 'Never mind, they will soon be dead, they have stopped calling now…'. I rushed back and reported and a rescue squad was sent at once. Our men were returning all from different

Notes

62 The subsequent reference to the Picture House (the Carlton) on the Stratford Road would strongly suggest this is actually Friday 25th October 1940.

63 Colour codes were used to indicate the level of risk of a raid occurring. These were: yellow, purple and red, the last being the signal for the public warning to be given. White was the code for the all-clear to be sounded.

places, and were all on the verge of collapse. Many did. One driver told me, only yesterday, that if he had been sent out again he would be in a lunatic asylum by now.

That terrible night has played havoc with our personnel. Such a lot have turned the job in since then, one of our men drivers had been four years in last war, yet said that all those years put together he never saw half as much as he saw in Bordesley Green that night. He has been off ever since and we hear he can never face it again. Every time he hears a bomb drop he shrinks into a corner on the floor and cries, and they dare not leave him. Yet he was a hardened old soldier. I got home about 3.30a.m. Dorothy and Peg were sleeping under dining room table. Pat in pantry. Father and Claude in bed. I felt like patting myself on back for coming through it so well, yet I could not sleep. I worried about those trapped people and wondered if they had been got out alive, and regretted I was unable to lift the tons and tons of bricks under gunfire and bombs. As the bombs fell I gripped on to back of ambulance and it was lifted, it just bounced. I had only been back a few minutes when the school, our depot, was actually struck. We all scuttled and lay down in the passage. It made a terrific row but only roof damaged and not badly.

The next night was inky black, no fires to light up Birmingham and I had to drive a patient to hospital. It was so black that when I got there I had to get out of car and feel for gates to drive in by, nothing at all to guide me, and no lights allowed on car. I had to wait 2½ hours for that patient, they hadn't a bed or would have kept her. While I was in, bombs were dropping. In all my life I shall never forget that drive back in the blackout. There was not a soul about, or a car, and it was so black you could not see the outline of buildings even to see where you were. Bombs had been dropped the way I had come and there was a white tape across a crater. If I had been going any faster than 5 miles an hour I could not have seen it. No one about to ask, and I tried several routes with the same result, all blocked until I found myself going round in circles. Surely some guardian angel took the wheel that night for after about two hours I got back to Stechford and safety. It was pouring in torrents all the time, but luckily no bombs dropped near although planes were over. But it was even worse than driving between fires and bombs the night before, for all Birmingham was ablaze then and we could see where we were going. I was feeling pretty rotten but went on duty next day as usual, but when the raid started about 7p.m. I just about collapsed and knew I could not go through another night of it, so just said I was going home, where I arrived in a state of collapse. Claude got me some brandy which helped to pull me together, and Peg was so glad I was home. We had a twelve-hour raid that night. It was dreadful, the bombs were so near. It seemed each one was for us. As soon as the all clear went I went to see Queenie and Dorothy, of course they and everybody had been up all night long. It had been a terrible raid and lot of people killed and trapped. They found arms, heads, limbs all shot away. Worst fate of all is to be trapped and so many are trapped for days sometimes and then found alive. After that I was away for 2½ weeks. I went to Campden for a rest alone and intended staying a week, but that first night I heard the deadly planes overhead going over, hundreds of them. I thought each was for

Birmingham and maybe Stechford and Yardley and I could not rest. I got up at 3a.m. and dressed and went back early. The terrible suspense was worse than being actually in the raid.

After 2½ weeks I came back to the depot yet felt I could never stand any more; the people here talking about the raids made me go all hot and trembly inside – I gave a week's notice. So many had left after that terrible week. I worked my week's notice out and here I am, still here. I was asked if I would give it another trial; orders had come from Headquarters that no women were to be sent out at night unless it was very urgent. So here am I hoping I can stick it and feel I have done something worthwhile in my life. With Norman a Captain and Alec doing so well in India, I feel I want to carry on this job until the end of the war, but when the raids start at night I go all of a tremble.

There was a bad raid last Thursday [11/12th December] and I was on duty from 2p.m. until 3a.m. and when I got back there was Peg sitting up for me. Father and Claude had gone to bed. We went to bed, but raid got very much worse so we got up and I made a fire in kitchen grate for all gas was cut off, and we sat by fire all the rest of the night. I should not fear doing anything during raids in the daytime but in the nights it is too terrible for words. The

morning after the Friday's raid I went to town. It took me two hours to get there and two to get back by car, for whole streets were bombed and it was a pitiful sight to see the homeless people just gathering what they could find of their homes. No water or gas for a week anywhere and people had to wait their turns in queues for water and water carts. The three nearest depots to ours have all been bombed down to the ground. They are Kings Road, Tyseley; Montgomery Street, Small Heath and Antony Road, Saltley. There are huge craters where these depots were, and a lot of casualties among the personnel. The cars in yard were turned completely over and the ambulance like a concertina. I prefer sitting in my car during a raid to sheltering in the cellars, but after seeing these cars, no more in cars for me.

There goes the bell time 7p.m. – yellow[63], so in a minute lights will go out and we must assemble in the hall with our kit and tin hats on ready to be called upon to go out if raid is around here. So once more I close and hope for the best and next week it will be Xmas – God save the King and all of us!

Thank you to the family of Claudia Frances Renton (1883-1968) for their kind permission to use these extracts from her diary.

Above and below: **Bomb damage to houses in Vera Road, Yardley during 1940.**

THE BLITZ PHASE THREE
SPRING 1941

Following the raid of 11/12th December 1940, the people of Birmingham enjoyed a period of three months' relief, only interrupted by minor nuisance attacks. With the worst of the winter weather behind them, in March the Luftwaffe renewed its night Blitz across Britain. Seaports continued to be the main objective but industrial cities like Birmingham and Sheffield were not overlooked. During the spring of 1941 Birmingham would be subjected to four sizeable attacks.

What was the thinking behind these raids of spring 1941? By this stage it was obvious that the night bombing was not going to force the British government to seek a peace settlement, because the nation was determined to press on with the war. Although the notion of tit-for-tat reprisals continued to be used for propaganda purposes, this was not the reason for the renewed vigour of Luftwaffe attacks. Hitler's mind was concentrated on more weighty matters than the vengefulness he had expressed in early September 1940.

The waging of economic war by bombing continued to make sense. Hitting centres of industry, ports and associated residential areas would hinder Britain's ability to strike any meaningful blows at Germany which might endanger Hitler's grand plans elsewhere.[64] These grand plans were supposedly known only to Hitler and a few of his privileged officers.

In early April Hitler called together all of the Luftwaffe commanders in France. In a two-hour long meeting he informed them that the second phase of the Battle of Britain was to commence. This would be an intensification of the night bombing. In attendance was General Adolf Galland who, after the war, when speaking of the spring attacks of 1941 said, 'Later he [Hitler] told two of us, my friend Mölders and myself, that these had only been to camouflage the offensive against Russia.'

The raids were to be a major feint, diverting the world's attention from Hitler's preparations for the forthcoming attack on the Soviet Union. Thanks to the work of the code-breakers at Bletchley Park, the British government was fully aware of these preparations and was keeping the Soviet leader, Joseph Stalin, informed. The latter chose to disregard the warnings. If Hitler had been aware that his secret intentions were compromised, would the air raids of spring 1941 have been less intense? Quite possibly.

During the winter months, much effort was expended on developing and increasing the number of RAF night fighter squadrons and ground control infrastructure.[65] This was not reflected in the number of German bombers brought down at night – three in January (the anti-aircraft guns claimed twelve) and four in February (the guns eight) but, due to the bad weather, Luftwaffe activity had been much reduced. In March night fighters were reckoned to have destroyed 22 German aircraft (the guns 17) and, from here on, as will be seen in the following pages, there was no looking back for the 'boys in blue'. No longer would the Luftwaffe crews be contemptuous of Britain's night defences.

On 11th March the Germans launched what they claimed was their fifth major attack on Birmingham. The raid commenced at 21:10 hours, when HE fell on Small Heath, and lasted until midnight. Three HE also fell on Redditch. Fire-raising was the German's main objective, with incendiary bombs falling on Bordesley, Stechford, Erdington, Sutton Coldfield, Handsworth, West Bromwich/Wednesbury and Walsall. As things turned out, the city escaped lightly with minimal casualties. Some bombs landed on industrial sites but it was residential areas which bore the brunt, with nearly 100 houses badly damaged but none beyond repair. For the influx of recent recruits to the civil defence, this was a baptism of fire. The fire brigades and other defence services responded quickly and minimised the damage.

The main attacking force came from *Luftflotte* 3 with *Luftflotte* 2 in support. About one third of the German bombers either diverted to other targets or aborted, leaving 135 which claimed to have reached the primary target. The force consisted of Heinkel He 111 and Junkers Ju 88 bombers, with the latter in the majority. The weather was not ideal and much bombing was done using radio navigational aids or dead-reckoning. Some crews were tasked with hitting industrial centres in the north-west of the city, but Birmingham as a whole appears to have been the target. Nearly 30,000 incendiaries and 122 tonnes of HE bombs were released according to German sources, although it is very doubtful that anything like this amount actually fell onto the city.

On 'All Fools Day' (1st April) there was extensive cloud and rain across much of the country,

The East – Hitler's Primary Goal

The acquisition of Austria (1938) and Czechoslovakia (1938-1939) had come easily enough. The invasion of Poland, in September 1939, presented no major problem, save that it caused Great Britain and France to declare war on Germany, so forcing Hitler's attention to be diverted westwards for more than a year.

With astonishing speed, the Germans occupied most of north-west Europe but failed to knock out Britain. Hitler made the fateful decision to go eastwards anyway, planning to attack the Soviet Union in May 1941. This had to be postponed another month whilst he dealt with pressing issues in the Balkans, as well as coming to the aid of Mussolini in North Africa.

The German attack on the Soviet Union, which was given the codename 'Operation Barbarossa', commenced on 22nd June 1941. With the exception of KGr100, all of the Luftwaffe bomber units known to have been involved with attacks on Birmingham in spring 1941, found themselves transferred to the East during the summer of that year.

making ideal conditions for a number of *Pirat* raiders. One such, a Junkers Ju 88 V4+BS from 8/KG1, headed for Birmingham. The poor weather may have offered the bomber crew protection from British defences, but it proved their undoing as the Junkers, with its bombs still on board, flew into high ground at Clee Hill. The aircraft disintegrated and all the crew were killed.

More raids occurred in Holy Week. On the night of 7th April at least one German aircraft dropped incendiary bombs on Kings Heath and the Austin factory at Longbridge. Also, in the Northfield area, the bomber made diving attacks, firing its machine guns. On the next night while Coventry was under heavy attack, Birmingham was on red alert for most of the night-time hours. No records of specific bombing have come to light, but 914 Sqn (barrage balloon) recorded, 'Enemy raid over Birmingham and districts,' and again after midnight, 'Enemy raid still in progress.'

These nuisance raids were followed by two bigger attacks. The double-blow struck on the nights of 9/10th and 10/11th. The 9th April was a Wednesday and, as on many previous occasions, the north-east, east and south-east districts, together with the city centre, were allocated to specified bomber units, gas works and railway facilities being considered of particular importance. *Luftflotte* 3 was given the task of providing the aircraft and mustered 282 for the job. Junkers Ju 88s were now being used in increasing numbers. In the event, 237 Luftwaffe crews reported that they had bombed Birmingham with no less than 40,000 incendiaries and 285 tonnes of HE. With springtime came shorter nights and so the raid did not commence until 21:45 hours. Shortly after 02:00 the last bombs dropped from a Junkers Ju 88 of II/KG1 and the various emergency services were left to, quite literally, pick up the pieces. Fatalities were around 330 and injuries were in excess of 800, half of which were deemed as serious. This would turn out to be the city's highest air raid casualty rate other than the raid of 19/20th November 1940.

After some initial incendiaries fell on Nechells, the raid developed as both HE and incendiaries were dropped. Areas affected included: Bordesley Green – including the Mulliners' factory, and then Sparkbrook, Small Heath – BSA at 22:30, Shirley – Deloro Stellite Ltd, Stechford – Parkinson Cowan Stove Co where the fire required the attendance of 14 pumps, Aston – Perfecta Steel Tube Co, Hockley, Ladywood, Spring Hill, Adderley Park – Morris Commercial Cars, Ward End – Wolseley, Saltley – Metropolitan-Cammell Carriage and Wagon Co and the Corporation gas works, Erdington – Birmingham Electric Furnaces at 22:30 and Dunlop at 00:50, Northfield, Kings Heath, Oldbury and Nechells – including the power station

and the nearby Corporation gas works. Birmingham City Transport tram depots at Miller Street and Washwood Heath were also hit, ensuring that around 30 trams would never carry passengers again. Public transport was crucial for getting workers to the factories engaged in essential war work. The railway network was badly disrupted and eight stations including both Snow Hill (GWR) and New Street (LMS) were hit. It would take some days to get roads unblocked and trains moving freely once more.

Around midnight the focus shifted to the city centre which was badly pounded. Fires took hold in Moor Street, Masshouse Lane, Holloway Head, High Street, New Street, Dale End, Edgbaston Street, Digbeth, Deritend, Highgate and the Bull Ring. The Midland Arcade caught fire from end to end i.e. from High Street to New Street. Marks & Spencer, C & A Modes and the Co-op were each caught up in the blaze. In the meanwhile, the fire on the corner of High Street and New Street got out of control and began to spread. Senior officers thought that the Royal Engineers should blast a firebreak, but before they could do so buildings collapsed anyway and the job was done.[66]

Amongst the churches hit were Birmingham Cathedral and St Martin's in the Bull Ring. With so many fires to deal with churches were left to burn, as priority was given to industrial and residential properties. Fire destroyed a number of buildings on the east side of the Bull Ring. The Prince of Wales Theatre in Broad Street was destroyed, as was Birmingham's oldest hotel, The Swan. The General Hospital was hit on this night and on the following one also. When its inability to cope with the influx of casualties was realised, an emergency annexe was pressed into use in the basement of Lewis's department store.

The fires in the city centre were well concentrated in a half mile square area. The Germans used a lot of explosive incendiaries, and the usual problem of having insufficient fire-watchers on duty in the city centre allowed fires precious minutes to kindle. Nevertheless, by 08:00 the following morning, the firefighters had all fires under control although 1 major, 20 serious and 40 medium fires were still burning in the afternoon, and damping down continued into the next day. Many residential, public and commercial buildings were damaged or destroyed. Although most factories escaped serious damage, production was adversely affected by interruption to water, gas and electricity supplies. West Bromwich in particular lost its electrical supply.

One factory hit, which has not been previously mentioned, was that of L H Newton & Co of Nechells, manufacturers of nuts, bolts and screws. The Nechells area suffered badly and a number of people from homes in the immediate

Notes

64 Hitler appears to have convinced himself that he just needed to keep Britain at bay until 1942 when, having dealt a swift, decisive blow to Russia, he could renew the offensive in the west.

65 By mid-February the disposition of night fighter squadrons was: 96 Sqn Hurricanes and 307 (Polish) Sqn Defiants (9 Group), 87 Sqn Hurricanes and 604 Sqn Beaufighters (10 Group), 85 Sqn Hurricanes/ Defiants, 219 Sqn Beaufighters, 264 Sqn and 141 Sqn Defiants (11 Group), 151 Sqn Hurricanes/Defiants, 255 Sqn Defiants (one section), 25 Sqn and 29 Sqn Blenheims/ Beaufighters (12 Group), 600 Sqn Blenheims (13 Group).

66 When eventually cleared this site became known as the Big Top.

The scene in Edgbaston Street following the raid of 9/10th April 1941. This street would become the location for a memorial to the victims of Birmingham air raids – see page 130. BirminghamLives

More damage, this time in Love Lane, Gosta Green. BirminghamLives

Opposite page: Damping down shops on the east side of the Bull Ring 10th April 1941. Mirrorpix/ Birmingham Mail

Prior to the outbreak of war, the city's fire brigade had taken delivery of a number of vehicles equipped with ladders of considerable extension. A demonstration of this equipment was conducted at Birmingham Central Fire Station. The following quote is from one fireman who was at the top of a 100 feet ladder over the burning Midland Arcade on 9/10th April 1941: 'It was a frightening experience up there, by myself, hearing bombs exploding and having no protection, thinking the next one could be mine. Was I scared! Somehow we struggled on until, towards dawn, the raiders dispersed, reinforcements arrived and water was relayed to the site.' via Transport Museum, Wythall

THE LUFTWAFFE OVER BRUM

area joined workers in the Newton's factory basement to shelter from the bombs. Incendiaries fell on the factory and while these were being attended to a high explosive bomb crashed through the four floors, exploding when it hit the ground floor and exposing part of the basement. With the spreading fire it was necessary to evacuate 400 people (some of whom were injured) from the basement shelter. The incident resulted in acts of heroism, some of which were recognised by the awarding of medals.

* * *

Although Birmingham was the principal target on this night, Tyneside also received a major attack and Coventry, along with other towns and cities, suffered to varying degrees. The Luftwaffe did not have it all its own way as the RAF's latest night fighting tactics began to bear fruit. Of the dozen or so air combats which occurred that night, some can be directly connected to the Birmingham raid. One of these, which resulted in a Heinkel crashing at Smethwick, has been described in great detail elsewhere in this book. Others are now referred to.

A Heinkel He 111H (w/n 3181) 6N+BK of 2/KGr100 was supposed to be one of the early arrivals over Birmingham. Patrolling off the south coast was a Beaufighter (R2187) from 604 Sqn. Its pilot, Flying Officer (Flg Off) Roderick Chisholm, was directed by his ground controller to climb to 17,000 feet and given a course to bring him on to the track of an incoming raid. His radar operator (RO), Sgt W.G. Ripley, quickly picked up a contact on his cathode ray tubes. The raider was 7,000 feet ahead and below. Ripley guided his pilot, bringing the Beaufighter in so that it was astern and slightly below, a now classic position for a night fighter to open its attack. The time was 21:17 and the two aircraft were over the New Forest in the area of Ringwood. Once Chisholm had a visual contact of the Heinkel, he closed in slowly to a distance of 50 yards. He opened up with his four cannons, and a three-second burst which discharged 57 rounds was enough to send the bomber spinning to the ground below with its tail detached. Chisholm was forced to pull up violently to the left in order to avoid debris from the Heinkel. As the RAF crew looked down, they saw the explosion of the impact and subsequent explosions as the incendiary bombs went off. The aircraft had come down at Cranborne in Dorset. The pilot managed to bale out successfully, but the rest of the crew were less fortunate; three died in the wreck and another was killed because, although he baled out, his parachute failed to deploy properly.

The Wittering-based 151 Sqn made a number of claims. At 23:12 hours Flt Lt Desmond McMullen and his gunner, Sgt S.J. Fairweather, took off in their Defiant (N3403 call sign 'Steeple 5') as part of a five-aircraft (A Flight) 'Fighter Night' patrol. They headed for Birmingham where they proceeded to patrol at 13,000 feet. They could see the fires below and in no time Fairweather, who was strapped into his cramped gun turret, spotted a bomber below and ahead at a distance of about 400 yards. Manoeuvring his Defiant so that they approached the enemy from below, McMullen took the fighter into point-blank range. Shooting upwards Fairweather put in a three second burst with his four machine guns from about 25 yards range. The fighter overshot and the bomber made the most of the opportunity and proceeded to take evasive action, making climbing and diving turns. McMullen was a seasoned pilot, having destroyed more than a dozen enemy aircraft to date, and so was able to stick with his prey. Further attacks were made again from below and to the port side of the bomber, which the RAF crew had identified as a Heinkel He 111. The German's port engine caught fire and the flames spread quickly. The Luftwaffe pilot apparently attempted to ram the British fighter but Fairweather put in one last burst causing the enemy to crash west of Bramcote, near Nuneaton. The Defiant landed back at Wittering at fifteen minutes past midnight. Fairweather, who had fought most of the action with just three of his four machine guns functioning, had expended 330 rounds.

In fact the downed aircraft was not a Heinkel but a Junkers Ju 88A (w/n 2170) 3Z+AL of I/KG77. The Junkers had crashed at 23:35. Three of the German crew successfully parachuted to the ground but the fourth crew member was killed.

A second 'Fighter Night' operation, again consisting of five Defiants (B Flight), got airborne shortly after 01:00. Sgt Lionel 'Jack' Staples with his gunner, Sgt K. Parkin, approached Birmingham in their Defiant (N3479) and soon saw a German bomber. Taking it to be a Dornier Do 17, Staples took up station below the right wing of the enemy and Parkin sprayed the fuselage with

Flt Lt McMullen (right) and his gunner Sgt Fairweather who brought down one of the Birmingham raiders on the night of 9th April 1941. Roddy McMullen via acesofww2.com

This 151 Sqn Defiant (N3387) is the aircraft in which Sgts Bodien and Jonas brought down a Heinkel He 111P on the night of 9/10th April 1941. *Courtesy of Amanda Low*

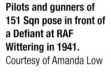

Pilots and gunners of 151 Sqn pose in front of a Defiant at RAF Wittering in 1941. *Courtesy of Amanda Low*

a long burst of fire from just 25 yards. The bomber turned towards the Defiant and dived, causing Staples to take avoiding action. As the German pilot dived his machine he also weaved in an effort to throw off his assailant. Staples was able to latch on to him, giving Parkin opportunity for a further three bursts. Smoke belched from the port engine and something dropped away from the bomber, which Staples and Parkin assumed to be a crew member. Convinced that the enemy was going down, Staples climbed to avoid getting in amongst the barrage balloons.

Arriving back at Wittering, the crew claimed one Dornier destroyed. However, the combat report was later altered to one Heinkel He 111 probably destroyed. It is nigh on certain that no Dornier unit was operating over Birmingham that night. It does seem that Staples' victim may have limped home as there is no unaccounted-

for wreckage that subsequently came to light.

Getting airborne soon after Staples was Flt Lt Donald Darling with his gunner, Plt Off J. Davidson, in another Defiant (N1808). While flying at 11,000 feet over the east of the city, they spotted a Junkers Ju 88 heading south-west. At about 01:40 (just when Müller's Heinkel was going down over Smethwick – *see Part One*) Darling brought his Defiant in underneath the Junkers and Davidson hit the belly with two two-second bursts from 50 yards. The enemy aircraft dived, followed by the Defiant, both machines braving the balloon barrage. In the mist and rising smoke over the city the Junkers was lost to view and so Darling headed for base. There is some doubt as to what became of the Junkers Ju 88, but there is reason to believe that it is the same machine which succumbed to anti-aircraft fire and crashed in Hertfordshire at 02:00.

Flt Sgt Edward Thorn, together with his air-gunner, Sgt Fred Barker, was the most success-ful Defiant crew of the war, accounting for 12 and one shared German aircraft destroyed. They served with 264 Sqn based during this period at Biggin Hill. They were airborne over southern England on this night when, at 10 minutes before midnight, they were vectored by their GCI station to bring them within the vicinity of a possible target. This turned out to be a Heinkel He 111P (w/n 1423) G1+DN belonging to 5/KG55, which was on its way to Birmingham.

The experienced crew was almost clinical in its approach to the job at hand. They com-menced their attack from about 100 yards on the starboard side of the bomber, from where Barker let off a two-second burst of fire. The Defiant was manoeuvred beneath the Heinkel to appear on its port side where a second burst of similar duration set the Heinkel's port engine aglow. Now, flying over the top of the Heinkel, Barker fired into the cabin. Thorn lowered his aircraft, going to the starboard side of his victim, allow-ing his gunner to deliver a fourth and final attack. The German bomber was now in a steep dive giving off white smoke. The Defiant followed it to 9,000 feet whereupon it disap-peared in cloud. The Heinkel's fate had been sealed and it crashed at Godalming, Surrey.

Another RAF fighter type airborne that night was the Vickers Supermarine Spitfire. The Spit-fire was not well suited to night fighter opera-tions. Its long nose, narrow-track undercarriage and tendency to overheat while ground manoeu-vring, meant that getting it on and off the ground at night could be demanding for the pilot. In addition, as a gun platform, it was less stable than the Hurricane, being better suited to dog-fighting with other fighter aircraft, rather than as a bomber destroyer. Nevertheless, some Spit-fire units were used to bolster the night fighter squadrons, one such being 266 Sqn, also based at Wittering. From a military history aspect, it is worth mentioning at this point an interception

which took place over Birmingham in the early hours of 10th April.

At 01:00 hours, 266 Sqn's Flt Lt D.L. Armitage took off in a Spitfire II (P8010). Along with two other Spitfires, Armitage was to patrol over Birmingham which was still under attack. Fly-ing south over the city at 15,000 feet, he saw a Heinkel He 111 silhouetted against the fires on the ground. The enemy was flying southwest and Armitage turned after it. The Heinkel, which was 200 feet lower, rapidly grew in his sights – he was coming in too quickly. Armitage pressed the firing button at 100 yards and continued to close in. His incendiary bullets struck the fuse-lage of the bomber. The flashes of the De Wilde ammunition exploding on impact dazzled the Spitfire pilot, causing him to break away vio-lently. Once out of immediate danger he looked to resume the attack, but the Heinkel had gone. Armitage returned to Wittering, putting his air-craft on the ground at 02:40. He estimated that his eight Browning machine guns had been fired

The Spitfire was not so suited for night operations but 266 Sqn, one of the Wittering-based units, flew 'fighter night' sorties over Birmingham in April 1941. Author's collection

for 2-3 seconds and that they had found their mark. A claim for one 'probable' was submitted.

A less conventional method of night defence which, unlike the Hampden Patrol, had not yet been abandoned, was the practice of laying a curtain of aerial mines suspended beneath parachutes.[67] At this stage in the Blitz, it was 93 Sqn which was given the dubious role of aerial mine laying. Initially they flew some obsolescent Handley Page Harrow aircraft, but these had been replaced by the American-built Douglas Havoc I twin-engined type. On this night Flt Lt Pat Burke, flying from Middle Wallop, was airborne in a Havoc (BT465). Under instruction from a GCI station, he sowed an irregular pattern of mines south-east of Portland Bill. A Heinkel He 111 flew into the screen of mines and Burke put in a claim for one Heinkel probably destroyed.

Another more conventional Havoc squadron was No.85 based at Debden, Essex. It was still in the process of exchanging its Hurricane fighters for the radar-equipped Havocs and this night was to be its debut with the new type. Wg Cdr Peter Townsend[68] engaged a Junkers Ju 88 and had to be satisfied with submitting a claim for one 'probable'.

* * *

During the previous weeks, there had been a drive to recruit more people to join the Civil Defence in order that they might quickly suppress the incendiary menace. Supplemented by personnel from local military units and members of the Home Guard, volunteers did excellent work in residential areas putting out fires and rescuing people from collapsed buildings. Their mortality rate, however, was three times higher than that of the general public.

On this night (9/10th April) 11,000 wardens had been on duty. The Lord Mayor publicly commended the work of the fire prevention wardens: 'Not only were they responsible for dealing in the first instance expeditiously and satisfactorily with countless numbers of incendiary bombs, many of which might well have led to serious fires, but when, in spite of their willing efforts, conflagrations developed, they rendered the fire services very valuable help.'

On the next night, both *Luftflotten* 2 and 3 made up the attacking force, with the former despatching 40 bombers and the latter 290. It is not known how many actually hit their primary target. The Luftwaffe crews reported dropping more incendiaries than ever – 41,608, together with 246 tonnes of HE. Far fewer bomber crews actually hit Birmingham on this raid than the Germans themselves believed. Coventry suffered this night due, no doubt, to a misidentification of the target city, while some 300 misplaced incendiaries fell on the small village of Wootton Wawen, about 20 miles south of Birmingham.

On the night 9/10th April 1941 Flt Lt Pat Burke was flying this Douglas Havoc I serial number BT 465 belonging to 93 Sqn. This squadron was tasked with laying aerial minefields. Although this type of operation had limited effect, on the night in question Burke was credited with one Heinkel He 111 'probable'. Simon Parry

Luftwaffe crews were briefed to attack along a line stretching from Castle Bromwich airfield to the city centre, along which they understood there to be many important factories connected to the aircraft industry. Returning crews reported seeing hits on the Dunlop factory. By the time the last aircraft departed the area at around 03:00 hours, fires appeared to be blazing all over the city and the airmen were confident that the raid had been a good one. In fact there were 70 fires of varying magnitude, compared with around 400 the previous night.

The two Pathfinder units *Gruppen* KGr100 and III/KG26, each using their specialist radio navigational aids, had dropped their fire-markers between 22:19 and 00:05. Whether it was according to plan or not, Junkers Ju 88s of KG76 and III/KG1 commenced their bombing earlier at 21:40. A typical example of a Luftwaffe crew attacking Birmingham on this night is that of aircraft commander Martin Reiser of 9/KG55. His crew took off from their base outside Paris at 23:48 in their Heinkel He 111 (G1+BT) with a bomb load of 3½ tonnes. Mission completed, they landed 3½ hours later at 03:18 (times BST).[69]

Notable fires were reported at Hall Green, Acocks Green, Solihull Lodge and Erdington. When bombs fell on the Dunlop factory roof, and many fires began, the works' fire brigade was elsewhere engaged. Some employees volunteered to go onto the roof and tackle the flames, which were illuminating the thick black smoke, smoke that was also visible to the Germans flying overhead. The brave volunteers were soaked with water and covered with black grime from the burning rubber. These workers eventually received compensation for their damaged clothing, which amounted to 7/6d (37.5p)! High explosive did much damage to five bays in the aero tyre shop. Another factory at Erdington, that of Con-

structors Ltd, suffered a roof collapse after being hit by an HE bomb. Elsewhere, unexploded and delayed-action bombs caused disruption to transport and the evacuation of W Canning and Co in Great Hampton Street, Hockley. Also at Hockley, the tool manufacturer John Rabone & Sons Ltd caught fire due to incendiary bombs.

In the light of the previous night's attack, people were not slow to use air raid shelters and, consequently, casualties were considerably fewer. Again, those branches of the Civil Defence tasked with fire prevention did good work. The worst and most tragic incident was in Smethwick, which resulted in the deaths of 22 people and two rescuers. This occurred when, at 01:55, a raider dropped bombs in the area of Windmill Lane. A row of four terraced houses was destroyed and 19 people perished in the basements where they were sheltering. More bombs from the same aircraft killed another three people. The two rescuers were fatally poisoned as a consequence of escaping gas.

* * *

Once more an encouraging number of bombers fell to the guns of RAF night fighters. The raid on Birmingham was expected and, to support 151 Sqn with its patrols over the city, 256 Sqn (whose normal task was to cover the ports in the north west) was called in to assist. So it was that nine Defiants of 256 Sqn left their home base of Squires Gate, Blackpool and landed at Tern Hill, Shropshire at 20:25 hours. With the first German bombs going down on Birmingham, the order was given for 256 Sqn to launch a 'Fighter Night' patrol.

The first ever victory for a 256 Sqn crew was the destruction of one of the pathfinder Heinkels of III/KG26. Flt Lt E.C. Deanesly and his gunner, Sgt W.J. Scott, were airborne at 21:55 in their

Notes

67 Due to the enthusiasm of the Prime Minister and the Admiralty, this experimental project, given the codename *'Mutton'*, was persisted with for many months. The 'long aerial mine' (LAM) consisted of 2,000 feet of piano wire with a small bomb at the bottom end and a parachute at the top. The idea was to unspool a number of these 'mines' from patrolling aircraft, in order to form a curtain in the predicted path of enemy bombers. If a raider struck one of the wires, the pull of the parachute would bring the bomb into contact with the aircraft causing it to explode. The project was not a success and was abandoned once the Blitz of 1941 had drawn to a close.

68 Peter Townsend hit the news headlines in the mid-1950s due to his close relationship with Princess Margaret. Marriage was denied the couple owing to the fact that he was a divorcee.

69 This same crew had operated over Birmingham on the previous night, taking off at 23:07 and landing at 02:30 (times BST).

During the evening of 10/11th April 1941, to assist with the defence of Birmingham, part of 256 Sqn deployed from its base at Blackpool (RAF Squires Gate) to Tern Hill in Shropshire. Within this contingent was Flt Lt Christopher Deanesly who, together with his gunner Sgt Jack Scott, attacked a Heinkel He 111 which came down at Radway, Warwickshire. Defiant T3981 JT-H of 256 Sqn was photographed over Blackpool.
via Les Whitehouse

Notes

70 After the war when speaking of this combat, Deanesly described the initial sighting as being a formation of three Heinkel He 111s, but the combat reports of the time do not mention multiple aircraft.

71 Some sources quote that this Heinkel was brought down by a Defiant of 264 Sqn, crewed by pilot Flying Officer Desmond Hughes and air-gunner Sgt Fred Gash. This assertion is unlikely to be correct.

72 Richard Plane Stevens shot down 14 – plus one shared – German aircraft during 1941. He served throughout the year with 151 Sqn, flying Hawker Hurricanes. It was in such an aircraft that he met his death, while flying on an intruder operation over Holland in December 1941.

Defiant (N1771) coded JT-U. The crew was told to patrol at the higher layer of 20,000 feet, but the order was soon changed to allow the fighters to operate independently. Although there was mist above the city at between 1,000 and 5,000 feet, the RAF crew observed flames on the ground through breaks in the cloud. Having spotted condensation trails above, Deanesly climbed to 20,000 feet and in the bright moonlight – it was almost full moon – the gunner alerted his pilot to a Heinkel He 111 on their starboard side.[70] Deanesly turned to chase his quarry, but lost it.

Then both Deanesly and Scott simultaneously saw another bomber on their port side. They made a quick turn and, aided by the Heinkel's condensation trail, they managed to keep the enemy machine in view. The Heinkel was about 600-800 yards ahead and 200 feet lower, going south. The Luftwaffe crew's mission had been to attack the aircraft factory at Castle Bromwich. Although the enemy machine appeared to be diving, apparently the crew had not seen the British fighter. Defiant interceptions were normally close-in affairs, but Scott delivered his first burst from a distance of 200 yards. They were at 13,000 feet and his pilot had positioned him on the port beam, slightly lower than the Heinkel. His aim was accurate and strikes were seen going into the engines. Scott fired again and the Heinkel caught fire. The bomber turned towards the Defiant coming as close as 50 yards, but no return fire was directed towards the fighter. More bursts from Scott's guns saw the enemy machine spiralling downwards with an engine on fire. Deanesly followed it to 10,000 feet but broke away at that height to avoid the balloon barrage. Climbing back to 15,000 feet the pilot radioed base for a homing. Deanesly later recalled that the return flight to Tern Hill was hazardous because of radio failure and cloudy conditions. Nonetheless, he touched down safely at 23:15. Another 256 Sqn Defiant (N3460) on a later patrol was not so fortunate. Low on fuel and lost, the crew baled out landing near Cannock at 03:00.

Deanesly's 'kill' was Heinkel He 111H-5 (w/n 3623) 1H+FS. Two of the crew were killed and two, although injured, survived, having taken to their parachutes. On fire and breaking up, the aircraft hit the ground at Radway, near Kineton in Warwickshire; wreckage was strewn far and wide. Crash investigators failed to spot any remains of the aircraft's *Y-Gerät* equipment.

About an hour earlier another III/KG26 Heinkel He 111H-5 (w/n 3592) 1H+JD had been intercepted and shot down by a Defiant of 264 Sqn as it crossed the south coast bound for Birmingham. The bomber was crewed by staff from the *Kampfgeschwader's* third *Gruppe* (Stab III/KG26). The Defiant (N3307) was being flown by Flt Lt Eric Barwell, and Sgt A. Martin was in the gun turret. The German pilot ordered his crew to take to their parachutes. Three got down safely but one other airman's parachute failed to deploy properly and he was killed. Meanwhile, the pilot, Lt Conrad, managed to put the Heinkel down on the golf course near Seaford in Sussex. The aircraft smashed into anti-invasion poles and wires. The pilot survived the wreck and joined his three comrades in captivity.

Later in the night, the same Defiant crew flew a second sortie and attacked another Heinkel He 111. They filed a 'probable' claim. A Beaufighter crew from 604 Sqn also attacked a Heinkel around the same time. From Luftwaffe loss returns it has been suggested that the two fighters had seen the demise of a I/KG55 machine.

Neither did KGr100 escape loss. Fw Otto Kunze and his crew from the third *Staffel* had

THE LUFTWAFFE OVER BRUM

taken Heinkel He 111H-3 (w/n 6929) 6N+HL to Birmingham in order to bomb a specified factory using their *X-Gerät*. Radio signals were not satisfactory and the crew attempted to bomb visually from 13,000 feet. They were frustrated by the cloud cover and became lost. The decision was taken to return to base, while hoping to find a worthwhile target on the way. No such opportunity had presented itself before they were intercepted by a Beaufighter (R2208) of 604 Sqn, flown by Flt Lt Georgie Budd, with radar operator Sgt Evans. Kunze put his laden aircraft into a series of evasive turns. These did not prevent cannon shells exploding in the cabin of the bomber which caught fire. Kunze ordered his crew to bale out, and three managed to do so but once more two of the parachutes failed to open properly. The Heinkel appeared to break up, the two burning pieces floating down and crashing on the Isle of Wight at 11:28, with two of the crew and the bomb load still on board.[71]

Two Junkers Ju 88As went down in the English Channel in the early hours. The first was from *Stab* III/KG1 (w/n 3207) V4+AD at 00:20 off Selsey Bill. The second was from I/KG54 (w/n 2185) B3+PH, which went into the water near Swanage at 01:45, having fallen victim to a Beaufighter of 604 Sqn. In both instances the crews were lost.

As with the previous night, 151 Sqn, which flew a mixture of Defiant and Hurricane fighters, put up aircraft to defend the skies in the Birmingham area. During 1941, Plt Off Richard Stevens was to excel as a night fighter Hurricane pilot.[72] On this night (10/11th April) he added two more victories to the four he had scored already.

Taking off from Wittering at 22:45, Stevens appears to have abandoned his search for the enemy in the city's immediate area as, one hour later, he engaged a Junkers Ju 88 at a height of about 16,000 feet north-east of Banbury. After he had poured 1,600 rounds of ammunition into the bomber, in two long bursts of fire, debris flew off the Junkers, drenching Stevens' Hurricane (V7120) with oil. The German machine dived straight into the ground, the impact point being between Bicester and Oxford. All members of the crew were killed. The investigators of the wreckage identified it as Ju 88A-5 (w/n 4203) V4+FV of 11/KG1.

Stevens landed back at Wittering at 00:25 hours, where his aircraft was refuelled and re-armed. He was up again less than two hours later heading westward and, in the moonlight, it only took 15 minutes for Stevens' sharp eyes to spot a Heinkel He 111 flying in the opposite direction and slightly higher than he was himself. He brought his fighter round to attack from the stern. At a distance of 150 yards he gave the bomber a three-second burst. Stevens was temporarily blinded by an explosion from

The Hawker Hurricane proved to be a satisfactory type when serving in the night fighter role. One of the Hurricane squadrons which switched from day to night operations was 87 Sqn. An example from this unit is seen in this rare colour picture.
RAF Museum

KGr100 – The Fire Raisers

The German bomber unit *Kampfgruppe* 100 played a significant role in the night attacks on Birmingham. Throughout the period August 1940-July 1941, according to the unit's own records, it carried out 24 separate night raids against the city.

KGr100 specialised in locating and then marking with incendiary bombs the target area so that other units could drop their loads onto the fire-markers. KGr100 did not restrict itself to this pathfinding function, but also dropped its own share of high explosive. Nor was it the only target-marking unit so employed; II/KG55 and later III/KG26 performed similar tasks, but it was KGr100 which dominated in this field, using the *X-Verfahren* radio navigational aid.

In 1938, 7 and 8 *Kompanien,* which had been experimenting with a secret radio navigational system, formed the basis of a new bomber unit *Luftnachrichten-Abteilung* 100 (Air Signals Section 100). The aircraft type used was the tri-motor Junkers Ju 52/3. Modern equipment, in the form of the Heinkel He 111, began to arrive at the start of the following year, going first to 8 *Kompanie*. Training with the *X-Verfahren* was stepped up in July and August in anticipation of the invasion of Poland. The proficiency of the unit was recognised and it was declared operational. Aircraft strength was: 7 *Kompanie,* 12 Ju 52s, and 8 *Kompanie,* 8 He 111s.

The unit participated in the Polish campaign of September 1939, bombing tactical targets by day and cities by night. The *X-Verfahren* was used and, although confirmation of bombing results was lacking, the German crews were confident that the system was up to the job. Flying back to its base at Köthen the unit's morale was high, boosted by the fact that there had been no losses. By the close of the month *Luftnachrichten-Abteilung* 100 (LnAbt 100), in keeping with regular bomber *Gruppen,* had its own *Stab* (staff flight) with two aircraft and 7 and 8 *Kompanien* were soon renumbered 1 and 2. By mid-October, both 1 and 2 *Kompanien* were flying the He 111, with 12 aircraft apiece.

On 18 November LnAbt 100 became KGr100, giving the unit the full status of an independent bomber wing. The two *Kompanien* were now 1 and 2 *Staffeln*. Three experimental flights were made over London during December, testing the *X-Verfahren*. No bombs were carried.

Early in the new year KGr100 moved to Lüneburg,

leaving some staff and a small training unit at Köthen. Disaster struck on 13th February when the *Gruppenkommandeur* of KGr100, Obstlt Joachim Stollbrock, was making an *X-Verfahren* trial flight over the Thames Estuary. His aircraft was intercepted in the fading light by Spitfires of 54 Sqn. The crippled bomber crashed into the sea off the north Kent coast. There were no survivors nor was wreckage of the aircraft 6N+AB found. As a consequence, the *X-Gerät* was removed from the unit's aircraft. As no attacks against the British mainland were imminent, it was prudent not to risk the equipment falling into the hands of the British any sooner than could be helped. One supposes that further trials were suspended for the present. Ten days later another loss occurred, this time to 'friendly' flak over the island of Borkum, north-west Germany.

KGr100's operational role was now armed reconnaissance over the North Sea and attacks against shipping, particularly around Scapa Flow. It was 30 miles south east of this naval base when, on 10th April, KGr100 lost its third aircraft.

It was around this time that the unit adopted its own emblem which was to be painted on its aircraft. This was a Viking ship with a black hull and a red and white striped sail superimposed on a blue disc. A most appropriate choice as KGr100 soon found itself heavily committed to operations in the Norwegian campaign of April and May. This campaign was a baptism of fire with the loss of five aircraft on operations.

The following two months was a time of expansion and further training. The *X-Gerät* was again installed in the aircraft and many new crews were introduced to it. There were plenty of new crews, as a third *Staffel* was formed. By the 20th July, KGr100 had three *Staffeln*, each with an establishment of 12 He 111Hs. The *Stab* had another three, with a further three spare. However, due to routine maintenance, repairs and modifications, only 12 were available for operations. Although 28.5% availability sounds low, it was typical of German bomber units at that time.

As the Battle of Britain commenced, KGr100 moved to its new home, a former civilian flying club field at Meucon, near Vannes in Brittany. Situated near the Atlantic coast, the unit's new home was spartan. The runways were grass and maintenance had to be performed in the open air. A small, open-ended hangar was available. This could just accommodate the nose section and engines of a single Heinkel and was used

for major maintenance, while an old barn became a workshop. A few wooden huts served the essential administrative needs. The aircrew were accommodated in nearby hotels. The only shelter for the aircraft was canvas covers for the engines and canopies, not ideal for the sensitive radio equipment on board the machines. Despite misgivings on the part of the Commanding Officer, Hptm Kurd Aschenbrenner, the airfield proved to be adequate.

Unlike most other bomber units then gathered in France, KGr100 was to concentrate on night attacks, in particular targeting factories involved in aircraft and armament production. KGr100's first bombing attack against Birmingham (and indeed England) was on the Castle Bromwich aircraft factory on the night of 13/14th August 1940 and its last against Birmingham is believed to have been on the night of 4/5th June 1941. In that month, six aircraft were lost on operations over England. It was at this time that KGr100 moved to Chartres, about 60 miles south-west of Paris, for a brief stay. A bigger move was imminent.

In July 1941 KGr100 left France in order to participate in bombing attacks against Moscow. In November, it moved back to Germany and was located at Langenhagen, where it rested and replenished. Here a full-blown *Kampfgeschwader,* namely KG100, formed, the existing KGr100 becoming the first Gruppe within that unit (i.e. I/KG100) on 20th December.[73]

The importance of the unit's contribution to the night Blitz was appreciated at the highest level by both the Germans and the British. Hermann Göring sent his prized bomber wing the following New Year message for 1941: 'I express to the CO and to the *Gruppe* my sincere thanks for an achievement unique in history.' He spoke of their effort and added, 'I am convinced, my comrades, that in 1941 as well, you will know only victory.' The *Reichsmarschall* wished each of them '…much luck and continuous success in the coming year. Heil Hitler!'

On the British side, Professor Frederick Lindemann, a scientific adviser to the Prime Minister, Winston Churchill, had briefed the latter in September 1940 regarding the importance of KGr100's contributions to the Luftwaffe's night air attacks. A commando raid, codenamed *Operation Savanna,* was planned whereby paratroopers would be dropped near to Vannes, with the intention of effecting an ambush of the aircrews as they travelled between their hotel billets and the airfield. It may be assumed that Churchill, keen as he was on commando raids, would have given his backing to the venture. However, the Chief of the Air Staff, Sir Charles Portal, shrank from having one of his aircraft involved in what he saw as an unethical operation, amounting to assassination. His objections were laid aside and, on 15th March 1941, five Free French Army paratroopers were dropped from a Whitley aircraft.

The following day, dressed in civilian clothes, the French paratroops made an information-gathering sortie, only to discover that the airmen travelled in a variety of cars and not, as was believed, en masse in buses. This rendered a single, surprise attack impossible. The mission was abandoned and the troops returned to England via submarine.

Heinkel He 111H of KGr100 with the unit badge visible beneath the cockpit. via Chris Goss

within the Heinkel before delivering a devastating attack which saw the engines and fuselage erupt in fire. The Heinkel He 111P (w/n 2827) G1+AT of 9/KG55 came down near Kettering. Of the Luftwaffe crew, three died and two survived to be taken as prisoners.

For the second consecutive night, a 93 Sqn Havoc released aerial mines over the English Channel. On this occasion the Havoc (BB894) was piloted by Flt Lt Dennis Hayley-Bell, who made a claim for one enemy aircraft probably destroyed.

Likewise, 85 Sqn's Peter Townsend was aloft in a Havoc coded VY-Y (BJ461) night fighter and got into a tussle with a Junkers Ju 88. Under instruction from his radar operator, he was brought to within 300 yards of the German. Townsend was approaching far too quickly and so executed a series of 'S' turns and closed down the throttle in order to kill the speed. At a distance of 100 yards he opened fire from behind and below. The flashes from his ammunition obscured the target and he was forced to break away. Townsend was fortunate to be able to rejoin the combat and again attacked the Junkers from below, only this time the German gunners responded with intense and accurate fire. A third attack failed to produce a decisive result and the high-ranking fighter ace could only claim a 'damaged'.

* * *

As with the major attacks of the previous November, in these April raids firefighters were hampered by insufficient water supplies. Even flooded bomb craters, which had collected escaping water from broken mains, were drawn from. The work and co-ordination of the fire services was again questioned by some city council-

Plt Off Richard Stevens with his 151 Sqn Hurricane. The horizontally mounted plate, below and ahead of the cockpit, was in order to protect the pilot's night vision from being impaired by the exhaust flames.

lors. On 29th May a special meeting was held and reports were heard from the chairmen of the ARP and Emergency Committees together with the Fire Brigade Committee. The identified inefficiencies were, however, to be resolved not at a local level but at a national one. The formation of the National Fire Service on 18th August 1941 saw the nationalisation of all fire services, resulting in the amalgamation of the Auxiliary Fire Service and local fire brigades. Under the new arrangement Birmingham, together with Coventry, Rugby, Redditch and some Black Country towns, was covered by number 24 Fire Force. Councillors and committees would have been more at ease had they known that whilst the Luftwaffe had not yet finished with Birmingham, the worst was over.

This Heinkel He 111 of III/KG55 displays its night camouflage.
via Creek

Note 73 (opposite page) Sister pathfinder unit III/KG26, the *Y-Verfahren* specialists, became II/KG100 at the same time.

Below left: **Fw Siegfried Rühle was the flight engineer aboard the Heinkel He 111 brought down by the searchlight crew at Earlswood in the early hours of 11th May 1941. He did not survive the crash.**

Below right: **The first time that British defences spotted one of the fender-equipped Heinkel He 111s was on 7th April 1941 when such a machine braved the balloon barrage in the Crewe area.**

Bottom right: **The extent of the balloon fender is shown in this picture of an He 111 which has made a forced landing.** RAF Museum

Opposite page, top: **Oblt Johann Speck von Sternberg – a *Pirat* raider.** via Glyn Warren

Another Heinkel Down

Saturday 10th May 1941 was notable for a variety of reasons. Firstly, it was one year to the day since the commencement of the rapid advance of German forces into France and the Low Countries. Also, on that same date, Winston Spencer Churchill replaced Neville Chamberlain as Prime Minister. Secondly, it was during this night in 1941 that Hitler's deputy, Rudolf Hess, made his flight across the North Sea and then landed by parachute near Glasgow. His solo initiative to bring about a peace settlement was not taken seriously by either side. Thirdly, the Luftwaffe launched a massive night attack on London. This involved 507 raiders, some crews flying two or even three sorties that night. An incident less likely to feature in historical accounts of the Second World War but noteworthy, in respect of the Birmingham Blitz, is the bringing down of a second Heinkel in the area.

While virtually all the attention was focused on the London attack, a single Heinkel was dispatched on a *Pirat* action, carrying one 1,000kg and four 250kg bombs. Its target was the rolling mills of Birmetals Aluminium works at Woodgate.[74] Less than 24 hours before, a Heinkel He 111 from III/KG55 had attempted a *Pirat* raid on the same factory. The crew had failed to identify it correctly, dropping their bombs in the vicinity of RAF Pershore, Worcestershire.

An experienced crew for the mission was selected, that of 27-year-old Oblt Johann Speck von Sternberg (pilot), 23-year-old Fw Fritz Muhn (observer), 24-year-old Fw Siegfried Rühle (flight engineer) and 21-year-old Gefr Rudolf Budde (wireless operator). Speck was the commander of the 9th *Staffel* belonging to KG55 based at Villacoublay near Paris.

The variant of Heinkel bomber used was unusual. It was an He 111H-8, a sub-type which featured a 550 lb balloon-cable fender/cutter. This device was a deflector rail of hollow, streamlined section, 8x2 inches, stretching from the wingtips to a point about 6 feet in front of the nose, supported on large, triangulated girders of hollow alloy. There were five supports – a very large one under the fuselage with two decreasing in size, outboard of each engine nacelle. The aircraft itself (w/n 3971) had been delivered to the Luftwaffe earlier in the year.[75] It was allocated the code letters G1+MT,[76] although only the individual identity letter 'M', which was painted yellow, was obviously visible, as most markings had been daubed over with black camouflage distemper.

The crew made landfall over Poole, probably around 23:25 hours. They would have kept west of the activity associated with the London raid, passing over the Cotswolds and along what the Royal Observer Corps in the Broadway area nicknamed 'Heinkel Alley'. German documentation, which came to light after the war, revealed that Luftwaffe bomber crews, seeking to locate the Austin aero works at Longbridge (and

THE LUFTWAFFE OVER BRUM

Birmetals at Woodgate was nearby), should first identify two reservoirs adjacent to a canal, with a railway line to the west that ran north to south. This railway line was to be followed northward to the target. The reservoirs were the Bittell Reservoirs. The canal was the waterway between Worcester and Birmingham and, likewise, the railway.

At two minutes past midnight an aircraft was reported flying through the balloon barrage to the south-west of the city on a north-north-east course and at varying heights. Operators on duty at 915 Sqn (barrage balloon) believed it to be an RAF Blenheim, as it appeared to be showing two orange navigation lights. The air raid warning sounded two minutes later. Sister Squadron 914, which covered the Wythall and Northfield area, reported a Heinkel He 111 entering their area from the south at 00:08 hours. It was noted that the aircraft was showing two red lights under the fuselage in line with the wing leading edge, and a white tail light.

In the moonlight visibility was good as Speck arrived at less than 500 feet over Wythall and Earlswood. The crew had apparently seen Earlswood Lakes. These comprise three separate lakes, two divided by a causeway and the third by a slim spit of land. The Stratford-upon-Avon Canal is adjacent and the Birmingham-Stratford railway line is to the west, running approximately north to south at this point.

The crew appeared confused by these features, being similar as they were to the navigational points they were seeking. They proceeded to circle around the vicinity and at one point the aircraft was certainly noted flying low over Acocks Green. Meanwhile the Royal Observer Corps had been tracking the Heinkel. The nearby observation post, known as E4, was sited about 2½ miles away at Solihull Lodge. Robert Jones was an observer at the post and remembered the reporting system functioning well as the track of the Heinkel was followed.

The local searchlight unit, 380 battery, was alerted and a number of beams probed the sky. According to the 914 Sqn operations record book, a number of sites opened fire on the enemy aircraft. One searchlight site in particular was well placed, that of site BG031 on open farmland at Fulford Heath. With the aircraft flying at an estimated 100 feet and approaching from the north-west at 00:18, this searchlight caught the Heinkel in its beam. The site commander gave the order to open fire with the Lewis machine gun. The gun jammed and by the time the blockage was cleared the aircraft had left the vicinity. Ten minutes later it returned flying even lower on a reciprocal course and again was fired upon, this time with machine gun and rifles. After an interval of five minutes it was back and then returned for a fourth and final time at 00:38.

Manning the site's Lewis machine gun was Lance Bombardier A.A. Hanson. He gave his version of events later:

'Just after midnight we exposed the beam and a few minutes later a plane…was flying very low…it couldn't have been much more than 100 feet…and we saw at once that it was a Jerry. The Sergeant in charge immediately ordered us to disperse the beam (that's to dazzle the pilot) and ordered machine-gun action. I'd been waiting for that moment for fifteen weary months… and I was almost petrified at my luck. The Heinkel didn't seem to be in any difficulties and as I opened fire I couldn't help wondering why he didn't have a go at us, either with a bomb or a machine gun. After a few rounds the Lewis gun jammed, but we put that right and blazed away again. Then Jerry flew away… Ten minutes later, when we'd practically forgotten him, the Heinkel flew back and circled over the site like a giant bat. I didn't have time to think…all I remember saying to myself is, "Well, I've been wanting action. Lad, you're going to have a basinful now." I blazed away and every rifle on the site was being fired in support. After two or three minutes the Heinkel flew away again, but

Notes

74 Interpretations of the German map found near the crash site (see page 102) suggest that the target was the Austin aero works at Longbridge, but this contradicts KG55 records.

75 The aircraft carried a manufacturer's plate stating that it was built by Ernest Heinkel of Rostock and dated January 1941.

76 There is a degree of confusion regarding the third and fourth code letters. One of the two official Air Ministry reports produced states, '…but the aircraft lettering had apparently recently been altered to G1+EM, and a compass card dated 29/4/41 bore this lettering.'

Below: **Fw Rühle, Fw Muhn, Oblt Speck von Sternberg and Gefr Budde on the occasion of their awards of the Iron Cross in early spring 1941. Budde was the replacement crew member when Ofw Martin Reiser moved on to command his own crew.** via Alfred Moos

Note

77 Martin Reiser flew operationally against the British in the First World War. In 1937, as a reservist, he did a 3 month refresher course before returning to his restaurant business. In 1939 he was mobilised and in July 1940, then aged 42, he joined KG55 becoming a part of Speck von Sternberg's crew, with whom he flew until March 1941. By coincidence, his wartime flying came to an end on the same night that his former crew mates were brought down at Earlswood. Reiser's aircraft, an He 111P (w/n 1619) G1+BT of 9/KG55, was participating in the London raid of 10/11th May 1941. During his second sortie of the attack, the Heinkel was brought down by a Defiant of 151 Sqn crewed by Flt Lt McMullen and Sgt Fairweather who also were on their second sortie of the night. The Heinkel crashed at Withyham, East Sussex. Martin Reiser was the only survivor, having safely baled out.

five minutes later it was back for the third time. By the fourth time we were getting a bit irritated. The Jerry plane was like a mosquito at a picnic. You couldn't brush the darned thing away. But this time was K.O. The plane crashed in a nearby field and burst into flames as it hit the ground.'

The site's Troop officer later reported that they had expended a total of around 260 machine gun and rifle bullets across the four actions. Speck had been hit in the head by a bullet. The Heinkel itself may have been crippled. It does seem that a crash-landing was attempted and almost successful. The aircraft came very low over a cottage in Rumbush Lane, then hit power lines, causing a large flash. Next it ploughed through young elm trees and a hedge, shedding pieces of wreckage before finally coming to a halt in a field, belonging to Kidpile Farm, on the north side of Rumbush Lane near to Fulford Hall. The aircraft had crashed about 300 yards north-west of the searchlight site, from where a number of soldiers were detailed to go and investigate the outcome of the action. The Heinkel had caught fire, with flames leaping 40 feet into the air; two of the crew perishing in the front of the fuselage. Another crew member was found dead a number of yards away from the wreck. The youngest crew member, Rudolf Budde, was met staggering out of a ditch with a leg wound and his clothes alight. Members of the Home Guard tore the burning clothes from him. Once the ambulance arrived he was taken to Solihull Hospital and would later be fit enough to be sent to a prisoner-of-war camp in Canada. He eventually returned to Germany. His stay in hospital meant that he avoided being interrogated by RAF intelligence officers.

The most aeronautically 'savvy' person to arrive on the scene was Geoffrey Alington who was then a test pilot working with Austin at Longbridge. When the Heinkel was circling around, he was at a friend's home in nearby Tanners Green. He soon arrived at the crash scene and, running across a field, spotted something white on the ground. He picked it up – a map showing the aircraft's track and destination. Later he passed on this document to the RAF at Wythall instructing them to forward it to Intelligence.

Alington was especially interested in the aircraft's balloon cutter which, in the moonlight, had been clearly visible when the aircraft was flying overhead. Having ascertained that the device was still intact on the wreck, he made sure that a guard was posted until an RAF recovery team arrived.

The story Alington picked up regarding the survivor, Rudolf Budde, is worth relating. Budde was supposedly blown into the air by an explosion, his parachute deploying and depositing him on the ground with his flying suit (just below the waistline) on fire. While this version of events seems quite incredible, it would account for the German parachute silk acquired by some local women for conversion into underwear – a story which made its way into national newspapers early in 2013, following an item on the television programme The Antiques Roadshow. Alington also returned home with some mementos – a machine gun together with a drum of ammunition and a pilot's compass.

Robert Jones at the Solihull Lodge observers' post said, 'We plotted this machine right down to crash-point, and then took the necessary action through our HQ Control to alert other services, including the fire service.'

The local fire brigade arrived to deal with the fire which was made all the more hazardous by machine gun bullets exploding. There is some uncertainty as to what became of the bomb load. Some claim to have heard the bombs exploding before the crash, others (notably the soldiers at the searchlight site) report explosions shortly after. There was evidence of several shallow craters in the field near where the trees were struck.

Once the fire was extinguished, two young members of the Home Guard, Colin North and Dennis Clayton, were posted to guard the site until relieved early next morning. RAF investigators arrived and took charge, with the remains of the aircraft being transported away for careful evaluation.

The subsequent crash report stated that there were signs of cannon strikes as well as machine gun damage to the Heinkel's upper surfaces. This would indicate that the aircraft had been attacked by an RAF night fighter. At that time the only type of night fighter equipped with cannon was the Bristol Beaufighter. There were many night fighter claims that night but only five by Beaufighter crews, none of which ties in with Speck's Heinkel.

It is quite possible that the apparent cannon strikes had been inflicted on an earlier occasion. As mentioned already, the previous night had seen an abortive attempt on the same target and by the same unit. It is quite plausible that this attempt had also been conducted by Speck in the same aircraft (G1+MT). Records show that on that particular night (9/10th May) two separate

incidents occurred when two Beaufighter crews of 604 Sqn each claimed to have damaged an He 111. Unfortunately no time or location is known. Such an explanation remains conjecture…

While a prisoner-of-war aboard the freighter *Rangitti (*sailing from Glasgow to Canada),

Rudolf Budde, the sole survivor, was debriefed by a fellow prisoner, Martin Reiser,[77] a superior officer, who was a former member of Speck's crew. Budde reported:

'I would like to describe our crash in more detail. We left in the evening and arrived

The grave of Fw Fritz Muhn and Fw Siegfried Rühle at the German Military Cemetery, Cannock Chase. Author

A couple of youngsters in the rear garden of a house in Eastfield Road, Little Bromwich. In the adjacent gardens can be seen Anderson shelters; also visible is the LMS embankment, which served as a navigational reference for Luftwaffe crews.
Ken Bird

FRITZ MUHN
FELDW.
28.9.17 +11.5.41

SIEGFRIED RÜHLE
FELDW.
22.12.16 +11.5.41

undetected up to the target. No defence, hardly any searchlights. At the target it got a bit tricky. We started to search, each time along the railway track. On the fourth and last approach a searchlight caught us from the front. At the same moment we were shot. The Oberleutnant was

hit immediately. What happened next was over in seconds. We hit the ground. Feldwebel Rühle who stood in the *Wanne*[78] was ripped apart. Just a cry escaped from him. Then I could only see fire and ammunition going off. I am struck and try to wriggle out. How I managed I cannot remember. In a badly burnt condition I was captured by the Tommies, and then taken to hospital, where I was operated on immediately. This was the course of events of my last enemy flight. I don't like to think about it. All my comrades are dead. It happened for Germany.'

It is noteworthy that Budde makes no mention of an attack by a night fighter, or any other defences, until the Heinkel's arrival over Earlswood.

The three dead crew were taken in the first instance to Fulford Hall. They were buried on 14th May at Robin Hood Cemetery in Hall Green, where they remained until they were exhumed between 18-25th May 1962 and transferred to the German Military Cemetery at Cannock Chase. Here they were allocated graves as follows:
- Feldwebel Fritz Muhn (born 28.9.1917) Block 3, Row 3, Grave No.81.
- Feldwebel Siegfried Rühle (born 22.12.1916) Block 3, Row 3, Grave No.82.
- Oberleutnant Johann Speck von Sternberg (born 15.7.1913) Block 3, Row 3, Grave No.80.

* * *

The last notable raid of the Blitz on Britain prior to the invasion of the Soviet Union was to be what the Germans termed a 'major' attack against Birmingham. This took place in the early hours of the 17th May. Things could have been much worse for the city, but events conspired to cause many of the bombers to drop their loads on another Midlands town, that of Nuneaton.

Brummies had been spared raids for more than a month and so there must have been some disquiet when the alert sounded at 13 minutes past midnight. Both *Luftflotten* 2 and 3 were involved. From each of these air fleets 53 and 58 crews respectively claimed to have reached and bombed the city, dropping 160 tonnes of HE including 14 x 250kg oil bombs and 2,076 incendiaries. As had been the case at the commencement of the air raids on Birmingham, the eastern and north-eastern districts, with their factories being involved in armament and aircraft production, were the main objectives.

The first bombers which arrived over the Midlands had difficulty in finding the target. Their usual visual reference for locating the east of the city – the LMS railway line – was denied them owing to the late moon rise and cloud cover. British interference to the *X-Verfahren* radio beam transmissions played havoc with the four Heinkels dispatched by KGr100 and quite probably the *Y-Verfahren* of III/KG26.[79] Of the former, two Heinkels gave up trying to use

the X-beams and diverted to their alternative target of Southampton. Bomber crews in the earlier stages of the attack tried using flares, but resorted to dead reckoning (in effect bombing blind) and were not optimistic about the outcome of their efforts. Weather conditions did improve and crews who arrived later saw fires on the ground and so bombed onto them. All of this explains why Nuneaton took an unplanned share of the attack – a night of tragedy for this Warwickshire town situated 15 miles to the north-east of the designated target area.[80]

Although the force reaching Birmingham was depleted, a number of important factories were damaged by fire including: Fort Dunlop, ICI (Kynoch Works) at Witton, ICI (Chemicals) at Perry Barr and Wolseley Motors at Ward End. Premier Motors Co (a vehicle supplier), just north of the city centre at Aston, was the site of a serious fire. Further bombs fell in Aston, Erdington, Saltley, Nechells, Sutton Coldfield, Stechford, Yardley, Sheldon, Shirley, Yardley Wood, Kings Heath and the city's central area. The inaccurate nature of the attack saw incidents being reported from the rural boundaries of Solihull – namely Hampton-in-Arden, Temple Balsall and Barston. As ever, utilities were disrupted and many hundreds of residential and commercial properties demolished or badly damaged. It was nearing dawn when the all-clear was sounded at 04:26.The death toll was 36 with a further 60 seriously injured.

A 'Fighter Night' patrol was mounted by 151 Sqn with only one Defiant crew making contact with the enemy. Plt Off G.A.F. Edmiston together with his gunner, Sgt A.G. Beale, took off from Wittering at 02:20 hours and set course for Birmingham. About 20 minutes later they engaged a Dornier Do 17Z, which they estimated to be 15 miles north-west of their base, heading towards Birmingham on a south-easterly course. They made a beam attack and the gunner registered hits on the Dornier's fuselage, with a flash being seen in the cabin. The German pilot executed a steep turn and he was lost to view in the region of Melton Mowbray. The Defiant crew continued their patrol and about half an hour later they were alerted by anti-aircraft bursts to enemy activity south-east of Derby. The RAF crew identified a Heinkel He 111 flying east, presumably on its homeward journey, and they were able to make a beam attack from 150 yards. Again, bullets were seen going into the fuselage of the bomber which, like the Dornier before it, went into a dive and was lost once it entered cloud. Another east-bound Heinkel He 111 was found 35 minutes later, in the process of dropping its bombs, to the east of Coventry. Edmiston and Beale must have thought 'third time lucky' as Beale opened fire, but they didn't see any hits on the Heinkel before it too disappeared into cloud. They had to be content with a claim for two enemy aircraft damaged.

Further south the air defences had more success when at least two bombers were prevented from reaching the Midlands. A Junkers Ju 88A (w/n 5230) V4+IR was intercepted and brought down shortly after midnight by a Beaufighter (T4628) from 600 Sqn based at Colerne, Wiltshire. The successful RAF crew consisted of

Three Beaufighters of 600 Sqn. IWM

Notes

78 The *Wanne* was the belly defence cupola.

79 The RAF's 80 Wing was responsible for radio countermeasures. On the previous night it had, for the first time, seriously affected KGr100's mission – an attack on the Westland aircraft factory at Yeovil.

80 In Nuneaton about 100 people were killed and 170 badly injured. Thousands of homes were damaged and industrial premises were hit. Many fires were started and the town's limited Civil Defence and fire brigade struggled to cope. Help was sent from nearby Coventry.

pilot, Flt Lt A.D.McN. Boyd and radar operator, Flg Off A.J. Glegg. It was their first 'kill' and the team would finish the war with a total of 10 victories. The Junkers which crashed north-east of Exeter was from 7/KG1 and none of its crew survived.

The second aircraft was a Heinkel He 111P from 7/KG55, which like the Junkers, was engaged and shot down around midnight, resulting in the death of all crew members. It had fallen victim to another Beaufighter (R2204), this time belonging to 219 Sqn which was based at the strategically placed Tangmere airfield near Chichester. The experienced pilot was Plt Off A.J. Hodgkinson with radar operator, Sgt B.E. Dye. This pilot, too, was destined to become a night fighter ace. The Heinkel (w/n 2801) G1+GR fell on the Sussex Downs in the Worthing area.

Luftflotte 3 units involved in the spring 1941 attacks on Birmingham were:

Unit	Aircraft Type	Base
II/KG1	Ju 88A	Rosière-en-Santerre
III/KG1	Ju 88A	Amy
III/KG26	He 111H	Le Bourget
I/KG27	He 111H	Tours
II/KG27	He 111P/H	Dinard
III/KG27	He 111P/H	Rennes / Orléans-Bricy
I/KG54	Ju 88A	Evreux
II/KG54	Ju 88A	St. Andre / Bretigny
I/KG55	He 111P/H	Dreux
II/KG55	He 111P/H	Chartres
III/KG55	He 111P/H	Villacoublay
Stab/KG55	He 111P/H	Villacoublay
KG76	Ju 88A	?
KG77	Ju 88A	Juvincourt/Beauvais ?
KGr100	He 111H	Vannes
KGr806	Ju 88A	Caen-Carpiquet

Although the people of Birmingham had no way of knowing it, the Luftwaffe would drop bombs on them just four more times in 1941, each of these attacks being considered minor. With the shorter nights the raids occurred after midnight.

The first took place on 5th June between the hours of 00:40 and 03:15 when a raid affected an area bounded roughly by Lichfield, Atherstone, Birmingham and Wolverhampton. In Birmingham, where at least 9 HE and a dozen incendiary bombs fell, casualties were few and damage was mainly to houses in Nechells. Incidents were also reported at Smethwick, Aston, Saltley, Duddeston, Yardley (cemetery), Edgbaston, Ward End and Sutton Coldfield. The small force of Heinkels and Junkers, however, suffered the loss of three Heinkel He 111s.

Wittering's only Beaufighter unit (25 Sqn) had success over the Wash, when one of its aircraft intercepted a Heinkel He 111. Sergeants Ken Hollowell (pilot) and Dick Crossman (radar operator) were flying in Beaufighter R2154, when they hit the Heinkel with just 41 cannon shells. The German machine went down in the mouth of the Wash at 01:45 and there were no survivors. Ironically, the Beaufighter crashed and was written off when it landed back at Wittering.

Another Heinkel was making its inbound flight westward over the Wash and was from 8/KG4, which was based at Leeuwarden, Holland. 25 Sqn had an aircraft orbiting the north side of the Wash at 12,000 feet. Its pilot was Sgt Horace Gigney and the radar operator was Sgt Gerard Charnock. The ground controller gave the pilot the course for a 'bandit' and subsequently the radar operator was able to see it on his cathode ray tubes, enabling his pilot to make an attack. Gigney positioned his Beaufighter (R2157) to the stern of the Heinkel and let fly with a short burst of cannon fire which was later counted as 44 shells. The bomber appeared to take evasive action and the RAF crew did not manage to stay with it. Actually, the Heinkel He 111H-5 (w/n 3793) 5J+FS was in trouble with one engine put out of action and the other failing. The German pilot, Oblt Hans Paas the *Staffel* commander, ordered his four crew members to bale out, which they did. Meanwhile, at 02:00, Paas managed to bring his machine down in a skilful wheels-up landing, north-west of Skegness. He was able to walk away from his machine into captivity. The relief that Paas must have felt would later be tempered when he was to learn that each of his crew members had drowned when they dropped into the sea.

A Beaufighter (R2190) of 604 Sqn, crewed by Flg Off K.I. Geddes and Sgt A.C. Cannon, was probably responsible for bringing down the third Heinkel He 111H-5 (w/n 4027) 1G+FL of 3/KG27 at 02:27. The machine went into the sea off Ventnor, Isle of Wight and the crew was lost.

One week later, on the 12th, the air raid alert was in place between 00:36 and 03:51 during which time a small force of Heinkel He 111s and Junkers Ju 88s penetrated the defences and dropped their bombs on mainly residential areas in Aston and Erdington. Damage and casualties were considered to be light. In Walsall a single HE bomb fell at 03:20 in Hospital Street, damaging 50 homes and the iron foundry of William Bates Ltd. Six people were buried in the debris of a foundry building, only one of whom survived.

In the early hours of 5th July, with most of the available Luftwaffe bomber units now committed to the war in the East, a small contingent managed to inflict some damage on houses in Yardley Wood, Kings Heath, Moseley, Small Heath, Hay Mills and Erdington between 01:45 and 02:10 hours. Two Heinkel He 111Hs and probably a Junkers Ju 88 were lost in the process.

Each of the Heinkels fell to the guns of Beaufighters belonging to 604 Sqn, the first coming down near Frome, Somerset at 01:07 hours. This was coded 1H+FR (w/n 4087) and belonged to 7/KG26. As the alert in Birmingham spanned 01:17 to 03:36, it is reasonable to assume that the bomber was on its way to this target. Three of the crew parachuted to safety but a fourth was killed. The crew of the Beaufighter was Flt Lt Patten and Flt Sgt Moody. They must have hit the Heinkel He 111H-5 hard, because it disintegrated in mid-air; the tail section hitting the ground 2½ miles from the main wreck. Of the crew, there were three survivors and one fatality.

The other Heinkel He 111 (w/n 5692) 5J+DS, an H-4 variant, belonged to 8/KG4. It was on its homeward journey when it was caught by Beaufighter T4623. The RAF crew, Flg Off I.K.S. Joll and Sgt R.W. Dalton, did not have it all their own way when they attacked the German machine, as they sustained damage to their own aircraft when an enemy gunner opened up. Nevertheless, the Heinkel succumbed and crashed on the edge of Exmoor at about 03:45. As with the other Heinkel, there were three survivors and one fatality. In each case the pilot stayed with the stricken aircraft while the rest of the crew jumped clear.

As the Junkers Ju 88, which was also shot down on this night, has not been identified, one cannot be certain that it was a bomber involved in the Birmingham attack. It came down in the

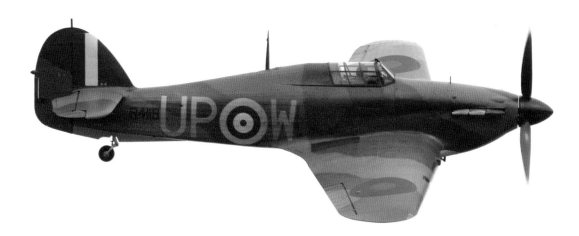

The crew of the Junkers Ju 88D was interned in Ireland where they carved and painted this model of their aircraft.
Oliver McCrossan/ Curragh Local History Group Collection

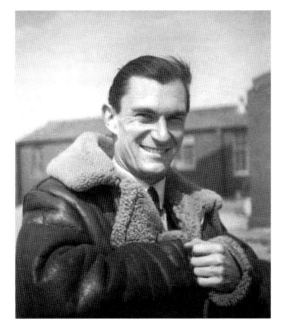

Flg Off René Mouchotte who led the attack on the Junkers Ju 88D reconnaissance aircraft which managed to limp to the Irish coast.
acesofww2.com

sea 25 miles east of Wells-next-the-Sea, Norfolk at 03:00. What the fate of the crew was has not been reported. The Junkers had the misfortune to be intercepted by Wg Cdr David Atcherley with his radar operator, Flt Lt John Hunter-Tod. As Commanding Officer of 25 Sqn, Atcherley was flying one of the Squadron's newer Beaufighters (R2251) which not only had four cannons, but carried an additional punch in the form of six .303 Browning machine guns.

In the early hours of the 9th July a few dozen bombs were scattered over Warwickshire. Minor incidents were reported at Sutton Coldfield, Cotteridge and Weoley Castle. Neither damage nor casualties was inflicted.

As will be readily apparent, during the spring of 1941, the RAF was progressively getting the measure of the enemy night bomber. This was just at the time that the raids across Britain peaked and then dwindled rapidly. Anti-aircraft artillery, with its gun-laying radar, was also having a degree of success. Undoubtedly, claims made at the time were over-estimated but sober analysis after the war reckoned that night fighters and anti-aircraft guns accounted for: March, 23 German aircraft; April, 45; May, 63. All were destroyed at night over the British Isles or around its coasts.

Birmingham was not to experience any more air raids for more than a year, though one or two reconnaissance flights over the city were made. On the afternoon of 26th August, a Junkers Ju 88D (w/n 0396) 4U+HH belonging to the reconnaissance unit 1(F)/123, launched a mission to Birmingham and Bristol. A pair of Hurricane IIs from 605 Sqn based at Baginton, Coventry, took off at 15:15 with a further pair at 15:20 but they failed to make contact with the Junkers. However, it was intercepted and damaged by a pair of Hurricane IIs from 615 Sqn at 18:16 hours over St George's Channel, at a position 40 miles north of Pembroke Dock. As a result, the reconnaissance machine made a wheels-up landing shortly afterwards in Eire, where the four crew were interned, but not before they had set fire to their aircraft. The Hurricanes were based at Valley on Anglesey and the two pilots credited with the victory were Flg Off René Mouchotte[81] and Sgt Hamilton. What was probably a replacement reconnaissance mission took place on the morning of the 30th and two Hurricane IIs from 605 Sqn were scrambled at 08:40 to intercept it. A second pair took off 10 minutes later but none of the Hurricanes made contact with the enemy.

Note

81 A very personal account from this Free French pilot relating to this action may be read in *The Mouchotte Diaries* published by Panther 1957. Mouchotte was shot down and killed in 1943.

THE BLITZ PHASE FOUR
FINAL RAIDS JULY 1942-APRIL 1943

Almost all of the air attacks mounted against Birmingham occurred in an 11-month period (August 1940-July 1941). Indeed, following the attack on Birmingham of 16/17th May 1941, there were no significant air attacks on Britain until the following spring. Once more it was an RAF attack on Germany which stirred up the hornets' nest only, this time, most of the hornets had flown elsewhere and the sting was less potent.

In order to give his bomber crews both experience and a taste of success, the head of Bomber Command, Arthur Harris, dispatched 234 aircraft to bomb the lightly-defended Baltic port of Lübeck on the night of 28/29th March 1942. The beautiful town, being mediaeval in origin, was of historic and cultural significance but of limited strategic value – some U-boat manufacturing was done there. When the fires were finally extinguished something like 80% of the old town had been lost.

Hitler was furious and ordered immediate retaliatory attacks to be made against British towns and cities noted for their architecture, historic and cultural appeal, and even health resorts. These attacks were dubbed the *Baedeker* Raids, being a reference to the *Baedeker* tourist publications. Others call them the 'Cathedral Raids'. Towns and cities which were bombed, often on numerous occasions, during the period April-June 1942 included Exeter, Bath, Norwich, York, Canterbury and Weston-super-Mare.

A notable departure from these attacks came on the night of 24/25th June. A few incendiaries

were dropped in the Bromsgrove/Droitwich area, but more critically Nuneaton was bombed by as many as 35 aircraft. The raid was spread across a one-hour period with the loss of 18 people. The Oram factory in Newtown Road was hit by HE and incendiaries. At the time, the factory was producing components for the Avro Lancaster B.II then in production at the Armstrong-Whitworth factory at Whitley, Coventry. As a result of the attack, production of the finished Lancasters was delayed for some weeks. Again, as on the night of 16/17th May 1941, the town suffered through misidentification, the most likely target being Birmingham or Coventry. This raid must have been something of a wake-up call for the people of Birmingham.

'Wake-up call' is an appropriate turn of phrase because at 06:12 on the morning of 27th July the air raid alert sounded. Around 06:30 a lone German bomber appeared over Solihull. Its

Birmingham City Transport employed gas producer trailers in an effort to save fuel as seen on AEC Regent, OG 392, in 1943, at the Kingstanding terminus, Finchley Road.
via Kidderminster Railway Museum

A wartime picture of Camp Hill, Birmingham; life goes on.
via David Harvey

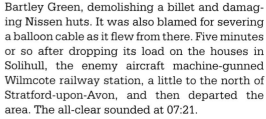

Above: **The Bull Ring as it appeared in 1942. The bomb damage on the east side has been tidied and, following the raids of spring 1941, Lord Nelson's statue has been removed from its plinth, the latter being encased by rough brickwork for protection (see inset).** IWM

target was either the Rover factory in Lode Lane, which was turning out aero engines, or the nearby gasworks. The bomb load missed the target by a few hundred yards and fell on houses in two adjacent streets. Homes were demolished or damaged, 10 civilians were killed and a further 19 seriously injured. The varying degrees of destruction to houses meant that 70 people had to be temporarily billeted elsewhere. Almost certainly this was the same aircraft which, minutes earlier, had bombed a barrage balloon site at

Bartley Green, demolishing a billet and damaging Nissen huts. It was also blamed for severing a balloon cable as it flew from there. Five minutes or so after dropping its load on the houses in Solihull, the enemy aircraft machine-gunned Wilmcote railway station, a little to the north of Stratford-upon-Avon, and then departed the area. The all-clear sounded at 07:21.

That night the sirens gave the warning at 01:43 and the bombers returned to Birmingham in force. With the limited resources available to the Luftwaffe it was, by the standards of the day, a big effort. The two-pronged attack, which lasted for two hours, consisted of about 40 bombers approaching from the east and around 15 (crossing over the Welsh mountains) from the west. The local element of the National Fire Service had its baptism of fire with many fires scattered across the city and its immediate suburbs, requiring the deployment of 468 pumps. Civilian casualties were heavy, no doubt due to complacency. After all, the city had been unmolested for more than a year. As a consequence, just over 100 people were killed and in excess of 130 seriously injured. To the east of the city, a balloon site suffered when it was hit, killing two servicemen and injuring others. Almost 1,000 homes were seriously damaged or destroyed including dwellings in Kings Norton, Harborne, Smethwick, Handsworth, Lozells, Small Heath and Bordesley Green.

Seven factories were permanently put out of action and another 65 notably damaged. Of those damaged by fire were the Castle Bromwich aircraft factory and Mulliners' (coachbuilders) two factory sites at Bordesley Green. Of the latter, which was also hit by HE, extensive damage and loss occurred at the company's Cherrywood Road site. A serious fire developed at Docker Brothers in Ladywood which saw 30 pumps in attendance. This company, a Category 2 key point, was producing 5% (15 tons per month) of the nation's crude phthalic anhydride. Loss of supply of this industrial chemical was considered serious by both the Ministry of Aircraft Production (MAP) and the Ministry of Supply (MoS). Jones & Rooke Ltd at Hockley suspended production after being hit by both HE and incendiaries. The Scribbans bakery in Smethwick went up in flames, as butter and sugar caught fire. Here, despite attendance by 15 fire pumps, a major fire developed and the factory was destroyed. Also at Smethwick, W & T Avery was bombed once again with HE and incendiaries affecting 50,000 square feet of floor space and 10,000 square feet of glazing. Serious fires developed particularly in the casting and pattern shops. Roof destruction occurred in other workshops and some plant was damaged. On the company's railway sidings ten railway trucks were burnt out. As on the previous occasion (the night of 11/12th December 1940),

repairs were made without delay and, even when still incomplete, 80-85% of normal production was being attained within a couple of weeks or so. The Moor Street GWR goods yard saw a serious fire develop, which required 30 pumps to attend, while phosphorus incendiary bombs fell in the vicinity of Birmingham Central Fire Station, Lancaster Street. Nearby at Duddeston, Gabriel & Co, which was producing gun mountings and tank track links, was hit by an HE bomb. In the Bull Ring, Smith's warehouse was reported as being burnt out. A further 100 offices and businesses suffered badly.

As ever, unexploded bombs (UXBs) caused disruption. Amongst the factories where the

Opposite page, bottom: **Solihull had been free from air attacks for more than 18 months when, shortly after 6:30 in the morning, a raider dropped bombs on houses in Alston Road and, as seen here, Cornyx Lane.** Mirrorpix/ Birmingham Mail

Above: **Female workers came from all over the country to work in Birmingham factories. This lady is seen in Rover's Lode Lane plant.** British Motor Industry Heritage Trust

Below: **A German map showing important factories to the south-east of the city.**

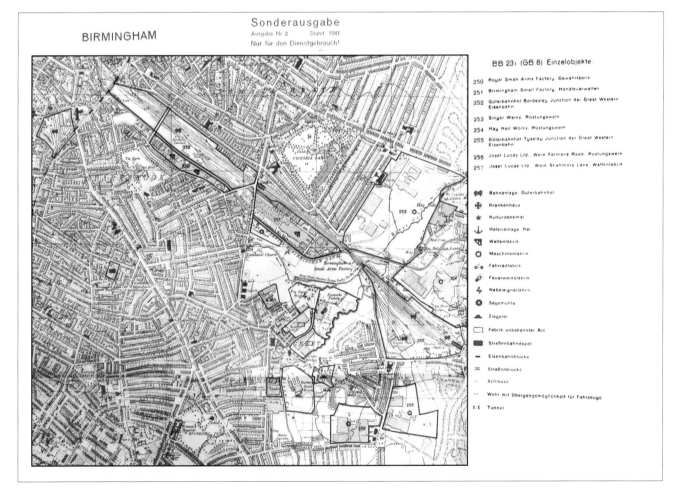

By July 1942 151 Sqn was flying Mosquito aircraft but a number of Defiants were still on strength. Shown here is a Defiant II from that time. RAF Museum.

workers were evacuated or prevented from entering were Wolseley at Ward End, MCCW at Washwood Heath, BSA at Marston Green and Webley & Scott of Weaman Street. Another UXB fell on the General Hospital where a number of patients had to be taken to safety.

A total of 131 fires was reported (4 serious, 9 medium and 118 small). It is a widely held view, perhaps emanating from German propaganda, that this attack was a direct reprisal for Bomber Command's 400-aircraft raid on Hamburg the previous night. This north German port saw 500 large fires which overwhelmed the city's defences and 337 people perished.

By this time Birmingham's faithful eastern sentinel, 151 Sqn at Wittering, was flying the superb de Havilland Mosquito NF.II night fighter. One, and most likely two, of the attacking KG2's Dornier Do 217Es coming in from Holland, were successfully engaged by 151's 'Mossies'. It is known that two of the German unit's Dorniers failed to return that night. One of these was U5+FL (w/n 5484), which went down in the sea off the north Norfolk coast, the crew being lost. At 01:00 and again at 01:30 two Mosquitoes attacked Dorniers, but neither crew actually saw the demise of their own target. The crews were: Sqn Ldr Dennis Pennington with Flt Sgt David Donnett and Plt Off Ernest Fielding with Flt Sgt James Paine, the latter in Mosquito

II DD629. The credit for the destruction of U5+FL is generally given to the former crew, based on the fact that the other crew saw an aircraft burning on the sea in the vicinity of Pennington's action. Fielding's own claim was for a Dornier brought down off Cromer at 01:30.

Seeking to reach Birmingham from the west was Heinkel He 111H-5 (w/n 3527) 5J+UU belonging to 10/KG4. It was intercepted and shot down by New Zealander Plt Off George Jameson in a Beaufighter II (V8136) of 125 Sqn based at Fairwood Common, Swansea. The Heinkel crashed into the sea 15 miles off Cemaes Head, Pembrokeshire at 02:08, but not before it had damaged its attacker with return fire. None of the German crew survived.

Two nights later, starting at 01:32, the reprisal continued and the bombers were back with around 55 aircraft, with 45 approaching from the east and 10 from the west. Most of the bombers attacked Birmingham, although some unloaded their bombs onto Coventry. Based on the statistics, the raid was even worse than the previous one, with more properties affected and 99 killed and 298 injured. Thirty or so factories were destroyed or seriously damaged. Incendiary fires caused consternation at a number of premises including: the General Hospital where there was a serious fire, Small Heath goods yard, the BBC in Broad Street, James Booth & Co at Nechells where two fires developed, United Wire Works Ltd and nearby George Mason Food Depot at Deritend, HP Sauce at Aston, MCCW at Washwood Heath, Wolseley Motors at Ward End, ICI (Kynoch Works) at Witton, Fisher & Ludlow (Rea Street) at Digbeth and BSA Guns at Small Heath. More fires occurred at Accles & Pollock Ltd (Paddock Works) at Oldbury where 10 pumps were in attendance, Phoenix Steel Tube Co at West Bromwich, Guest Keen & Nettlefolds (Heath Street Works) at Smethwick and Mitchells & Butlers brewery also at Smethwick. At the Nechells gasworks a gas holder caught fire when an HE exploded and another HE started a small fire at Dunlop, Erdington. Other districts affected included: the

Mosquito NF.II DD609 of 151 Sqn. IWM

City Centre, Great Barr, Handsworth, Gravelly Hill, Warley, Little Bromwich, Greet and Acocks Green. Taking the two nights together, the large number of fires amounted to 380 and was testimony to the effectiveness of the phosphorus incendiary bombs being included in the bomb loads at this stage in the Blitz.

Again on this night, the Luftwaffe certainly did not have it all their own way, losing seven of the attacking force to the defences, an attrition of about 12%. Such losses were unsustainable. Of these losses, five were on their way to Birmingham, the first of which was Heinkel He 111H-6 (w/n 7544) A1+GR from 7/KG53. It was brought down 42 miles west of Lands End at 13 minutes past midnight by Beaufighter IF (V8274) of 604 Sqn, crewed by Flt Lt William Hoy and his radar operator Plt Off Dalton. None of the five German crewmen survived.

The second victim crashed into The Wash at 01:06 and there were no survivors. It was Dornier Do 217E-4 (w/n 5469) U5+GV from 11/KG2. It had been downed by a Mosquito II (DD669) of 151 Sqn, flown by Australian Flg Off Alex McRitchie who had his navigator/radar operator Flt Sgt E.S. James sitting alongside. Next, having been alerted by ground defences in the form of searchlight activity, James picked up a contact coming straight for them. His pilot deftly turned and was on to the tail of the Dornier Do 217.

Searchlight illumination helped McRitchie in locating the enemy. The Dornier jettisoned its bombs while return fire holed the wooden wing of the attacking Mosquito. The German pilot took violent evasive action as McRitchie clung to him, pouring in cannon shells and machine gun bullets, as the Dornier jinked around the sky. Both aircraft were losing height and ended up at 1,500 feet. The RAF pilot was struggling to see the camouflaged aircraft against the dark ground and, with ammunition expended, broke off the engagement and returned to base, submitting a claim for one enemy aircraft destroyed and one damaged. However, Dornier Do 217E-4 (w/n 5470) U5+ET of 9/KG2 crashed at 02:00, five miles south of Peterborough. The crew were killed. At the time it was assumed that this wreck was the result of anti-aircraft fire but it is almost certainly the result of McRitchie's attack.

The fourth was Heinkel He 111H-5 (w/n 3962) F8+LW from 12/KG40, which crashed on the beach at Pwllheli at 01:35. It fell to the guns of a Beaufighter VIF (X8251) of 456 Sqn based at Valley, Anglesey, with Wg Cdr Edward Wolfe at the controls and Plt Off Ashcroft as radar operator. Two of the five German crew survived.

The fifth bomber, which was prevented from dropping its bombs on Birmingham, was shot down by Flg Off Raybould and Flt Sgt Mullaley, in a Beaufighter of 68 Sqn based at Coltishall,

KG4, based at Leeuwarden, Holland, contributed a number of its Heinkel He 111s to the attacking force which hit Birmingham on the night of 27/28th July 1942. He 111 5J+AC of this unit is in night camouflage. ww2.com

The superb de Havilland Mosquito NF.II was entering squadron service in 1942. This air-to-air study shows NF.II DD750. de Havilland Aircraft Museum

82 The manufacturer's designation was Fieseler Fi 103.

Norfolk. The bomber was another Dornier Do 217E-4 (w/n 1213) U5+DP of 6/KG2. The aircraft was flying in from its Dutch base at Eindhoven and came down on the foreshore at Sheringham, Norfolk, at 02:00. Three of the crew perished and one baled out safely.

Two Junkers Ju 88s which were beating a hasty retreat across the Fens at low level, having bombed Birmingham, were shot down by anti-aircraft fire. The first of these was a Junkers Ju 88A-4 (w/n 3810) 1T+KT from 9/KG26. It was flying at just 50 feet when it was hit in the tail by anti-aircraft fire from Caister and crashed into the sea one mile off Hemsby, Norfolk at 02:30. The four crew survived, to be taken prisoner.

The second, from 7/KG26, was Junkers Ju 88A-4 (w/n 2086) 1T+CR. It was hit by light anti-aircraft fire and then flew into a 25,000 volt power line at Thorney, Huntingdonshire. At 02:45 the aircraft hit the ground and disintegrated, killing the four crew.

This attack of 29/30th was the last large raid anywhere on Britain until the 'baby Blitz' of January 1944. Also known as the *Steinboch* raids, this series of attacks would not affect Birmingham.

On the 30/31st July, Walsall and Wolverhampton were the principal targets. At the former there was a large fire at Hawley, Mills & Co where 25 pumps attended, with notable fires at two transport depots, one belonging to Walsall Corporation Transport. At Willenhall a 14 pump fire ensued at Samuel Parkes & Co (Pretoria Works). Some bombs fell on Birmingham where the alert lasted from about 01:00 to 03:30. Casualties were light in comparison with the previous two raids, with seven people killed. These fatalities were the last attributable to the German Blitz on Birmingham. Damage was restricted to a dozen or so homes mainly in the Little Bromwich, Yardley, South Yardley and Hall Green areas, where HE and incendiaries fell, a few of the latter also dropped in Shirley. One factory known to have been hit by incendiaries was that of Halladays Drop-Forgings Ltd of Witton where production ground to a halt.

Long gone were the nights when Luftwaffe crews considered missions over Britain to be mere 'milk runs'. For them British airspace was a dangerous place and efforts were made by German planners to limit the amount of time spent over the British mainland. To this end, some German bomber units would deploy to jumping-off or forward operating bases to enable them to make circuitous routes to their target. A typical routing was to fly low over the sea (to minimise radar detection), tracking west of Lands End, up St George's Channel, then proceeding northwards close to the Irish coast before turning east and flying across mid-Wales at high speed and so to Birmingham. Having disgorged their load on the city at a little above barrage balloon height, the bombers would dive to low level, continuing eastwards and taking advantage of the lowlands as they exited the danger area. Having crossed Norfolk they would head across the North Sea to Holland, where they might refuel or continue full circle to their French bases.

The final air raid on Birmingham took place on 23rd April 1943. The alert commenced at 23:00 hours and lasted less than 30 minutes. During this time a single raider dropped bombs on Drummond Road, Little Bromwich, where damage was inflicted upon scores of houses, while others fell on playing fields in Saltley. There were no fatalities but 8 people were seriously injured and a further 13 slightly.

Hitler had for some time spoken of his forthcoming secret vengeance weapons, one of which was the pilotless aircraft ('flying bomb') with its nearly one ton warhead – the FZG-76[82]. The flying-bomb campaign of 1944 did not affect Birmingham. Although the city was out of range of the continental launch sites, Heinkel He 111s were adapted to launch these indiscriminate weapons from positions over the North Sea. By using these stand-off techniques, many British towns and cities were potential targets for the flying bomb and Birmingham may have been targeted on three occasions, namely: 24th December 1944, when the bomb actually fell near Kettering; 3rd January 1945, when the bomb fell west of Peterborough and a few days later on 13th January when once more it reached as far as the Kettering area.

The Dornier Do 217E was a superior aircraft to the earlier Do 17. KG2 operated Do 217Es against Birmingham in the raids of July 1942. From this unit is U5+NT. ww2.com

THE FINAL ANALYSIS

How may we sum up the story of German air attacks on Birmingham? To 'sum up' is not too difficult as there are numerical statistics available to the researcher. Numbers are useful as far as they go; they give a sense of scale and present us with an opportunity for comparison. For example: how many people were killed in Birmingham by bombing, as compared with London, Hamburg or Hiroshima? Similarly, what proportion of Birmingham was levelled to the ground in comparison with Clydeside, Dresden or Caen?

One inadequacy of numbers is that they are a cold and soulless mechanism when it comes to understanding the effect that bombing had on actual individual lives. Joseph Stalin may have been speaking cynically when he said something like 'The death of one person is a tragedy; the death of one million people is a statistic', but we know that, unfortunately, there is some truth in those words. It is impossible to measure the pain and sorrow, the physical and mental suffering and the short and long-term psychological effects which bombing had upon each person at the receiving end.

Neither are numbers themselves an accurate indicator of strategic value; for example, just because in February 1945 a large tonnage of bombs and incendiaries caused massive destruction to the German city of Dresden, it is unlikely that the attack shortened the duration of the war or reduced Allied casualties.

Comparisons also need to be treated with caution. Between November 1940 and May 1941, while the tonnage of bombs dropped on London was 10 times that dropped on Birmingham, 14 times as many civilians were killed in London (28,000 as against 2,000).

Nevertheless, despite the limitations of bare statistics and comparisons, I shall endeavour to give some sort of perspective for the Birmingham Blitz.

At the outset it can be safely said that the German bombing of British towns and cities (even London) was nowhere near as devastating as pre-war analysts had feared. In 1925 the Air Staff estimated that on the first day of war London could expect casualties in the order of 1,700 killed and 3,300 injured; then on the second day 1,275 killed and 2,475 injured. Each subsequent day having reducing numbers leading to a levelling off to 880 killed and 1,650 injured. Over the following years these figures were revised – upwards. It was assumed that bombing would create panic and a migration of millions of people to the countryside. Food, water supply and sanitation would be severely impacted. It was said that the loser in any modern European conflict would be the one whose population cracked first. During the 1930s, newsreel footage of the bombing of civilian towns in China, Abyssinia and Spain only served to fuel anxieties. In the late 1930s those with a particular axe to grind painted an even bleaker picture. In 1938 the Marxist writer, J.B. Haldane, declared that 270 aircraft could drop 400 tons of bombs in 30 seconds. This would result in the deaths of 8,000 people and the wounding of around 15,000. Gas attacks were also considered a real possibility. The public perception was that, within hours of the outbreak of war, enemy bombers would drop their lethal loads on London.

The predictions that massive casualties would be swiftly inflicted from the air proved false. Instead, the momentum of the war grew progressively; the quickest events being the *Blitzkrieg* launched against Poland in September 1939 and against France and the Low Countries in May 1940.

When the bombing did start, families experiencing the immediate effect would have gained cold-comfort from the fact that things were not as widespread and intense as predicted. However, for all of those in positions of responsibility, who were required to limit the effects of bombing attacks, there must have been a degree of relief that the Armageddon-like predictions were not realised.

In many instances the tonnage of bombs the German crews believed they had dropped on given targets is known. Claims, even though sincerely made, do not necessarily equate to fact. Then again, knowing the size of a raid in terms of the tonnage of bombs dropped does not provide an accurate indication of those bombs' overall strategic value. To make the point, take the extreme case of the Ruhr dams raid by 617 Sqn in May 1943. The small tonnage of bombs – less than 65 tons, dropped by 16 aircraft – was out of all proportion to the large amount of devastation and the resulting death toll of 1,300 people. On the other hand, the Luftwaffe believed it had carried out a major follow-up attack (i.e. over 100 tonnes of HE dropped) against Birmingham on the night of 10/11th April 1941. The number, however, of casualties sustained and houses and factories seriously affected on this night was relatively small and easily surpassed on other raids, raids which the Germans would have considered only moderate in scale.[83]

Birmingham's Blitz, which spanned three years, produced the following approximate statistics: Total air raid casualties for the entire war was about 9,150 comprising: 2,406 killed, and about 3,050 seriously injured and a further 3,700 injured to a lesser extent.[84] In respect to property: 4,650 houses were never to be lived in again; 25,500 required considerable repair work and a further 74,000 were recorded as damaged; nearly 300 factory buildings had been destroyed or needed to be demolished and about 950 had been repaired; more than 400 offices and business premises fell into the destroyed or in

Notes

83 Using rounded figures to emphasise the point that German claims to have dropped high tonnage did not always equate to high casualties or destruction: the major raid on 9/10th April 1941 killed 300, whereas the 'major' attack the next night killed 50. The non-major raid of 29/30th July 1942 killed 100. Quoting figures relating to collateral damage would make the same point.

84 These figures are based on known fatalities within Birmingham (2,207), Bromsgrove (3), Oldbury (6), Smethwick (91), Solihull (34), Sutton Coldfield (4), Walsall (7) and West Bromwich (54). In the immediate post-war period, the Ministry of Home Security compiled its own figures concerning civilian war dead *viz* Birmingham (2,151), Bromsgrove (7), Oldbury (10), Smethwick (93), Solihull (38), Sutton Coldfield (19), Walsall (12) and West Bromwich (63). What criteria the Government were using to calculate its figures is not clear, as a few deaths are included which occurred in each of the three years 1943-1945; in these years only one air raid took place in the Birmingham area and it caused no fatalities.

Right and below: **These two photographs taken c. 1946 show a bustling city centre with no evidence of the Blitz. Lewis's department store identifies Bull Street. The other picture shows Corporation Street.**
D Harvey collection

Bottom: **Bomb sites were, of course, in evidence in the city centre, notably the 'Big Top' on the corner of High Street and New Street and the Market Hall in the Bull Ring together with, as seen here, buildings on the east side.**
D Harvey collection

need of demolition category and a further 1,250 required repair; finally, 1,900 other properties were either destroyed or notably damaged.

Lest these statistics give the impression of a city devastated by aerial bombardment (as seen in newsreel footage of wrecked German cities), this was not the case. Once the dust had settled and rubble tidied, bomb damage was not obvious, but had to be looked for. Referring to the areas which, before the outbreak of war, had been identified for redevelopment, the City Engineer at a Council Meeting in July 1943 observed that the task of redevelopment was little altered since 1939. In other words, the Luftwaffe had not assisted him as much as it might have! Photographs of Birmingham's city centre, taken soon after the war, could be mistaken for pre-war scenes.

Neither did the bombing come near to disrupting war production. In late 1940 neutral observers from America and Sweden reckoned that production was only being adversely affected to the tune of a few percentage points. This was surely correct; with the exception of BSA at Small Heath, and Fisher & Ludlow, none of the most important factories in Birmingham was very badly damaged or set ablaze. In any case, the policy of utilising dispersal factories was well advanced by early 1941[85]. It is interesting to note that, of the dozens of air attacks on Birmingham, only four raids resulted in more than 100 houses being completely destroyed and only three raids demolished more than 10 factories.

At this stage neither the Germans nor the British realised the shortcomings of bombing factories and what a poor return the effort yielded. By way of example, in 1944, despite the massive bombing attacks on German targets by the British and Americans, more fighter aircraft than ever were being manufactured for the Luftwaffe.[86] Post-war analysis claimed that only 1% of war production was affected for every 15,000 tons of bombs dropped on German industrial targets.

Notes

85 Nonetheless, to quote the *Official History of the Royal Air Force 1939-45, Vol.II* the air attacks of 1940 did adversely affect the nation's aircraft industry as a whole: 'British aircraft production had been seriously impaired, both by direct damage and enforced dispersal of plant: not until February 1941 did output again approach the level of the previous August.'

86 Total German war production was as high in March 1945 as it had been in December 1941 (six months after the invasion of the Soviet Union). Compare these German aircraft production figures for the years 1939: 1,928; 1940: 7,829; 1941: 9,422; 1942: 12,822; 1943: 20,599; 1944: 35,076. It was want of fuel and trained pilots, and not shortage of aircraft, which drove the Luftwaffe from the skies. After D-Day this lack of air power allowed allied ground forces to move around at will, while their German counterparts were constantly harassed from the air.

THE LUFTWAFFE OVER BRUM

Above left: **This Witton street scene could be mistaken for bombed ruins. Although the area was a prime target for the Luftwaffe, most of the homes were not demolished until redevelopment in the early 1970s as depicted here.** Author

Above right: **The attention given to the inner city by the Luftwaffe did not expedite slum clearance. Again, some thirty years after the Blitz, this Witton scene shows a newly-built, high-rise block with the derelict Victorian terraces still in evidence.** Author

Above and far left: **The Bull Ring underwent a transformation in the early 1960s with the whole area (except for St Martin's church) being demolished and then rebuilt.** Author

Left: **At the beginning of the 21st century the Bull Ring was rebuilt once more, although the iconic Rotunda from the 1960s was retained.** Author

As part of the latest Bull Ring development, St Martin's church was given a thorough clean. The architecture of the church building makes something of a contrast to the Selfridges' building (to the left) with its multitude of 'Allegro hub caps'! Author

Notes

87 The most affected area stretched from Aston in the north to Small Heath in the south and Winson Green in the west to Ward End in the east.

88 By way of comparison, the Home Office's Air Warfare Analysis Section, in its post-war work, reckoned that 4,500 bombs (including 49 parachute mines) had been dropped on the County Borough of Birmingham. It was impossible to count the scores of thousands of incendiary bombs dropped during the Blitz.

The Luftwaffe's efforts to hit specific factories within Birmingham were, on a number of occasions, spectacular near-misses, e.g. the Windsor Street gasworks, Fort Dunlop, the Austin factories and the Castle Bromwich aero factory. Most of these were attacked at night, and although only a small proportion of bombs found their mark, many others fell in the immediate vicinity. This was no mean feat when it is remembered that the entire country was blacked out. It must be acknowledged that, at that time, RAF Bomber Command was not in the same league, struggling as it was to find designated German cities, let alone particular areas within those cities. German crews certainly benefited from the use of radio navigation beams, employing to good effect the fire-marker units KGr100 II/KG55 and later III/KG26. The Luftwaffe managed to find, with some ease, specified districts, such as Small Heath/Bordesley/ Tyseley, Erdington/Washwood Heath/Nechells/ Saltley, Aston/Witton, Smethwick/West Bromwich and, of course, the city centre. In this way some bombs were always going to find factories, which were the principal targets, but the consolation prize was the nearby homes of the workers.

The majority of bombs dropped on the County Borough of Birmingham fell within an area amounting to 30% of the city's total land area.[87] Of the 5,129 high explosive bombs, which were recorded by the civil defence as being dropped within the city boundary, 930 did not detonate, a failure of 18.7%.[88] The unreliability of German munitions was demonstrated even further by the much-feared parachute mines, of which 48 were recorded as being dropped within the city boundary, but one third failed to detonate. These 'duds' resulted in casualty figures being lower than they otherwise would have been.

The German Air Force had not been established with a strategic bombing campaign in mind and so lacked heavy bomber aircraft. Such aircraft would have been required in substantial numbers to form a credible, strategic bombing arm. Even if Germany had possessed such heavy bombers, hindsight strongly indicates that bombing for the purpose of critically damaging a nation's industry and economy, with conventional bombs, was unlikely to produce the desired knockout blow. Furthermore, bombing in order to cause the collapse of civilian morale simply did not work. Needless to say, the use of atomic weapons would have been a different story…

Hitler appears to have realised this more quickly than did the Allies. An entry in the diary of Joseph Goebbels (head of German propaganda) dated 27th April 1942, quotes Hitler as saying: 'The munitions industry cannot be interfered with effectively by air raids. We learned that lesson during our raids on English armament centres in the autumn of 1940 and had a similar experience when, vice versa, the English attacked German munitions plants. Usually, prescribed targets are not hit. Often the flyers unload their bombs on fields camouflaged as plants and in both countries the armament industry is so decentralised that the armament potential cannot really be interfered with.'

BIRMINGHAM'S BLITZ IN PERSPECTIVE					
	Birmingham* for the entire war	London's worst raid 10/11 May 1941	Hamburg 24 July to 2 August 1943	Dresden 13/14 February 1945	Hiroshima and Nagasaki 6 and 9 August 1945
Tonnage	2,000	800	9,000	2,660	37,000 equivalent
Killed	2,400	1,450	42,600	24,000	160,000 minimum

* including the adjacent boroughs/districts: Bromsgrove, Oldbury, Smethwick, Solihull, Sutton Coldfield, Walsall and West Bromwich.

WHO SHOT DOWN THE SMETHWICK HEINKEL?

Until recently, published information offered by local history groups concerning the Heinkel He 111 which crashed in Smethwick, credited its destruction to a Defiant aircraft crew, Flt Lt Christopher Deanesly and his gunner Sgt W.J. Scott of 256 Sqn.

Two sources appear to be at the heart of this claim: a dissertation which was written in 1994 by local historian, Peter Kennedy, entitled *The Air Raids on Smethwick 1940-1942* and, secondly, an amazingly detailed work, *The Blitz Then and Now volume 2*, published in 1988. Referring to the latter, there is a reference (page 520) where Deanesly is cited as being responsible for bringing down the Heinkel which then crashed onto houses in Hales Lane, Smethwick. Mention is made of the fact that the RAF pilot was a 'local' Wolverhampton lad. It is, however, the Kennedy work which seems more authoritative.

Kennedy reproduces what he describes as an extract from Deanesly's logbook which tells of the action against a Heinkel. Actually what he cites is a copy of the RAF combat report submitted to Fighter Command HQ, RAF Stanmore.

The Smethwick Heinkel came down in the early hours of 10th April 1941 at 01:40 hours. That Deanesly was in action over the Birmingham area on this date is confirmed by the report and, indeed, by the squadron's operations record book. Crucially, his take-off time is recorded as being on the evening of the 10th at 21:55 and his return to base was at 23:15. In other words Deanesly's combat took place on the night of 10/11th (not the early hours of the 10th). On this night he brought down a Heinkel which crashed at Radway, Warwickshire. It is to this combat that the report related by Kennedy refers, and is not connected to the Smethwick Heinkel. In fact, 256 Sqn had no contact with enemy aircraft on the night of the 9/10th.

In later years aviation historians, Christopher Shores and Andrew Thomas, were each able to interview Deanesly on separate occasions and inspect his logbook which showed that his first night victory was on the 10/11th April 1941. However, it is most likely that Deanesly was under the misapprehension that his Heinkel had crashed at Smethwick. Apparently the word through unofficial channels had reached him about a Heinkel going down at Smethwick on the 10th and he, not knowing any different, seems to have assumed this was his. Even the writer of the squadron's record book adds to the confusion by mentioning a bomber down at Smethwick in connection with Deanesly. The fact remains that the Heinkel which crashed at Smethwick had come down 21 hours earlier.

The Defiant crew who did, in fact, deliver the critical attack on the Heinkel were Sgt Harry Bodien and gunner Sgt Dudley Jonas of 151 Sqn. This squadron put up several aircraft in response to the large raid on Birmingham on the night of 9/10th. Bodien took off at 01:10 and, following his engagement with a Heinkel, landed again at 02:10. The Defiant's gunner, believing his pilot to be dead, bailed out after they had made three attacks on the enemy machine. Jonas saw the Heinkel going down in flames and the impact as it hit the ground. Having safely descended by parachute, he was taken care of by E Flight of 915 Sqn (barrage balloon). Here he was informed that reports were coming in saying that a bomber had gone down on houses killing as many as 12 people.

On the 12th, which was Easter Saturday, Bodien wrote to his sister who lived on the Isle of Wight. He described in great detail how, in the early hours of the 10th, he and Jonas brought down a Heinkel over Birmingham. His story mirrored his formal combat report. Towards the close of his letter he wrote:

'My gunner has just got back and tells me our Heinkel crashed on some houses in Castle Bromwich killing about 12 people. Hope the weather is good tonight. Cheerio and all the best, Harry'

References to Castle Bromwich and 12 people killed were inaccurate, but serve as an illustration to how half-truths and rumour were rife in the heat of battle.

The Smethwick Heinkel was the only German aircraft to crash onto houses in the West Midlands during the war. Just one other came down in the immediate vicinity of Birmingham and this was the Earlswood Heinkel which crashed in a field one month later.

H.E. Bodien DFC DSO

Henry Erskin Bodien was born in Hackney, East London, in 1916. The family called him 'Snowball' (on account of his white-blonde hair) or Harry but not Henry. It was while he was an infant that the family moved to live on the Isle of Wight.

In September 1933, he joined the RAF as an aircraft apprentice and trained as a fitter. He was later accepted for pilot training and subsequently flew Avro Anson aircraft with 48 Sqn Coastal Command, on one occasion having to ditch in the English Channel.

In response to the need for fighter pilots after the Battle of Britain, he transferred to 6 OTU at Sutton Bridge, Lincolnshire, for conver-

sion training to single-engine night fighters. A posting to 151 Sqn followed. In May 1941 he received his commission as a Pilot Officer. His biggest difficulty in securing officer status was the need to raise £60 to pay for his uniform! He did this by obtaining a loan from a relative. The rank of Flying Officer was soon attained.

In April 1942 'Joe' (the name which he picked up in the RAF) Bodien received his DFC and one year later was promoted to Flight Lieutenant. His career as a night fighter pilot was over; he had been credited with five enemy aircraft destroyed and one damaged.

A period as a flying instructor followed when he became a Squadron Leader. In February 1944 Bodien resumed operational flying, joining 21 Sqn as a Mosquito fighter-bomber pilot. The Mosquito was a familiar type to him, as he had previously flown the night fighter version with 151 Sqn. His second 'gong' was awarded in September 1944 in the form of the DSO.

After the war was over he stayed in the RAF, receiving various postings including duties in Palestine, Rhodesia and Hong Kong and was attached to the United States Air Force (1950-1951). With the USAF he flew in Korea, flying the B-26 Invader aircraft on night interdiction sorties. He received a U.S. Air Medal.

On returning to the RAF, Bodien then commanded 29 Sqn, which was flying Meteor NF11s from Tangmere. This posting lasted from August 1951 through to June 1952.

In 1954 the Royal Canadian Air Force was seeking pilots experienced in night interdiction

to assist in the setting up of its new Avro Canada CF-100 Canuck units. Along with fellow night fighter ace Wg Cdr Bob Braham, Bodien transferred to the RCAF. He was required to relinquish his then current rank of Wing Commander, dropping to Squadron Leader for a period before being reinstated. Initially he served with 428 Sqn and then, in 1957, 410 Sqn where he regained the rank of Wing Commander.

Four years later in 1961, Bodien and his wife Phyllis became Canadian citizens. In that same year, as part of the RCAF's NATO commitment in Europe, he was posted to RCAF 1 Wing at Marville in France, where he served as Chief Operations Officer. It was from here that Wg Cdr Joe Bodien retired in 1965. The family returned to Canada, but came back to Europe in 1970. Following a spell of touring, Bodien worked as a civilian in Europe 1972-1978. Once again he moved back to his adopted home of Canada, and after a few moves settled in British Colombia. Henry Erskine Bodien died in 1999.

E.C. Deanesly DFC

Edward Christopher 'Jumbo' Deanesly was born in 1910 in Wolverhampton. At the age of 27 he joined the Auxiliary Air Force, flying with 605 (County of Warwick) Sqn. He received his commission in March 1937. Upon mobilisation in August 1939, Deanesly soon found himself posted to a new Spitfire squadron, number 152. Twice during the Battle of Britain he was shot down and had to be fished out of the English Channel. On the credit side he part-shared in the destruction of two German aircraft.

After the second ditching there followed a spell in hospital and a short time as a Fighter Controller. At the beginning of 1941 he was posted as a Flight Commander to one of the new Defiant night fighter squadrons, number 256. During the spring of that year, together with his gunner, a New Zealander named Scott, he brought down four German bombers. For these actions Deanesly received the Distinguished Flying Cross and Scott received the Distinguished Flying Medal (DFM).

In September he became Commanding Officer. Further postings as a Commanding Officer followed after April 1942, including duties in West Africa. Back in England he became Chief Flying Instructor with 107 OTU at Leicester East. The unit was training Dakota pilots for paratroop drops and glider towing duties. At the start of 1945 Deanesly found himself commanding 575 Sqn, which was flying Dakotas. The one-time fighter pilot flew a Dakota glider tug in the Rhine Crossings of March 1945.

With the end of hostilities, Deanesly was demobbed with the rank of Wing Commander. He returned to civilian life and established a plastics company. At retirement he lived in Edgbaston, Birmingham. Deanesly died in 1998.

ROYAL OBSERVER CORPS SITES

The map below shows the disposition of observation posts in the 5 Group (Midlands) area as at October 1939. There were more than 30 sites grouped into 10 clusters.

Inkberrow (site E1) and Broadway (site D3) being located in hilly areas, later had the distinction of becoming 'Granite' sites. When visibility was poor these Granite sites had the responsibility of alerting aircraft to their proximity to high ground. Upon receipt of the instruction 'Granite' from the Control Centre, an array of red flares would be activated. Such posts were also permitted to light the flares on their own initiative if deemed appropriate.

Observer Corps site map showing observer posts in the 5 Group (Midlands) area as at October 1939. ROC Trust

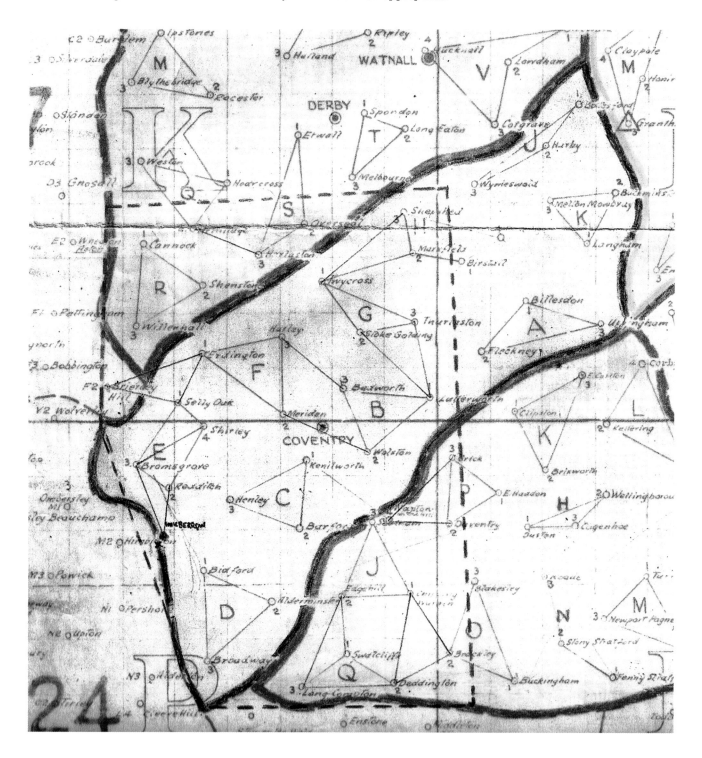

ANTI-AIRCRAFT GUNS – BIRMINGHAM AREA

The unit tables which follow are not definitive. Corrections and additions are welcome. The raising of the 11th Division came at the time when the Blitz was at its highest. With the reorganisation, different regiments appeared on the scene, the transition presumably occurring over a period of time.

4th Division 34th Brigade August-November 1940

Regiment	Batteries	Based at
69th Heavy Anti-Aircraft	190th, 191st	Edgbaston
	192nd, 199th	Kings Norton
95th Heavy Anti-Aircraft	204th	Saltley
	293rd	Washwood Heath

4th Division 54th Brigade August-November 1940

Regiment	Batteries	Based at
45th Searchlight*	378th	Maxstoke Castle
	379th	Halesowen
	380th	Shirley
	381st	Pendeford Hill
59th Searchlight*	399th, 427th, 428th	Birmingham

* Initially, upon formation, both the 45th and 59th were designated Battalions and their Batteries were Companies.

11th Division 34th Brigade November 1940-1942

Regiment	Batteries	Based at
6th Heavy Anti-Aircraft†	3rd, 12th, 15th	?
60th Heavy Anti-Aircraft	168th, 169th, 194th	?
95th Heavy Anti-Aircraft	204th, 293rd	?
110th Heavy Anti-Aircraft	?	?
112th Heavy Anti-Aircraft	?	?
134th Heavy Anti-Aircraft	456th, 459th, 460th, 461st	?
22nd Light Anti-Aircraft	70th, 72nd	?

† 71st HAA (Batteries 227th, 229th, 335th) replaced 6HAA, arriving Sept 1941 from Scotland before moving to Clacton in December 1941.

11th Division 54th Brigade November 1940-1942

Regiment	Batteries	Based at
45th Searchlight	378th	Sheldon/Shenstone
	379th	Halesowen
	380th	Shirley
	381st	Shenstone/Wightwick Hall/Weston Park/Arbury Park
80th Searchlight‡	?	?

‡ Took over from 45th Searchlight Dec 1941-Jan 1942

Deployment of Heavy Anti-Aircraft guns May 1940-May 1941

Date	4.5	3.7 (Static)	3.7 (Mobile)	Total
29.05.40	16	4	11	31
26.06.40	16	24	11	51
24.07.40	16	29	24	69
21.08.40	16	31	24	71
18.09.40	16	32	16	64
23.10.40	16	32	16	64
20.11.40	16	32	16	64
18.12.40	16	32	47	95
22.01.41	16	32	48	100*
19.02.41	16	32	48	96
19.03.41	16	32	16	64
23.04.41	16	32	16	64
21.05.41	16	32	16	64

*For this month an additional four 3.0 inch guns were allocated.

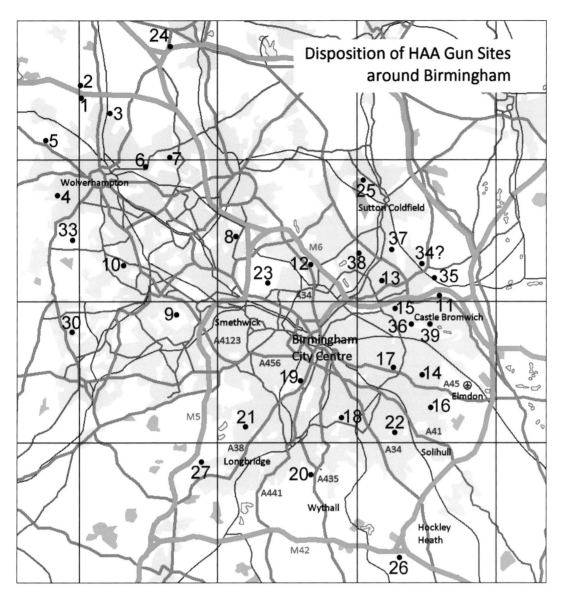

Disposition of HAA Gun Sites around Birmingham

KEY TO DRAWING

No	Site No (early/late)		Site Name	Location	No	Site No (early/late)		Site Name	Location
1	A	-	Coven Heath	N of Wolverhampton	21	S	H58	Welsh House Farm	W of Weoley Castle
2		H1	Coven Heath	N of Wolverhampton	22	T	H59	Langley Hall Farm	Robin Hood Golf Course
3	B	H50	Bushbury Hill	NNE of Wolverhampton	23	U	H60	The Uplands	N of Handsworth
4	C	H18	Merry Hill	WSW of Wolverhampton	24		H2		SW of Cannock
5	D	H51	The Elms	NW of Wolverhampton	25		H5		E of Streetly
6	E	-	Wednesfield	S of Wednesfield	26		H11	Nuthurst	WSW of Hockley Heath
7		H52	Wednesfield	E of Wednesfield	27		H13	Rubery	N of Rubery
8	F	H3	Stoke Cross	S of Walsall	28		H14		
9	G	H17	Turners Hill	ESE of Dudley	29		H15		
10	H	H53	Mons Hill	NNW of Dudley	30		H16		SE of Kingswinford
11	I	H6	Park Hall	N of Castle Bromwich	31		H19		
12	K	H4	Perry Park	Perry Barr	32		H20		
13	L	H10	Erdington	E of Erdington	33		H49	Upper Penn	NW of Sedgley
14	M	H55	Sheldon	Sheldon	34		H54	Walmley Ash ?	Walmley Ash?
15	N	H56	Castle Bromwich	S of Fort Dunlop	35		H61	Castle Bromwich	S of Minworth
16	O	H9	Olton Hall	Rover, Solihull	36		H62	Glebe Farm	NE of Stechford
17	P	H7	Oaklands	Yardley	37		H63	Wylde Green	Walmley Golf Course
18	Q	H57	Swanshurst Park	SE of Moseley	38		H64	Short Heath	SW of Wylde Green
19	R	-	Edgbaston	Edgbaston Golf Course	39		H65	Shard End Farm	S of Shard End
20	R	H12	Kingswood Farm	SW of Maypole					

ANTI-AIRCRAFT EXERCISES

It was necessary for the anti-aircraft gun and searchlight batteries to have training exercises. From the spring of 1939 to the outbreak of war, civilian aircraft operators were contracted by the Air Ministry to provide aircraft for day and night training exercises for the batteries. Once hostilities commenced, these army co-operation contracts were terminated as all civilian flying was suspended. Henceforth, only the RAF dedicated army co-operation units (such as 7 Anti-Aircraft Co-operation Unit, based at Castle Bromwich) and operational squadrons were involved in such exercises.

Based at Baginton, Coventry was 605 Sqn (County of Warwick), a Hurricane-equipped fighter unit. The following extract from the squadron's operations record book dated 4th August 1941, makes interesting reading: 'A combined exercise to provide air co-operation for the AA gun defences of Birmingham was carried out between 11.00 hours and 13.00 hours today. The squadron afforded a close escort and a protective screen to two Blenheim aircraft of No.9 Group AA Co-operation Flight. The formation was led by F/Lt Ingle at the head of a section of three aircraft, and made a rendezvous over Nuneaton at 11.00 hours. Close escort consisted of four aircraft on each flank, and high cover was provided by a further section of three aircraft, led by F/Lt Wright, "A" Flight Commander. From Nuneaton, a sweep was made over the whole of the Birmingham, Walsall, Wolverhampton area. Just east of Birmingham, an interception was effected by No.457 Squadron. While their whole object was to achieve this, their success came about rather too suddenly for their liking, for they broke from cloud and unwittingly flew right across our front at 400 yards range, and Alec Ingle, with his two accompanying "Bombers", neatly disposed of the majority in a few seconds. Dog fights ensued, and some valuable tactical experience was gained by our newer pilots. The Blenheims, still escorted by our Squadron, then dive-bombed Nuffields factory [Castle Bromwich aircraft factory], and the Hams Hall power station, vital points which were both heavily defended by AA guns. The Squadron landed at 11.55 hours, and at 12.15 hours 6 aircraft set off to complete the programme after refuelling, by attacking and machine-gunning four AA heavy gun sites in the Wolverhampton area. "Watty" Watson in particular put in some hair-raising dive attacks, scattering a large number of enemy personnel round the site at Wednesfield, who fled in terror to any temporary cover they could find. Our aircraft returned from this mission at 13.38 hours. The whole exercise was described by the 34th AA Brigade as a good show in every way, and the Squadron work was enthusiastically appreciated. Later in the day a Flight formation of 6 aircraft flew to Warwick Castle, giving a short display to a large number of Boy Scouts gathered there. The usual day state was assumed at 13.00 hours and the night state of 6 aircraft at 30 minutes [readiness] at 22.35 hours. A really good day's work.'

605 (County of Warwick) Sqn flew the Hurricane from Baginton, Coventry between May-September 1941. The squadron transferred to the Far East but was captured by the Japanese in March 1942. Author's collection

Appendix E

THE BARRAGE BALLOON

The elephant-like barrage balloons were suspended in the skies over many British towns and cities from September 1939 until late in the war. They were looked upon with some affection by the civilian population and the crews who operated them, even to the point where 'their' local balloon was christened with names such as Matilda, Annie, Susie, Barry and Romeo.

The streamlined balloons were large, 63 feet long and 31 feet high, and made of specially treated, rubber-proofed cotton fabric. The gas bag had a capacity of 19,150 cu ft and weighed 550 pounds. The balloon was flown on a flexible steel cable of 0.31 inch diameter and it was this cable, rather than the balloon itself, that deterred aircraft from flying in the vicinity of balloons. A collision with the cable almost invariably meant that the aircraft would not make it back to base.

As barrage balloons were inflated with hydrogen gas, which is much lighter than air, the balloons were able to rise thousands of feet into the air, tethered by their lethal cables. As the balloon gained altitude, the atmospheric pressure diminished and, as a result, the hydrogen gas expanded. For this reason the balloon was designed to make allowances for the expansion of the gas. A false bottom permitted the lower cavity to be filled with air which, as the hydrogen gas expanded, was expelled. This false bottom was called the ballonet and the flexible wall which separated it from the upper (gas) chamber was referred to as the diaphragm.

When the balloon was inflated the upper compartment was not filled to capacity with the hydrogen gas. The ballonet was filled with air through its wind scoop. As the balloon ascended, the atmospheric pressure dropped, the hydrogen gas expanded pushing down on the diaphragm and so expelled the air. When the balloon descended, the ballonet scooped in air as the gas contracted, so that the shape of the balloon remained constant. Three air-inflated stabilisers ensured that the balloon flew at an even keel always head to wind.

Maintaining and flying a barrage balloon was heavy and demanding work. Normally a balloon site was manned by two corporals and eight men.[89] Preparing a balloon for flight took between 20 and 40 minutes, while bedding down times were very much dependent upon weather conditions. When in flight, balloons were vulnerable to lightning strikes, as the steel cable acted as a conductor. With hydrogen gas being particularly inflammable, a lightning strike would invariably destroy the balloon by fire. Snow and ice were a problem, making the balloon heavy. Wind was the biggest challenge, especially when trying to bed down. As the war progressed, new equipment and techniques ensured a more efficient operation.

Balloons were also vulnerable to attacks by enemy aircraft and shrapnel damage from exploding anti-aircraft shells. Although some German aircraft fell victim to balloons, their primary purpose was to act as a deterrent. The passive role of the balloons meant that the operating crews had little to encourage them, despite much hard work.

Note

89 From 1941, many balloon sites were 'manned' by the women of the WAAF.

Appendix F

LUFTWAFFE AIRCREW

Luftwaffe Ranks	RAF equivalent Ranks
Oberst (Obst)	Group Captain
Oberstleutnant (Obstlt)	Wing Commander
Major (Maj)	Squadron Leader
Hauptmann (Hptm)	Flight Lieutenant
Oberleutnant (Oblt)	Flying Officer
Leutnant (Lt)	Pilot Officer
Stabsfeldwebel (Stfw)	Senior Warrant Officer
Oberfeldwebel (Ofw)	Flight Sergeant
Feldwebel (Fw)	Sergeant
Unteroffizier (Uffz)	Corporal
Gefreiter (Gefr)	Aircraftman 1st Class (AC1)

Luftwaffe crew roles	
Flugzeugführer (Ff) Pilot	On multi-crewed bombers the Flugzeugführer's role was to fly the aircraft and, in the early years, he took his orders from the Beobachter.
Beobachter (Bo) Observer	During the early years the Beobachter was the Commander and often Senior Officer, his role being navigator, bomb-aimer and forward gunner.
Bordfunker (Bf) Wireless Operator	Apart from operating the wireless equipment the Bordfunker also doubled as a gunner.
Bordmechaniker (Bm) Flight Engineer	This role is difficult to translate literally. While he could turn his hand to a number of trades, primarily he took the role of a qualified gunner.
Bordschütze (BS) Gunner	Tended to be the lowest and least trained of all aircrew, with few qualifications, often having been transferred from the infantry.

GERMAN BOMBS AND BRITISH BULLETS

German bombs

The Luftwaffe dropped an array of ordnance on Birmingham during the Blitz. German high-explosive (HE) bombs utilised TNT, amatol or tri-alen. They were of two main types: thin-walled general purpose weapons designated SC (*Spreng Cylindrisch* or explosive cylindrical) and thick-walled fragmentation bombs designated SD (*Spreng Dickenwand* or explosive thick-walled). Their type designation was used as a prefix, followed by a number indicating their weight in kilograms, e.g. SC-250, SD-50.[90] The thinner-cased SC yielded a greater blast effect, while the thicker-cased SD type could penetrate deeper into strong points before exploding. The SC-250 was the most common HE bomb dropped on Birmingham; it measured about 5 feet long by 18 inches in diameter. Bombs bigger than the 250kg were carried on external racks beneath the bombers fuselage or wings, which impaired the aircraft's performance.[91] Larger bombs were dropped on the city; these included the SC-1000 (*Hermann*), the SC-1500 and the SC-1800 (*Satan*). The last was 13 feet 6 inches long and was first used over Britain on 7th September 1940 during an attack on London. In 1941 the SC 2500 (*Max)* appeared, but this large weapon could only be lifted by specific Heinkel variants. These variants, namely the He 111H-5 and He 111H-6, were not widely available although III/KG26, a regular visitor to Birmingham, was so equipped. It is, however, doubtful that these large bombs were ever used against the city.

Much disruption was caused by the tactic of fitting delayed-action fuses to bombs. The delay time could be anything from a few hours to several days. This feature was indicated by the suffix LZZ (*Lange Zeit Zünder*). Hence, for example, the designation SC 250 LZZ (sometimes abbreviated further to LZZ 250) indicated a thin-walled 250kg HE bomb fitted with a long delay fuse. Bombs could also have a short delay fuse in place of an impact fuse, to allow penetration into a building before exploding. Such bombs had the suffix mV (*mit Verzögerung*).

Anti-shipping sea mines were adapted and dropped by parachute. These were not the familiar, spherical mine with spikes sticking out, but were akin to torpedoes. The parachute allowed little, if any, penetration and, together with the impact fuse, guaranteed maximum blast effect. These *Luftminen,* as dropped on Birmingham, were either 500kg or 1,000kg, designated LMA and LMB respectively. The LMA was 5 feet 8 inches long and the LMB 8 feet 8 inches. The civilian population held these devices in contempt as they were blatantly indiscriminate

and were capable of destroying a row of houses with a single blast.

There were numerous types of incendiary bomb. The most prolific were of two basically similar types: the B 1 E (*Brandbomb*, 1kg *Elektron*) and a derivative fitted with a small explosive charge, the B 1 E-ZA. Incendiaries of both types utilised magnesium and were dropped in containers known as the BSK 36 which, as the designation implies, carried 36 1kg bombs. After leaving the aircraft the container opened in mid-air to disgorge its contents. A 2kg bomb was an option (16 of these could be carried in the BSK container). Some incendiaries were fitted with a seven-minute delay fuse intended to deter interference by civil defence personnel. Also available were two large incendiary weapons known as the Flam C 250 and Flam C 500 (Flam: from *Flammen-bomben* or 'fire bombs'). Similar in size to the 250kg and 500kg HE bombs, the Flam casing weighed less because it was of light, thin, pressed-steel. The bomb contained a central 'burster charge' of about 1.5kg of TNT. The main charge was a heavy, highly-inflammable mixture consisting of benzene, tar and raw rubber, making for a sticky concoction. These bombs were fitted with impact fuses. A failure to detonate on impact was not uncommon and resulted in the case splitting to spill its contents without igniting.

In the raids of 1942, phosphorus incendiaries were dropped on the city. These highly effective fire bombs (*Phosphorbrandbomben*) were either 50kg or 250kg (C 50 and C 250). In appearance they were similar to the HE bombs of comparable weight.

Indeed, it was incendiary bombs which were the greatest threat. Firstly, they were used to mark the target at the onset of a raid. The main force then dropped their loads onto the fires started by the fire-raising (or pathfinder) units. Secondly, the vast number of such devices employed was in danger of overwhelming the civil defences. By spring 1941, however, the number of available fire-watchers had been increased and the enlarged force proved equal to the task.

RAF bullets

The small variety of projectiles fired by RAF fighters at German aircraft, intent on bombing Birmingham, is a more straightforward subject. The guns used by the relevant fighter aircraft (Defiant, Hurricane, Beaufighter and Mosquito) were either the .303 Browning machine gun or the 20mm Hispano Cannon.

The Browning machine gun as used in British aircraft was based on the American designed Colt and, after considerable modification, was produced under licence by BSA and Vickers-Armstrongs. Unlike day fighters, the night fighters did not employ tracer ammunition as it compromised the position of the attacking fighter. Night fighters were normally provided with a mixture of bullet types. As well as ball and steel-cored armour piercing, the much-favoured de Wilde ammunition was also used. The latter was the painstaking invention of a British designer – a soldier named Captain Aubrey Dixon – working at the Woolwich Arsenal. An explosive incendiary bullet, the de Wilde had a chemical tip which ignited upon impact. Having penetrated the target's outer skin, the incendiary properties were so controlled and retarded that the bullet could cause any inflammable material or liquid, located within the target aircraft's structure, to catch fire or explode. Additionally, the flash of the igniting de Wilde, as it found its mark, confirmed to the pilot the accuracy of his aim. This last benefit could also be a hindrance for, as has been noted earlier in this book, pilots who delivered a close-in attack at night were likely to be blinded by the flashes of the de Wilde as it hit home.

The name de Wilde was something of a subterfuge on the part of the British. It was intended that the Germans should believe that it was a product being manufactured under licence from a Swiss munitions company, owned by the Belgian-born designer, one Paul René de Wilde. This was a product which was utterly unsuitable for mass production.[92]

The 20mm Hispano cannon was of French origin, modified and produced under licence for the RAF from 1940. Initially it was problematic, resulting in frequent jams. The guns were fed by drums, each holding 60 rounds. Once the rounds were expended, drums had to be changed. In the Beaufighter this necessitated the radar operator vacating his position, manoeuvring himself into the aircraft's belly, lifting the fresh and, therefore, heavy drum from its rack and locating it into position. All of this in the dark and while the aircraft might be twisting and turning. Things improved when the drums were abandoned in favour of belt-feed.

The performance of the rounds themselves was disappointing. It was found that the fuse of the standard explosive shells was too sensitive, causing them to burst on the aircraft skin rather than penetrating the structure where they would inflict most damage. Plain steel practice shells often proved more effective.

By 1941, a high explosive incendiary (HEI) shell had been developed. The shell had a delayed-action fuse and an explosive with added incendiary filling. The practice rounds remained in use alongside the HEIs. A new, semi-armour-piercing incendiary round (SAPI), which was essentially an HE shell filled with an incendiary compound and capped with a hard steel tip instead of a fuse, was soon introduced to replace the practice round. From 1942 the standard loading for the Hispano was 50% HEI and 50% SAPI.

Notes

90 The SC weights in kilograms were: 50, 250, 500, 1,000, 1,200, 1,800, 2,000 and 2,500. The SD weights were: 50, 70, 250, 500 and 1,700.

91 The Dornier Do 17 could not carry anything larger than the 50kg bomb in its internal bomb bay. The much-improved Dornier Do 217, which was used against Birmingham in 1942, could carry up to four 500kg bombs internally.

92 In early 1939, the British entered into a contractual arrangement to produce the de Wilde incendiary ammunition under licence. It then became apparent that the bullet was impractical. However, the British Government more than honoured their contractual payments to the Swiss company, in part to perpetuate the deception directed at the Germans.

An example of the 500kg LMA parachute mine which the Admiralty designated **TYPE D.** via Nigel Parker

Appendix H

THE RAIDS IN SUMMARY

Over the years various figures have been quoted in respect of the number of air attacks suffered by Birmingham. Most common are 77, 65 and 63. The highest figure includes some bombs falling in the Sutton Coldfield area (on occasions when none fell within the Birmingham County Borough boundary), and also counts multiple raids in one night separately (e.g. 11/12th December 1940, when there was a gap of more than one hour between the two waves of bombers). In the table below multiple raids in a single 12 hour period are counted as one raid.

In line with some wartime reporting, this table and the one in *Appendix I* divide the 24 hour day into two 12 hour periods. Daytime commences at 06:00 and finishes at 18:00. Night-time commences at 18:00 and finishes at 06:00

the following morning. Hence in the table a daylight raid is represented by a single date and a night raid by a dual date (e.g. 27/28).

With many of the raids it is not possible to know exactly how many German aircraft actually reached and bombed the city. In the vast majority of cases, we are reliant upon incomplete German records. In the table, which has been laid out to give an overview, an informed guess has been taken in a few instances. In the main, such estimation has been restricted to whether a minor raid is entered in the first column (1-5) or the second (6-25). It should be borne in mind that some entries in the first column may refer to a single bomber and even an attack where a solitary bomb was dropped (refer to the main text).

Date of Raid	Number of Aircraft Involved			
August 1940	1-5	6-25	26-99	100+
8/9	✓	-	-	-
13/14	-	✓	-	-
15/16	-	✓	-	-
17/18	✓	-	-	-
19/20	✓	-	-	-
23/24	-	✓	-	-
24/25	-	✓	-	-
25/26	-	-	✓	-
26/27	-	✓	-	-
27/28	-	✓	-	-
28/29	✓	-	-	-
31/01	✓	-	-	-
September 1940				
2/3	✓	-	-	-
12/13	✓	-	-	-
14/15	✓	-	-	-
16/17	✓	-	-	-
27	✓	-	-	-
27/28	✓	-	-	-
October 1940				
15/16	-	✓	-	-
16/17	-	✓	-	-
17/18	-	✓	-	-
18/19	-	✓	-	-
20/21	✓	-	-	-
21/22	✓	-	-	-
22/23	✓	-	-	-
24/25	-	✓	-	-
25/26	-	-	✓	-
26/27	-	-	✓	-
27/28	✓	-	-	-
28/29	-	-	✓	-
29/30	-	✓	-	-
31	✓	-	-	-
31/01	✓	-	-	-
November 1940				
1/2	✓	-	-	-
4	✓	-	-	-
4/5	✓	-	-	-
5/6	-	✓	-	-
6/7	✓	-	-	-

Date of Raid	Number of Aircraft Involved			
7/8	✓	-	-	-
8/9	✓	-	-	-
9	✓	-	-	-
9/10	✓	-	-	-
10/11	✓	-	-	-
13	✓	-	-	-
14/15	✓	-	-	-
15/16	✓	-	-	-
18/19	-	✓	-	-
19/20	-	-	-	✓
20/21	-	-	-	✓
21/22	✓	-	-	-
22/23	-	-	-	✓
28/29	✓	-	-	-
December 1940				
3/4	-	-	✓	-
4/5	-	✓	-	-
11/12	-	-	-	✓
12/13	✓	-	-	-
16/17	✓	-	-	-
21/22	✓	-	-	-
22/23	✓	-	-	-
1/2 January 1941	✓	-	-	-
4/5 February 1941	✓	-	-	-
11/12 March 1941	-	-	-	✓
April 1941				
7/8	✓	-	-	-
9/10	-	-	-	✓
10/11	-	-	-	✓
16/17 May 1941	-	-	✓	-
June 1941				
4/5	-	✓	-	-
11/12	-	✓	-	-
July 1941				
4/5	-	✓	-	-
8/9	✓	-	-	-
July 1942				
27	✓	-	-	-
27/28	-	-	✓	-
29/30	-	-	✓	-
30/31	-	✓	-	-
23/24 April 1943	✓	-	-	-

Appendix I

CIVILIAN AIR RAID CASUALTIES

The casualty figures relating to the actual County Borough of Birmingham, which are presented below, are taken from returns passed by the Medical Officer of Health to various branches of the Civil Defence. The remainder are based upon the Civilian War Dead Roll of Honour, which is on display in Westminster Abbey.[93]

The author has had to use some discretion in adjusting the figures, as the Civilian War Dead Roll of Honour lists people under the local authority in which they died. Therefore, by way of example, someone severely injured in an air raid on Smethwick who died later in a Birmingham hospital, is listed in the Roll of Honour under Birmingham. For the purposes of the tables immediately below, if such instances have come to light, the death has been included under the local authority in which the air raid incident occurred and not where the death took place.

Some people who were seriously injured in an air raid died of their wounds days later. Where this is known, the individual has been listed as 'killed' on the date the raid took place. The figures for Birmingham, however, have only been adjusted marginally, in accordance with the previous paragraph, with no attempt being made to shift any 'seriously injured' to the 'killed' category.

For our purposes here, Home Guard personnel have been classed as 'civilian'. Military personnel have not knowingly been included in the following figures, but, where known, are mentioned in the main text of this book.

Note

93 The content of the Civilian War Dead Roll of Honour may be viewed at www.cwgc.org

Birmingham County Borough

Date	Killed	Seriously injured	Slightly injured
August 1940			
8/9	1	2	5
13/14	7	29	113
15/16	11	13	16
17/18	?	1	?
23/24	1	7	4
24/25	17	10	3
25/26	25	19	20
26/27	20	36	46
27/28	5	3	15
28/29	?	1	1
September 1940			
2/3	2	3	18
12/13	1	?	7
16/17	1	2	5
27/28	12	7	9
October 1940			
15/16	59	43	135
16/17	8	14	16
17/18	17	14	83
18/19	10	22	51
20/21	3	35	27
20-27 October 1940*	210	176	255
28 Oct-02 Nov 1940*	43	41	91
November 1940			
3-10*	11	18	24
11-17*	19	13	26
18/19	15	9	24
19/20	301	518	533
20/21	14	94	234
22/23	113	470	416
19-24†	254	42	18
28/29	3	?	1
19 Nov-04 Dec 1940†	114	3	?
December 1940			
3/4	36	60	129
4	3	30	31
To 15 Dec*	263	245	298
To 22 Dec*	15	4	16

Date	Killed	Seriously injured	Slightly injured
To 29 Dec*	?	1	?
January 1941			
To 5 Jan*	?	12	13
11/12 March 1941	6	22	15
April 1941			
7/8	?	?	4
9/10	290	408	423
10/11	25	43	96
9-11†	31	22	?
16/17 May 1941	36	60	35
June 1941			
4/5	3	4	6
11/12	1	2	4
4/5 July 1941‡	-	-	-
July 1942			
27/28	73	130	160
29/30	95	289	215
30/31	7	16	19
23/24 April 1943	?	8	13

Notes to table:
* Weekly totals only reported. During these weeks raids occurred on the following dates: October 20/21, 21/22, 22/23, 24/25, 25/26, 26/27, 27/28, 28/29, 29/30, 31, 31/01. November 1/2, 4, 4/5, 5/6, 6/7, 7/8, 8/9, 9, 9/10, 10/11, 13, 14/15, 15/16, 18/19. December 11/12, 12/13, 15/16, 21/22. January 1/2 1941.

† Due to the intensity of the raids during these periods, daily record-keeping was impractical. Later, when things quietened a little, additional casualty figures were reported. These would, for example, include deaths occurring at a later date as a result of serious injury sustained nights earlier. The majority of these additional numbers may be attributed to the two heaviest raids, i.e. 19/20 November 1940 and 9/10 April 1941.

‡ Casualty figures not recorded.

Bromsgrove Urban District

Date	Killed	Injured
22/23 November 1940	1	?
9/10 April 1941	2	2

Oldbury Municipal Borough

Date	Killed	Injured
19/20 November 1940	3	?
9/10 April 1941	1	2
4/5 June 1941	1	?
29/30 July 1942	1	?

Smethwick County Borough

Date	Killed	Injured
25/26 October 1940	5	1
November 1940		
19/20	21	11
22/23	12	?
11/12 December 1940	3	7
April 1941		
9/10	7	?
10/11	24	4
July 1942		
27/28	15	29
29/30	4	9

Solihull Urban District

Date	Killed	Injured
November 1940		
19/20	9	40-50
22/23	10	?
11/12 December 1940	5	?
27 July 1942	10	31

Sutton Coldfield Municipal Borough

Date	Killed	Injured
25/26 August 1940	1	?
? November 1940	1	
July 1942		
29/30	1	?
?	1	

Walsall County Borough

Date	Killed	Injured
14/15 November 1940	1	?
11/12 June 1941	5	10
30/31 July 1942	1	?

West Bromwich County Borough

Date	Killed	Injured
19/20 November 1940	54	?

The Tree of Life Memorial located in Edgbaston Street is in memory of the civilians who died in Birmingham air raids.
Carole Richards

AIR RAID FATALITIES

There follows a series of lists of civilians known to have been killed in the county boroughs/ municipal boroughs/urban districts covered by this book, each of which resulted from German air raids.

Birmingham County Borough

Abbot Alfred
Abrahams Hyman
Adams Doris
Adams Thomas
Adams William Edward
Addicott Alan John
Addicott Cecelia Ann
Alderton Esme
Alderton Lizziet
Aldington Howard Burnaby
Aldridge Elton Edwin
Allen Arthur Abraham
Allen Clara
Allen Edith
Allen Percy Frank
Allen William
Allsopp Arthur Edward
Allum John
Allwood Elsie Elizabeth
Amos Vera
Amphlett George Henry
Amphlett Jamesina Mary Robinson
Anderson Annie
Anderson Henry
Anderson Lily
Andrews Leonard Cecil
Ansell Peter Benson
Anslow Albert William
Anslow Alice Annie Elizabeth
Anslow Gertrude Annie
Appleton Edith Jane
Arkell Horace
Armson Herbert
Armson Lily

Armstrong Elizabeth
Armstrong Eva
Armstrong Eva
Arnold Alfred Edward
Ashford Daisy Elizabeth
Ashford Edith Mary
Ashford Emma Eliza
Ashford Walter
Ashmead Betsy
Ashmead Sara Annie
Ashmore Ada
Ashmore Ellen
Ashmore Jean Mary
Ashmore Lucy
Ashmore Raymond Albert
Ashmore Sylvia
Ashmore Violet
Ashmore Walter
Ashurst Margaret
Astle David
Astle George
Astle Horace
Astle Leah
Astle Maureen
Astle Raymond
Astle Susannah
Astle Thomas
Astley Maud Mary Elizabeth
Aston George Edward
Atkins Frederick Kenneth
Atkins Henry
Austin Annie Maud
Austin George Alfred
Austra Christina
Avery Frederick Charles

Bach Cecil Arthur
Backman Samuel
Badger Eva Gertrude
Bagshaw Edward Orlando
Bagshaw Ernest
Bailey Agnes Genevieve
Bailey Agnes Margaret
Bailey Arthur Alec
Bailey Elizabeth
Bailey George Edwin
Bailey Harry Ernest
Bailey Jane Elizabeth
Bailey John
Bailey John Thomas
Bailey Joseph
Baker Albert Henry
Baker Christine Mary
Baker Frederick Herbert
Baker Jean Iris
Baker Joseph
Baker Leo
Baldock Frances Mary Mallaber
Ball Ada Emma
Ball Edith May
Ball Eileen Mary Marguerite
Ball Elsie Elizabeth
Ball Florence Elizabeth
Ball Joan
Banks Annie Elizabeth
Banks Florence
Banks Helena Rose
Banks Selina Rose
Banner Catherine
Banner Dorcas
Banner Dorcas Annie
Banner Hilda

Banner William
Barber Ernest Joseph
Barley Sidney
Barnard Charles Henry
Barnes William
Barnsley Rose
Barratt William Henry
Barrett James
Barrett Patrick
Barrett William Oswald
Barrier Joan
Barrier John
Barrier Rose Ann
Barrow Harold
Barsby Harriet Anne Lloyd
Barsby Nina
Barsby Ruth
Bartlett Leslie Harold
Bassett Jane Maria
Bastianelli Anthony
Bastianelli Carolina
Bastianelli Laura
Batchelor Ada
Batchelor Barbara
Batchelor George
Bates Francis Arthur William
Bates John Joseph
Bates Maurice Edwin
Battista Bertram Olaf
Bauer Pauline
Baum Harry
Baxter Joseph
Baxter Laura
Baxter Sylvia Gladys
Bayley Vidah Blanche
Bayley William Henry Smyth

Bayliss George
Bayliss Walter Howard
Baynham Alfred
Baynham John Henry
Beach Ann Elizabeth
Beale Stanley William
Bean Annie
Bean Norman
Beard Doris
Beasley Albert
Beddowes Joseph
Beech Oliver Samuel
Beech Kenneth
Beet Robert George
Belcher Thomas
Bell Annie Elizabeth
Bell Gladys June
Bell Iris Jean
Bell Lily Minnie
Bell Pauline Elsie
Bell Daniel Hubert
Bellamy Edwin Walter Thomas
Bellamy Lily Prudence
Bembridge Francis Edgar Ernest
Bennett Margaret Augusta
Benson Ellen Louisa
Benson Joseph Henry
Berry Walter
Best Beatrice May
Best Phyllis Margaret
Betham Samuel
Bethel Joseph
Bevan Alfred
Bibb William Ernest
Bibbey Constance Mary
Bibbey Doris Adelaide
Biddle Allen Frederick
Biddle Elsie Valerie
Biddulph William John Sydney
Bidmead Horace
Birch Annie Selina
Bird Albert Burton
Bird Albert Montague
Bird Clara
Bird Sarah Elizabeth
Bishton Ada
Bishton Charles Henry
Bishton Margery Ada
Black Kate Hinsley
Blake Charles Harold
Blake Thomas
Blakemore Albert
Blakemore Ethel Irene
Blakemore Kitty
Blum Robert
Blunt William
Boddington Samuel Joseph
Bodenham Charles William
Bodenham Charlotte
Bohemia Elizabeth
Bond Joseph
Bond Martha Bella
Bond Mary Jane
Bond Richard
Bonelle Ada Jane
Booth Daniel
Booton William Frederick
Bott Harry
Bott Joan Kathleen
Bott Nellie
Bott Phyllis Marjorie
Bourne George Albert
Bowen Lilian
Bowen Margaret Alice
Bower Sarah Kate
Bowerman Maude Blanche
Bowyer Ellen
Bowyer John William

Bowyer Stanley
Boyd Elizabeth Hatch
Boyd Elsie Mabel
Bradley Doris Corbett
Bradley Ethel Florence
Bradley Peter John
Bradnock Elsie Heath
Bradshaw Mary
Bragg George
Bragg George
Bramham Charles
Bramham Eleanor
Bramham Joan
Bramwell Elsie
Bramwell Henry Howard
Bramwell James Henry Howard
Bramwell John Alfred David
Bramwell Reginald Arthur
Branaghan Thomas Jeremiah
Brant Stanley Charles
Brazier Arthur Victor
Brennan Mary
Brennan Michael John
Bretherick George
Briant Arthur Mcalister
Bridgland Emma
Bridgwater John Thomas Charles
Briggs Maud
Brittain Thomas Lambert William
Britton William Edward
Broadhurst Arthur Lewis
Broadhurst Florence
Brogan James
Bromhead Nellie
Brookes Alfred
Brookes Alfred John
Brookes Joseph Victor
Brookes Marjorie Ivy Irene
Brooks Georgina Elizabeth
Brooks Leslie
Broome John
Brotherton Emma Matilda
Brown Bernard
Brown Frances
Brown Frank
Brown Ivy
Brown James
Brown Wilfred Stanley
Bruce Andrew
Brunner John Frederick
Brunner Winifred Florence
Bryan Albert Ernest
Bryan Bertie Leonard
Bryan Ernest
Bryant Clara
Bryant Henry Charles
Bryant Marion
Buck Robert
Buckland Philip Sidney
Buckley Kathline
Budd Alfred Sidney
Budd Barbara
Budd Dennis
Budd Doreen
Budd Ethel
Budd Minnie
Budd Ronald Sidney
Buffery Henry
Bull Mary Irene
Bull Vera
Bull William
Bull William Albert
Bullock Charles
Bullock Hilda Muriel
Bullock Mary
Bullock Olive Nancy
Bundy George Edward
Bunford Caroline

Bunford John
Bunford Ruby Maureen
Burdett Thomas Twine
Burdett William Charles
Burford Albert Edward
Burford Dorothy May
Burford Ellen Ann
Burford John
Burnett Mavis
Burnett Rose Elizabeth
Burrows Joseph Henry
Burrows Raymond Arthur
Burton Harold Charles
Bushell Charles Bennett
Bushell Ethel Blanche
Butler Albert
Butler Beatrice Florence
Butler Emma
Byram Mary Emma
Byrne Edward

Caine Albert
Caine William
Caines Clara
Callaghan Frederick
Canter Walter
Capewell Ernest Stanley
Carey Frederick
Carey Joyce
Carey Raymond
Carless Edward
Carlin Reginald Davis
Carroll Florence
Cartwright Cecil
Cartwright John Simmonds
Casey Eric
Cash John
Caterer Edwin William
Cerrone Dennis
Chadney Bessie Matilda
Chancellor George Frederick
    Raymond
Chapman Louisa
Chapman William
Chare Beryl
Charley Augustus
Charley Bertha
Cheslin Harriett
Chick Mary Ann
Church Frederick
Clark Albert
Clarke Albert Edward
Clarke Charles Herbert Wreford
Clarke Doris Joan
Clarke George Samuel
Clarke Howard
Clarke John Thomas
Clarke Stephen
Clarke Teresa
Clarke Thomas William
Claytor Audrey Hilda
Claytor David Arthur
Claytor Hilda
Claytor Kathleen Margaret
Clews Victor Leonard
Clifford Delia
Clifford Dennis
Clifford John Peter
Clifford Leah Elizabeth
Clifford Louisa
Clifford Walter
Clifton Doris Harriet
Clifton Emily
Clive George Ralph
Clover Joseph Albert
Coates Philip Francis
Coates Raymond Walter
Coen Franciscus

Coen Pauline Matilda Julia
Cogin Doris
Colder Selina
Cole Margaret Ellen
Coleman Alfred
Coleman Esther
Coleman John William
Coleman Laurence William
Coles Margaret Jane
Coley Doris Winifred
Coley Frederick Dennis Rhys
Colley Edith
Collingswood Sydney Thomas
Collins Frank
Collins George
Collins Jane
Collins Jessie May
Collins Lily
Collins William Joseph
Collins William Robert
Constant Francis Charles
Cook Frank James
Cook Geoffrey Frederick
Cook Mabel Esther
Cooke Arthur Ernest
Cooke Ethel Emily
Cooke Frederick
Cooke Joseph
Cooke Kate Cissy
Cooke Maud Ivy
Coombes Alan
Coombes Albert William
Coombes Alice
Coombes Alice
Coombes Barbara
Coombs Harry
Cooper Horace Edward
Cooper Mary Ann
Cooper William James
Cope Alfred
Cope John
Cope John Alfred
Cope Mary Theresa
Cope Stanley
Corbett Elsie
Corbett Nellie
Corfield Annie
Corfield Ralph Henry
Cotton Charles
Cotton Hilda
Cotton Jane
Cotton John
Court Mildred
Courtnell Ernest
Courtnell Minnie
Courtney Christina
Cox George
Cox Harry
Cox Stephen George Gladstone
Craddock Albert Edward
Cragg Emily
Cragg Frederick
Cragg Frederick Harold
Crebbin James
Crichton John Kennedy
Cridge Frank William
Crisp Thomas
Crockett Lily Rose
Crockett Sidney
Crompton Ronald Michael
Cross James
Crowther John
Crozier John Phillip
Crozier Millie
Cumbey Mary Anne
Curley Margaret
Curley Nellie
Curley Thomas

Curran William
Curry Eric Victor

Daeman Petrus
Dale Constance Mary
Dalgetty William
Dandy Albert
Dandy James Leslie
Daniels Frances Magdalene
Daniels Thomas
Danks Florence
Danks William Thomas
Darby Alfred John
Darby Olive Violet
Darbyshire Harry
Darlison Alfred Frank
Darlison Chrystabel Irene
David Doris May
David Heman Llewellyn
Davies Arthur John Thomas
Davies Charles
Davies Dorothy
Davies Fred
Davies George Richard
Davies Gilbert
Davies Joyce
Davies Mildred Lilian
Davies Pearl Sylvia
Davies Sarah Hannah
Davies Stanley Charles
Davies Stanley Job
Davies William Ernest
Davis Arthur Reginald
Davis Elizabeth
Davis Eric
Davis Frank Latham
Davis Harriet Matilda
Davis Laura Helen
Davis Maud
Davis Reuben
Davis Sarah
Davis William Charles
Dawes Charles Edward
Dawes Ronald Frank
Dawkes Rose Annie
Day Ellen
Deakin Ann Court
Dean Ivor
Deane George
Dearn George Edward
Deebank Brenda
Deebank Elizabeth
Denham Alfred Albert
Denning Joseph
Denny Bertie Alfred
Dent Annie
Derry Frank Charles
Dickens Charles Reginald
Dillon Edward
Dillon Matilda
Dix Stephen
Dixon Albert
Dobbins William George
Dodsley Frederick
Donnelly Dennis
Dooling Ada
Dooling Patrick
Dorey Ernest George
Dorney Amelia
Doughty Harriet
Doughty Muriel
Douglas William
Dowman Albert Edward
Downes Arthur
Downes Leonard
Downes Mary
Downes Norman
Downes Samuel Albert

Dowse Sarah
Dowse Thomas James
Dowson Minnie Evelyn
Drakeley Alfred
Draper Alfred John
Drew Ernest William
Dudley Arthur Robert
Duggan Nellie
Duggan Robert Evan
Dunn Ada
Dutton Arthur Augustus
Dutton Laura Ellen
Dwyer Dennis
Dyer William

Eagle William
Eastlake John
Eaton James Harry
Eccleston James
Eddleston Jannete Ann
Eden Frederick William
Edge Marjorie
Edgerton Charles Henry
Edgerton Grace
Edwards Brian John
Edwards David William
Edwards J. H.
Edwards John William
Edwards Louisa
Edwards Matilda Ellen
Edwards Matilda Grace
Edwards Sydney Thomas
Eeles Helen Gertrude
Egginton Ernest
Elder Clara
Ellerker Isaac Sydney
Ellgood Annie
Ellgood Frank Augusta
Elliott Florence Emma
Elms Montague Bertie
Elvins Walter Edward
Endean William
Essex John
Estill Beatrice
Evans Annie Ada
Evans David John
Evans Emily
Evans Harry Stanley
Evans John Rowland
Evans Lily
Evans Marjorie
Evans Patricia Anne
Evans William Everett
Everitt William Ernest
Everton Albert
Eyre Dorothy Lilian
Eyre Elsie Elizabeth
Eyre George Henry
Eyre Jack
Eyre Patricia May
Eyre Roland David

Facer John
Facer Robert
Facer Sidney Joseph
Fahy Joseph
Farrell James
Farrell John Thomas
Farrell Sarah
Faulkner George Richard
Faux Alice Mary
Felix Mary Dorothy
Fenner Agnes
Fenner Walter
Fenton John
Fenton Sarah Ann
Ferguson Violet Beatrice
Fern Gladys

Fidoe Norman Edward
Field William Joseph
Fieldhouse Charles
Finch Bryan
Finch Leslie Harold
Finch Nellie
Finch William James
Findlay James
Finnegan William
Firth Annie
Firth John Alfred
Firth Lilian Mary Edith
Firth Sheila
Fisher Charles Redgrave
Fisher Frederick William
Fisher Harold Hubert Edward
    James
Fisher Ivy
Fisher Lottie
Fisher Sarah Ann
Fitter Alan John
Fitter Norma Olive
Fitter Winifred Olive
Fitzpatrick Philip
Fitzpatrick William
Fletcher Cecil George
Fletcher Ida Summerfield
Fletcher Joan Eileen
Fletcher John Charles
Flowers Harry
Floyd Ernest Midlam
Follis Albert
Follis Annie
Ford Henry Thomas
Forrest Charles George
Forrest Charles William
Forrest Edna May
Forrest Laura Ada
Forrest William
Foster Beatrice
Foster Clara
Foster Elizabeth
Foster George
Foster Mary
Foster Samuel Ambrose
Foulston Roy
Fowler Maurice Allan
Fowles Frederick
Fox Daniel
Francis Archibald George
Francis Betty
Francis David William
Francis Emily
Francis Maud Harriett Lucy
Francis Walter
Franklin Annie
Franklin James Mills
Free Sydney William
Freeman Arthur Augustus
Freeman Gladys Edna
Freeman Louisa Harriet
Freer Doreen
Freer Frederick Arnold
Freer Iris
Freer Isabella
Friar George Thomas
Frost James
Frowen Albert George
Frowen Ernest Henry
Fry Edna
Fry Elizabeth
Fry Vivian Ronald James
Fryer Lily
Fulbrook Elsie Caroline
Fuller Harold Joseph

Gadd Arthur William
Gadd Ellen Maria

Gadd Florence Louisa
Galloway Swanton Agnes
Gambell John Alfred
Gardner Dorothy
Gardner Ethel
Gardner George William
Gardner Gwen
Gardner Phyllis
Garey William
Garner Albert Herbert
Gaskin Annie
Gaskin Edward
Gaskin Margaret
Gateley Robert William
Gauder Ernest William
Gauntlett Florence Maud
Gaylord Arthur Edwin Reginald
Gaynham Percy
Gell John Vernon Pritchard
Gennoe Bertram Ernest
Gensberg Charles
Gibbins Arthur
Gibbons Charles
Gibbs Ashley Maria
Gibbs Bertha Winnie
Gibbs James
Gibbs Thomas Charles
Giblin John
Gilbert Louisa
Gilbey Stanley George
Giles Thomas Henry
Gilliver Lilian Florence
Gilliver Rose
Gilliver Sarah Ann
Gilmor John
Glover Albert
Godson Harriet
Goldberg Ann
Goldberg Maurice
Gombrich Else
Goodby John Henry
Goodchild Jack Frederick
Goode Ernest Alfred
Goode Mary Ann
Goodson Barbara Ann
Goodson Winifred Emily
Goodwin Alfred John
Goody Rose
Goolding Annie
Gorman John
Gorth Frank
Grady John
Grainger Albert
Grainger Alfred
Grainger Ellen
Grainger Flora Elizabeth
Grainger Harold James
Grainger Leonard Charles
Granner Henry
Grant Arthur
Grant Mary
Gray Alice Laura
Gray Derek
Gray Robin
Gready Bertie
Greasley Ann
Greaves Gaious
Green Arthur
Green Arthur Leonard
Green Ethel Kate
Green George
Green James Walter
Green John Albert
Green Mary Josephine
Greenhill Mary Ann
Greenway Jane
Greenway Winifred
Greer Reginald Ernest

Gregory Harry
Gregory Louisa
Griffin William Henry
Griffiths Joseph Joshua
Griffiths Mary Eleanor Nellie
Griffiths Peter Llewellyn
Grimley Clara
Grimley Dorothy Georgina May
Grimley William Edward
Grinsell Emily Lilian
Grinsell Norma
Groom William
Groome Alice Beatrice
Grundy Joyce
Grundy Maud
Guest John
Guest Leonard
Gumbley Walter
Gunn Mary Elizabeth
Gupwell Emma
Gupwell Frederick James
Guscott Dorothy
Guscott Ernest Charles
Gwinnett David Cyril
Gwinnett Winifred Violet

Habberley Ernest Frederick
Hackett Harry Reginald
Haddon George William
Hadley Ada
Haines Oliver Alfred
Hale Avril Cynthia
Hale Ellen Maria
Hale Stanley Lawrence
Hale William James
Hall Alice Catherine
Hall Amy
Hall Frank James
Hall Frank Joseph
Hall Harry
Hall John Ernest
Hall John Ernest
Hall Lilian Mary Edith
Hall Walter Reginald
Halpin Dermot
Halpin Julia
Hamilton Frederick Douglas
Hammett Alice
Hammett James Edward
Hammond Howard
Hammond Hugh
Hammond Louie
Hampton Frederick Donald
Hand George
Handley Edith Florence
Handley Edith Maria
Handley Sarah Ann
Hands Bertha Winnie
Hands Reginald
Hanks Alice
Hanks Beryl Ann
Hannon Richard
Harbutt Ada
Hardwick Archibald Thomas
Hardwick Marion Frances
Hardy Arthur
Hardy Valerie
Hardy Vera Mary Elizabeth
Hare Ellen
Hare John Charles
Hare Mary Ann
Harman Rowland Thomas
Harrey Frederick Edward Hyde
Harrington Edith Ellen
Harrington Herbert Walter
Harris Adelaide
Harris Bert
Harris Clara Eliza

Harris Elizabeth
Harris Francis
Harris George James
Harris Harry
Harris Ivy Mary
Harris Ivy Priscilla
Harris Joan
Harris John Clifford
Harris Margaret Rose
Harris Marianne
Harris Norman John
Harris Richard
Harris Walter
Harrison Ada Maria
Harrison Donald Arthur
Harrison Edward
Harrison Florence Irene
Harrison George
Harrison George
Harrison George Joseph
Harrison John
Harrison Kenneth
Harrison Robert William
Harrison Thomas Edgar
Harrison Thomas John
Harrison William Frank
Hart Florence
Hart Henrietta Madeline
Hartill Martha
Harvey Basil
Harwood William
Haseler Helen Mary
Hassall Charles Henry
Hastings Bertie John Charles
Hastings Rose
Hatton Thomas
Hawes Fanny
Hawes Harold James Crisp
Hawkes Elsie
Hawkins Arthur
Hawkins Emily Beatrice
Hawkins William Charles
Haycock Harry Cyril
Hayfield Henry Edward
Haywood Edward Thomas
Haywood Polly
Haywood Victor William
Healey Daniel
Heath Dorothy
Heath Emily Jane
Heath Joan Molly
Heath Mary Ann
Heath Sydney
Heath William Edward
Hemming Albert Thomas
Hemms William John
Henley Alice Gertrude
Henley Doris
Henley Mary
Henley Sheila
Henn William
Henson Cyril John
Henson Dorothy Jean
Henson Frederick John
Henson Raymond Harold
Henty Eileen Margaret
Henty Kathleen
Hewer Robert Henry Henchley
Hewitt Albert Edward
Hewitt Albert James
Hewitt Audrey Kathleen
Hewitt John
Heynes Ivy
Heynes Louisa
Heynes May
Heynes Samuel
Hibbard Joseph E
Hicken Gladys

Hicken Gladys
Hicken Henry
Hicken Robert
Hicks Rose
Higgins Leonard
Higgins Winifred
High Harry Gilbert
High Rosa May
Higham Susannah Emma
Hill Albert Edward
Hill Charles Ernest
Hill David William
Hill Esther Margaret
Hill Frank
Hill Hilda Maud
Hill James
Hill Lucy Jane
Hinton Annie
Hird Albert Edward
Hitchen Catherine
Hobbs Clarence
Hodges Charles William Victor
Hodges Richard Baden Powell
Hodgetts Herbert John
Hodgetts William
Hodgkins Frederick
Hodgkins Harry
Holdaway Arthur Edmund
Holdom Irene Kitty
Holdom Margaret Ann
Hollis Valerie Margareta
Hollyoake Kathleen
Holmes Albert George
Holmes George Henry
Holmes Nellie
Holmes Thomas
Holmes Walter
Holt Albert Henry
Holt Annie May
Holyland Adelaide
Homer John William
Honick Henry Robert
Hood Alice Elizabeth
Hood Frederick James
Hood Rosalind Ethel Lilian
Hood Thomas Arthur
Hood Winnie
Hook Ronald Edward
Hooper John Walter
Hopkins Arthur
Hopkins Ethel Mary
Hopkins Sarah Ann
Hopkins Walter Joseph
Hopkinson Charles
Horne Harold
Horton George
Houlson Ethel Florence
Houlson Harold
Houlson Violet Hilda
Howard Richard Vincent
Howard Samuel
Howe Edward James
Hudson Gladys
Hudson William Alfred
Hughes Alice
Hughes Audrey Joan
Hughes Charles Thomas
Hughes Charles William
Hughes Elsie Maud
Hughes Emma
Hughes George Owen
Hughes Herbert Victor
Hughes Maud
Hughes Nathan Brookes
Hughes Nellie
Hughes Neville
Hughes Peter
Hughes Ronald Percy

Hulme Barbara Nina
Hulme Florence May
Hulse Harry Jerome
Hunt Charles
Hunt Joseph Henry
Hunt Maud Bevis
Hyatt Annie
Hyde Agnes Mary

Ilsley James Thomas
Inman Charles Henry
Inns Frederick
Inwood Gc George Walter
Isaacs Florence
Isaacs Gertrude May
Isaacs Jean
Isaacs Peter Philip
Islip Arthur
Islip Eva

Jacks John
Jackson Amy Marguerite
Jackson Elizabeth
Jackson Joseph
Jackson Maurice Denton
Jackson William
Jackson William Isaac
Jacobs Samuel
James Dorothy Irene
James John William
James Phoebe Harriett
James Sylvia
James William Henry
Jarman Florence May Violet
Jarvis Herbert
Jauncey Charlotte
Jenkins Albert
Jenkins Geoffrey Thomas
Jenkins James Hugh
Jenkins Richard Gwilym
Jenkins Ronald Colin Frederick
Jenkins William Evan
Jennings Benjamin
Jennings Charles
Jennings Lionel William
Jenson Anne Clarissa
Jenson Clarice
Jenson Phillip
Jervis Elizabeth Ann
Jessop Emily Lucy
Jevons Alfred George Isaac
Jinks May
Johnson Annie
Johnson Annie Steedman
Johnson Benjamin
Johnson Frederick
Johnson Gladys Winifred
Johnson Gordon Donald
Johnson John Henry
Johnson Lily
Johnson Mary
Jones Arthur
Jones Charles
Jones Clara
Jones Ernest Paul
Jones Islwyn Michael
Jones Kenneth Bertram
Jones Leonard
Jones Thomas Francis
Jones Thomas Howard
Jones Thomas Isaac
Jordon Pamela
Joseph Alfred Reuben
Jukes Agnes
Jukes John Albert

Kaufmann Bernard
Kavanagh Harold Alexander

Kavanagh Peter
Keasey Daisy
Keasey Hilda
Keasey Marjorie
Keeling William
Keight Ernest Reuben
Kelly Edward
Kelly John Edward
Kelly Kathleen
Kelly Thomas
Kelway Kathleen Dorothy
Kemp Albert
Kemp Jane Amenda Olive
Kendrick Dennis George
Kendrick Emily Beatrice
Kendrick George
Kendrick John
Kendrick Leslie Samuel
Kendrick William George
Kennedy Ada Winifred
Kennedy Emma Llewellyn
Kennedy Maureen
Kenny James
Kenny Rose Victoria
Kent Albert Edward
Kent Philip
Kettlewell Thomas Sykes
Kidd Roland Garner
Kidd Thomas Brand
King Arthur
King Maud
King Robert
King Robert
Kirby Wilfred
Kirk Alfred
Kite Philip George
Knight Lily
Knowles Albert Bertram
Knox Bridie
Knox Joseph
Knox Marjorie

Lacey Emma
Lake Florence Annie
Lambert Edgar
Lambert Elizabeth
Land Fred Raymond
Lane Gladys
Lane Samuel Richard
Lane William Henry
Langford Nellie
Langley George Henry
Langley Mary Ann
Larbi Ahmed
Larkin Thomas
Lawley John William
Lawlor Elizabeth
Lawrence Esther May
Lawrence F. G.
Laws Margaret Campbell
Lawson Dora Mary
Laxton William Henry
Layton Horace Alfred
Lea Aubrey Edgar
Lea Gilbert
Lee William Alfred
Lees William
Leigh Marjorie Kathleen
Lemmon Jean Agnes
Lemmon John William
Lemmon Maria
Lemmon Ramon
Lemmon Stanley William
Lemon M.M. Edwin Thomas
Leonard John
Lewis Ernest
Lewis George Reynolds
Lewis Harold Gilbert

Lewis Joan
Lewis John
Lewis Margaret
Lewis Thomas
Lewis Thomas
Lewis William John
Liddall Amelia
Lilley Alfred Ernest
Lilley Ellen
Lilley Ellen
Lilley John
Lilley Joseph Ernest
Lilley Kathleen
Lilley Kathleen
Lilley Phyllis Ellen
Lilwall Patty
Lines Alan Colin
Lines Annie Elizabeth
Lines Margaret
Ling Joseph Edward
Linton Leslie Bernard
Lister Elizabeth
Lister Maurice
Little John Michael
Llewellyn Edward Edgar Mannock
Lloyd Clara Jane
Lloyd Katharine Ann
Lloyd Lewis
Lloyd Rene Llewella
Lloyd Suzanne
Lloyd Valerie Doreen
Lloyd Violet
Loftus Edith
Lombard Charlotte
London Herbert William
Long Arthur Ernest
Long Dennis Henry
Long Donald Roland
Long Hazel Nellie
Long Ernest John
Long Katie Ellen
Long Leonard William
Long Samuel John
Longford Ada
Longford James Thomas
Longman William
Lord Ernest Edward
Louch Leonard Robert Charles
Lough Grace
Lough Thomas
Loveday Audrey
Loveday Ernest George
Lovedee Edith Alice
Lovsey Arthur John
Lownes William James
Lucas Alice
Lucas John William
Lugg Hubert Victor
Lydiatt Agnes Mary
Lydiatt Dennis Thomas Charles
Lynch James
Lynes May
Lyness Thomas

Maclean Alexander Murchison
Maclean Donald
Maclean Ian Alister
Maclean Mary
Maclean Mary Muir
Macnaughton Elizabeth Mabel
Maddox George
Maddox Leslie Arthur
Mahon Henry
Maiden Elsie
Maiden Elsie Louise
Maiden Herbert
Maiden Irene Eva
Malin Alfred Thomas

Malvern Cyril
Mancini Anthony Paul
Manley Albert Kenneth
Manley Beatrice May
Manley Brenda
Manley Cyril James
Manley Gilbert Terrence
Mann Annie Elizabeth
Mann Clara Amelia
Mann Florence Alice
Mansfield Charles Henry
Mansfield Clara
Mapp Constance Edith
Marburg Suzanne
Mark Euphemia Mary
Mark Phoebe Ann
Markland Joseph
Marklew William
Marriott Walter John
Marris Daniel
Marsh James
Marson Patricia Valerie
Marson Violet
Marsters Gertrude
Marsters Thomas Lewis
Martin Agnes Elizabeth
Martin Albert Edward
Martin James
Mason Eric Leslie
Mason James Henry
Masters Alice Helen
Masters Colin Thomas
Masters Doris Elizabeth
Masters Jean Anne
Masters May
Masters Philip
Matthews Arthur Bernard
Matthews Bridget
Matthews Elizabeth
Matthews Mary Jane
May Frank
Mayall Arthur John
Maybury William
McCarthy Anne
McCarthy Desmond
McCarthy Ellen Nellie
McCarthy Honora
McCarthy John
McCarthy John Peter
McCarthy Mary Josephine
McCarthy Patrick
McCarthy Thomas John
McClean Frederick William
McDonald John
McGrail James
McGrail Mavis L
McGrail Rose Elizabeth
McGreevy Joseph
McGuirk Henry Edward
McHugh Bernard Thomas
McLaughlin Annie Selina
McPherson David
Mead Leonard Arthur
Meakin Alfred Harold Charles
Meakin Doris
Meakin Frederick Thomas
Meakin Susan Elenore
Meanwell Alfred Edward
Mellor Ernest
Melville Mary
Merrett Albert Edward
Metcalf Kate
Metcalfe Matthew
Middleman Christopher
Miller Benjamin John
Miller Minnie
Mills Alice Louise
Mills Allen William

Mills Charlotte
Mills Edith
Mills George Edward
Mills Harry Bertram
Millward Beatrice Louise
Millward Gladys Annie
Millward Mary
Milner Douglas Donovan
Milroy Alice Maud
Minikin Herbert Price
Minor William Charles
Minott Sylvia
Mitchell Albert Edward
Mitchell Amy
Mitchell Diana Winifred
Mitchell Emma Ethel
Mitchell Frank Stanley Noel
Mitchell Kathleen
Mitchell Patricia Margaret
Mitchell William
Mitchell William Philip
Mitchinson William Alfred
Mitton Thomas
Mogg Brenda
Mogg Rosalind
Mogg Thomas Charles
Mohan John
Moody Barbara
Moody Edith Ellen
Moore Dorothy
Moore Henry
Moore June
Moore Thomas Anthony
Moore William
Moorhouse George Kaye
Moran Sheila
Morgan David John Edwin
Morgan Elsie
Morgan Harry
Morgan John William
Morgan Maureen Patricia
Morgan Selina Elizabeth
Morley Roland
Morrall Doris Ida
Morrall Thomas Edward
Morris Howard Fisher
Morris Lilian Florence
Morris Walter
Morris William Ernest
Morsley Richard William
Mortimer Eva
Moseley Arthur
Moseley Arthur
Moseley Clifford
Moss Ellen
Moss Elsie
Mould George Herbert Neville
Mountford Edith
Mountford Ernest Hope
Mucklow Joseph
Muddyman Edward
Mugleston Edward Stanley
Mulhall Christopher
Mullervy John
Mullins Edwin
Mullins Sarah
Mulliss Charles George
Munn William Henry
Murcott Joyce
Murray Esther
Murray John
Mutchell Alfred Edward

Nash Leslie Josiah
Nash Linda Florence
Navarre Alexander
Neal Mary
Neale Herbert John

Neil Joseph Harold
Nel Adrian
Nend Louisa
Neville Evelyn Mary
Neville William Allen
Nevitt Richard
Newall Jesse Arthur
Newman Amelia
Newman Joyce
Newman Kenneth
Newman Phyllis
Newton Arthur James
Newton Charles Arthur
Nicholls Henry
Nokes Ada Kathleen Leonora
Nolan Jerrard
Nolan Mary Ann
Nolan William
Nolte Ada Annie
Norgrove Harry
Norman William
Norridge Arthur Francis
Norris Florence Gertrude
Norris William
Northern Mary Elizabeth
Norton Edith
Nowell John Alfred
Nunn George
Nutting Jane
Nutting Lilian Joan

O'Donell Lilian
O'Leary Jeremiah
O'Neill Christopher Joseph
O'Neill John Joseph
O'Neill Margaret
O'Neill Neal
O'Neill Thomas
Onions John
Orme Alice May
Orme Joseph
Orme Thomas Joseph
O'rourke Thomas
Orton Howard Charles
Osborn Peter John
Osborn Winifred Gladys
Osmond Florence Louisa
Overend Hubert
Owen Ada
Owen Maud Beatrice
Owen Walter Thomas

Page Horace Albert
Page Mabel Florence
Page Thomas
Painter Ellen
Painter Marjorie
Palfreyman Jack
Palmer Eliza
Palmer Harry James
Palmer Leonard James
Palmer Norman
Pardoe Christine
Pardoe Joyce
Pardoe May Gertrude
Parfitt Douglas John
Parish Eliza
Parish George Kitchener
Parker Beatrice Alice
Parker Daphne Audrey
Parker Evelyn May
Parker Harry
Parker Ivy Grace
Parker Jean Lilian
Parker Joseph
Parker Leonard William
Parker Philip Henry
Parker Richard William

Parker Richard William
Parkes Martha
Parr Gwendoline
Parsons Alexander Raymond
Parsons Amy
Parsons Charles Henry
Parsons Dennis
Parton Albert
Parton George
Parton Henry
Partridge Phoebe
Patrick Albert Edward
Patrick Beatrice Maud
Patrick Mary Jean
Patrick Maureen
Paul Horace
Payne Douglas Harry
Payne Edgar Charles
Payne Ernest William
Payne Frank
Payne Lawrence
Payne William
Paynter Gladys Edith
Paynter Henry James
Peake Doris Patricia
Peake Elizabeth
Peake William Edward
Pearce Elsie June
Pearce Emily
Pearce James
Pearson Ann
Pearson Beatrice Mary
Pearson Frederick Charles
Pearson June Mary
Pearson Vera
Pearson William Charles
Peat Nellie Martha
Pemberton Frances Emily
Pemberton Gwendoline Evelyn
Pendleton Elizabeth Ann
Pendrey Roland Ernest
Penson Catherine
Perry Charles Arthur
Perry Daisy
Perry Eliza Ann
Perry Jane
Phillips Albert Arthur
Phillips Albert Edward
Phillips Edith Annie
Phillips Elsie Elizabeth
Phillips Ethel Annie
Phillips Gladys
Phillips Janet Alice
Phillips Raymond James
Piccioni Angela
Piccioni Doris Mary
Piccioni Gina Edvige Ernesta
Piccioni Phyllis Maud
Pickering Ernest
Pickering Ronald
Pierpoint Amy
Pierpoint Cornelius
Pitcher Iverina May
Pitman George Stanley
Pitt Alfred
Pitt Sarah Ellen
Pitt William
Pittaway Arthur
Plant Norman
Plumpton Jemima
Pollock Elizabeth
Poole Matilda
Pooley Lily
Poolton George Edward
Potter William James
Powell Edith Maria
Powell Frederick George
Powell George Edward

Powell Gordon Harry
Powell Kathleen May
Powell-Tuck Ethel Clara
Poxon Samuel Morley
Pratt Herbert Charles
Pratt Joan Winifred
Pratt Patricia Irene
Pratten Evelyn May
Prest Cicely
Price Douglas Ernest
Price Walter Robert
Price Wilfred Thomas
Priestman Lily Edith
Priestman Lucy Elizabeth
Prince Beatrice Wilhelmina Maude
Prince Jack Delworth
Prince Norman Delworth
Prince Sylvia Olive Janet
Pritchard Pauline
Pritchard Susannah
Proctor Frederick Leslie
Pugh Emma
Pugh Mabel
Purser Cecil Edwin
Purshouse Albert Edward
Pym Joan Irene
Pym Kenneth Arthur

Quercia Joseph
Quiney Bryan George
Quiney Elizabeth Jane
Quiney George
Quiney Olive
Quinn Eric Francis
Quinn Hilda Nora
Quinn Irene May
Quinn Louisa
Quinn Norman

Rabone Frederick Mitchell
Radd William
Radford Ernest James
Rainsford Annie May
Rainsford George
Rainsford George Henry
Ralph Joseph Henry
Randall Arthur Allister
Ranger Frederick Thomas Victor
Ravyts Jeanne
Rawlins Edith Ellen
Ray June
Rayworth Iris
Rayworth John Stewart
Rea May
Rea Norman Philip
Reacord Charles Henry
Reddall John Norman
Reed Wallace Nelson
Rees John
Reeves William
Reid Alfred
Reid Elizabeth Ann
Rendle Elsie
Resuggan John Henry
Reynolds Leonard
Reynolds Thomas George
Reynolds William
Rhodes John
Rhone Florence Ada Lucy
Richards Alice Margaret
Richards Charles Douglas
Richards Howard Walter
Richards John Garbett
Richards May
Richards Ronald
Richards William Frederick
Richardson Louisa
Rickards George Samuel

Ridgway Howard Percy
Riley Albert
Riley Albert Harry
Riley Douglas
Riley Janetta
Riley Jean
Riley Joan Lilian
Riley Laura Elizabeth
Riley Nora Vera
Rimell Albert Leslie
Roach Frank
Roberts Annie Avarina
Roberts Annie Mary
Roberts Arthur
Robinson Frances Patricia
Robinson Georgina Amelia
Robinson Hilda Daisy
Robinson Kenneth Edward John
Robinson Peter Maxwell
Robinson William Henry
Rockett Beryl Kathleen
Rockett Horace Frederick
Rockett Kate
Roddy Nellie
Roddy Thomas
Rodway Harold
Rodway Minnie
Rodway William Alfred
Roe Sarah Ann
Roe William
Roe William John
Rogers Alfred Thomas
Rogers Annie
Rogers Barbara May
Rogers Edith
Rogers Elizabeth
Rogers Elsie
Rogers Hannah Matilda
Rogers John William
Rogers Mary Ann
Rogers Minnie
Rogers Richard Lewis
Rogers Sybil Barbara
Rollason Maurice Stanley
Rollings Harry
Rooke Eliza
Rooke Sarah
Roper Edward
Roper Maurice Edward
Rose Harold
Rose Josephine
Rose Kathleen
Rose Nellie
Rosenberg Emmie Eliza
Rosenberg Isaac
Ross Rebecca
Round Emma Elizabeth
Round Martha
Rowan Frederick
Rubery James
Rudge Albert Arthur
Rumbold Arthur
Russell Joan Gertrude May
Russell William
Russell William
Rutter Edwin
Ryland Edith
Rymill William

Sallis Felix
Salmon Ella Alice Louisa
Sambrook Clara
Sambrook John
Sambrook Ronald
Sanders Hilda Maud
Sanders Thomas
Sanderson William John
Savage Denis Sidney

Savage William James
Savin David Thomas
Savin Kenneth Joseph
Savin Raymond John
Savory Frederick Lionel James
Scott Annie Elizabeth
Scott Edith Elizabeth
Scott Elizabeth Jane
Scott Ernest
Scott James
Scott Kenneth Sidney
Scott Sidney
Scott William Henry Richard
Scragg Alfred
Scriven Audrey Jean
Scriven Elsie Mabel
Scriven Lily
Scrivener Albert George
Scrivener James Henry
Scrivens Florence
Sealey Minnie
Seaton Rosetta
Sellek Mark William
Selvey George Allen
Senior Eric
Severn Luke
Seymour Barbara Florence
Seymour Divinia Edith
Seymour William Alfred
Seymour William Barry
Shakespeare Charles Henry
Shakespeare William Henry
Shamsudi Allah Ditta
Shapter Charles Edward
Sharp Clara
Sharp Herbert Walter Thomas
Sharpe Alfred
Sharpe Dennis H
Sharpe Edith Maud
Sharpe Jesse
Sharpe John
Sharples Harry
Shaw Brian
Shaw Edward
Shaw Joan
Shaw Joan
Shaw Louis
Shaw Marion
Sheffield George
Sheffield Ida
Sheldon Leslie
Sheldon William
Shenton Annie Amelia
Shepherd Amy
Shepherd Cyril
Shepherd Dorothy Louise
Shepherd Howard
Shepherd John
Shepherd Joseph Charles Lea
Shepherd Lorna
Shepherd Molly
Shepherd Thomas Henry
Shepherd William Charles
Sherrin Thomas Edward
Sherwood William John
Sheward Will
Shingler Monica Agnes
Shipley Eunice Lilian
Shotton Alfred
Showell William Arthur Harry
Shutt Annie
Shutt John
Shuttleworth Eric
Silk Robert Bernard
Silk William
Simmons Eric Samuel
Simpson Elizabeth Rose Edith
Simpson Frank Philip

Simpson Harold Sidney
Simpson Joseph Ernest
Simpson Sidney
Sinclair Louise
Singh Mehnga
Singleton Alfred John
Skermer Drucilla
Skermer Leonard
Skermer Patricia
Skermer Reginald
Skermer William James
Skett Mary
Skinner Leonard Richard
Skinner Reginald George
Slater Leslie
Slater Lydia
Slater Walter Byron
Sleet Betsy
Sleet Charles
Sleet George
Smallwood Annie
Smallwood Edith
Smallwood Gladys
Smallwood Hilda Mary
Smallwood Thomas Edward
Smart Alice Frances
Smart Muriel Dorothy
Smart William Charles
Smith Ada
Smith Albert Edward
Smith Albert Ellis
Smith Alfred
Smith Alfred Ernest
Smith Alfred John
Smith Alice
Smith Alice
Smith Alice Marie
Smith Annie
Smith Anthony John
Smith Anthony John Mackenzie
Smith Arthur John
Smith Catherine
Smith Edith Alice
Smith Edward Arthur
Smith Elsie
Smith Ernest Evatt
Smith Ernest Henry
Smith Ethel Dora
Smith Evelyn Gladys
Smith Florence
Smith Florence
Smith Florence Hannah
Smith Florence Lilian
Smith Frank Pearson
Smith Frederick
Smith Geoffrey William
Smith George William
Smith Harriet Ann
Smith Harry
Smith Hilary Margaret
Smith Horace Charles
Smith Ida Mary
Smith Irene
Smith John
Smith John
Smith John James
Smith John James
Smith John Kemp
Smith June
Smith Mary Ann
Smith Ralph
Smith Rose Ellen
Smith Sheila
Smith Sidney John
Smith Violet Annie
Smith Wallace
Smith Walter Alfred
Smith William

Smith William Albert
Smith William Arthur
Snow John Beverley
Soden Colin
Sollors William Frederick
Spalton Joseph Newbould
Sparrow Reginald William
Speed Annie Elizabeth
Speed Sarah Florence
Speller Eustace Lionel
Spencer Arthur Edward
Spencer William Beasley
Spink James
Spooner Harry
Spooner Joseph Henry
Spooner Rose
Sprague Frank
Squires John Gordon
Stafford Alfred Smith
Stagg Clara Beatrice
Stanley Albert Edward
Stanyard Rosanna
Staples Drusilla
Starkey George
Steedman Edna
Steedman Elsie
Steedman Joan
Steedman Vera
Stephens Mary Teresa
Stevens William Thomas
Stevenson Gertrude May
Stevenson Henry
Stevenson William
Stimpson Alfred Edward
Stockley Eric Norman
Stringer Bertram
Strophair Anita Josephine
Strother Richard Edward
Stryke George
Stuckey Harriet
Summerfield William
Sumner William Joseph
Swadkins Harry
Swadling Ernest
Swales Henry
Sweet Herbert James
Swindale Florence
Swindale Kathleen Ethel
Swindale Michael John
Swingler Henry

Talbot Emma Eliza
Talbot Harry
Tandy Phyllis Valentine
Tankard Laura
Tankard Mary Ann
Tanner Isabella
Tarnosky Ida Mary
Tatchell Bertha May
Tavinor Herbert
Taylor Albert Edward
Taylor Dorothy Rose
Taylor Florence
Taylor Gordon
Taylor Henry
Taylor Joan Ethel
Taylor John
Taylor Norman
Taylor Olive Aline
Taylor Samuel
Taylor Sarah Ann
Taylor Sarah Elizabeth
Taylor Sidney Arthur
Taylor William
Taylor William Charles
Teagle G.E.
Teague Bertha Annie
Teague Joan Margaret

Teague Mary Dorothy
Teague Nellie Edith
Teale Bryan
Teale Dorothy Jane
Teale Kenneth John
Teale Patricia
Teale William Joseph
Tennant Alice Maud
Tennant Susannah Jane
Terrell Charlotte
Terry Norman
Tetley Samuel Frank
Thomas Daniel Smedley
Thomas Evan Owen
Thomas George Lionel
Thomas John Penry
Thomas Thomas John
Thomas Trevor
Thomas William Henry Charles
Thompson Albert Edward
Thompson Annie Elizabeth
Thompson Edith Elizabeth
Thompson Edwin
Thompson Mary
Thrasher George
Tilly Arthur
Tilt Samuel
Timmins Harry
Timmis Kate Alice
Tims Edmund Percy
Tirrell Albert
Tomkinson Gertrude Ellen
Tongue Charles Arthur
Tonks Ivy Catherine
Tooth Gladys
Tovey Hannah
Towers Thomas
Townley Alma Eileen
Townley James
Townley Jessiemine
Townsend Albert Edward
Townsend Doris Mary
Townsend Mary Ann
Tozer Augustus Cyril
Tranter Gordon
Tranter Peggy
Tranter Rose
Traves John Henry
Trentham Susannah
Trickett Reginald Louis
Troman Nellie Elizabeth
Tropman Sidney Charles
Trueman Evelyn Annie
Trull Gladys Bertha
Tuby Gladys Anita
Tucker Ernest Edward
Tucker John Ernest
Tudor Dorothy
Tudor Elsie Annie
Tudor George
Tudor Georgina
Tulk Brian Keith
Tulk Frederick Ivor Harris
Tunney Florence
Tunney John
Turland Alfred Ernest
Turland Hilda Kate
Turland John Alfred
Turland Margaret Victoria
Turland Maureen
Turnell Amy Vera Dumolo
Turner Arthur Richard
Turner Harry Rowland
Turner James Francis
Turner Kathleen
Turner Mary
Turner Maud Gladys
Turner William Thomas

Turvey Norah Isabel
Tustin Frank Thomas
Tyler Elizabeth Ann
Tyler Elsie
Tyler Henry John
Tyler Stanley Horace

Ullaha Rafie
Underhill Edgar Albert
Unitt Benjamin Stanley
Upton Mabel Charlotte

Van Asten June
Vann Emma
Vaughan Ada
Vaughan Agnes Boyd
Vaughan Conrad
Vaughan George
Vaughan Hilda
Vaughan Jane
Vaughan Michael Roy
Vaughan Noreen
Vaughan Robert Daniel
Vaughan Thora
Vaughan Winifred Elizabeth
Vicary Adrian John
Villers Sidney
Vine George
Viney Emily Mary
Vogan Lily
Vogan Molly
Vogan Thomas
Vowles Ivor

Wadhams Emily Elizabeth
Wadhams William
Waight Elsie
Wainwright Arthur Frank
Wainwright Brian John
Waite Thomas
Wake Walter Harry
Wakeling Alfred James
Wakeling Mabel
Wakeman Eileen Florence
Walden Alfred William
Walden Arthur
Walden Carol Ann
Walden Melville
Walden Nora
Waldron Henry Charles
Waldron Phyllis June
Walewski Waclaw
Walker Arthur Albert
Walker Douglas Henry
Walker Edith Sarah
Walker Elizabeth
Walker Gertrude
Walker Isaac Rufus
Walker John
Walker John Henry
Walker John James
Walker Margaret Audrey
Wall Charles Henry
Wall Dora Eleanor
Wall Sarah Helena
Wall William Edward
Wallace Henry Clement
Wallace James Charles Thomas
Wallington Albert Edward
Wallington Albert George
Wallington Charles
Wallington Edith
Walmsley Alfred Edward
Walmsley Caroline
Walmsley Doris
Walsh Daniel
Walton Walter William
Ward Ann Matilda

Ward Charles William
Ward Spencer Littleton
Ward Thomas
Waring Ivy May
Warner Patricia Rose
Warner Shirley Barbara
Warr Rose
Warren Mary Jane
Warwick-Mcclave William
    Frederick
Waterhouse Austin
Waters Edith
Waters Edith Gertrude
Waters Harry Seymour
Waters Winifred Mary
Waterson Fanny Elizabeth
Waterson Jean Elizabeth
Waterworth Sarah Jane
Watkins Alice
Watkins Alice May
Watson Annie
Watson Henry
Watson William
Watson William Howard
Watton Jesse
Watts George
Weaving Annie
Webb Algernon
Webb James Frederick
Webb M.M. Samuel
Webb Thomas Walter
Weeks Arthur John
Welch James
Welch Nancy
Welding Harold
Wells Arthur Pinfield
Wells Doris Eileen
Wells Nellie Susannah Whiteman
Welsby Clara
Welsby Herbert
West Bertram Edward
West Florence Eunice Bessie
Westley Thomas
Westwood Arthur Edward
Westwood Arthur Thomas
Wheeler John Francis
Wheeler William Joseph Patrick
Whitbread Frederick William
White David Oliver
White Howard
White Mary Ann
White William
Whitehead Thomas
Whitehorn Wilfred Thomas
Whitehouse Adelaide
Whitehouse James Henry
Whitehouse Joseph Frederick
Whitehouse Leonard
Whitehouse Mabel Eliza
Whitehouse William John
Whitlock Arthur
Whittingham George
Whittingham Harold
Whittingham Rose
Whitworth Norman
Wiedemann Herbert Joseph
Wilcox Walter
Wilford Kathleen Annie
Wilkes Irene
Wilkins Alice
Wilkins Alice Maud
Wilkins Frances
Wilkins Joan
Wilkins William
Wilkinson Edith
Wilkinson Henry
Wilkinson Ralph George
Williams Alfred Neander

Williams Charles Henry
Williams David
Williams Doreen
Williams Ernest George
Williams Frederick
Williams Lily Mary
Williams Mary Ann
Williams William
Willmore Stanley Walker
Willmott Alfred George
Wills Dora
Wilson John
Wilson Samuel
Wilson Stanley Frederick
Windsor Dorcas Hilda
Windsor Margaret
Windsor Mary Jane
Winfield Jessie
Winkett William Wilberforce
Winter Joseph
Winwood William George
Witts Leonard
Wood Alfred John
Wood Alice
Wood Charles Henry
Wood Frank Howard Job
Wood Lucy
Woodard Reginald
Woodbridge Alice Lilla
Woodbridge David Leonard
Woodbridge Leonard
Woodcock Charles Henry
Woodcock Gertrude
Woodhall Maggie Sarah
Woodhall William Benjamin Gold
Woodley Harold Frank
Woodley John Charles
Woodward Robert Alfred
Woolaston Elizabeth
Woolley Gertrude Annie
Wootton Arthur Howard
Wormall May Louise
Worrell Ellen Louisa
Would Harold Temperton
Wren Mary
Wright Alexander
Wright Christy
Wright Frederick George
Wright Thomas Edgar
Wright Thomas Edgar
Wright William Frederick
Wrigley Annie
Wyatt Wilfred Victor
Wynne Frank Wilson
Wynne Rose
Yarnold Edgar
Yates Dorothy Eileen
Yates Edna Joan
Yates Mary
York William
Yorke Charles
Young Daisy

Bromsgrove Urban District
Haynes Lionel Leslie

Waldron Florence Queenie
Waldron George Arnold

Oldbury Municipal Borough
Hadley George Arthur

James Eric Hubert

Kendrick Harry
Kendrick Ivy Eileen

Pickerell Horace

Wheildon Florence Ivy

Smethwick County Borough
Bahauddin Tunku
Beardsmore Joseph Thomas
Best John
Billing Elizabeth
Bladon Thomas
Briant Arthur Mcalister
Brookin Edna
Brown Thomas Leslie
Bunch John Thomas

Chambers Aubrey
Clancey Brenda Margaret
Coles Ernest Harry
Cooper Horace

David Thomas Charles
Digger Clifford William
Digger Margaret

Farnell Horace
Farnell Josephine
Foulds Terence Leslie
Fry Elizabeth
Fry Edna
Fry Eric John
Fry William

Gardiner Pamela
Gardiner Philip Vincent
Goodman Dorothy Maud

Hanson Amy
Hanson Doreen Joan
Hargrave Glays May
Hargrave James Charles
Harper Florence Ada
Hill John Henry
Hudson George William

James Elizabeth
Johnson Frederick
Johnson Jean Ruth May
Johnson Ronald Arthur
Johnson Ruth Mary
Johnson Thomas Henry

Kent Florence Ada
Kent George
Kent Leonard
Kent Lillian Elizabeth
Kent Minnie Beatrice
Kent Rachel Ellen
Kent Sarah Ann
Kent Sidney

Lindberg Charles Thorley
Lindberg George William Lowe
Lindberg Lily
Lindberg Lily Jean

Marsh George Frederick
Martin Arthur
Mason Eliza

Norgrove Lizzie

Owen Howard

Padfield Leslie
Phayre John Charles
Poole Christine Dorothy Annesley
Poole Geoffrey Dudley
Poole Gertrude Dorothy
Poole Grace Jacqueline
Pritchard Brian
Pritchard Eileen
Pritchard June
Pritchard Margery Emma

Richards Albert
Richards Albert Walter
Richards Daisy
Richards Edna Elizabeth

Roper Maurice Edward

Sargent Edith
Selvey George Allen
Share Dorothy Rose
Smart Albert Frederick
Smart Alfred Leslie
Smart Brian Roy
Smart Doris Evelyn
Smart Malcolm Leslie
Smith Harriet Ann
Smith John James
Steele Norman Joseph
Stockley Eric Norman

Tongue Selina May

Waterfield James Thomas
Webster Roy William
Wolfe Ada Elizabeth
Wolfe Cyril
Wolfe Daniel
Wolfe George Edward
Wolfe Marguerite Ada

Solihull Urban District
Allen Cyril
Atkinson George

Bushell Patricia Ann
Bushell Winifred Irene

Clark Lilian Muriel

Foster Beatrice
Frith Ivy

Gumbley Margaret

Harrington Ernest Harry
Harrington Joan Margaret

Johnson Violet
Jones Cyril

Moore Charlotte
Miller Jane
Myatt Beatrice May

Pearse Mary Elizabeth
Pinder Alice Lizzie
Pinder Doris Muriel
Pinder Edgar
Pinder Edith Mary
Pinder Neville
Pinder Ralph

Rawlins Edith Ellen
Robbins Ethel Frances
Robbins William

Scragg (Mayne) Eveline
Sealey Bertie
Sealey Gwendolen

Tucker Betty
Tucker Robert Huntley Everest
Tucker Violet May

Whitehead Reginald Philip
    Mansfield
Woods Martha Amelia
Woods Tom Sainsbury

**Sutton Coldfield
Metropolitan Borough**
Bunford
Ruby Maureen
Brown Charles Edmund

Hayward William Ralph Philip
Holcroft William Frederick

Walsall County Borough
Baker Thomas Arthur
Bayley Norman Leonard

Edwards Richard
Emery Emily

Gee Raymond

Partridge Ralph Charles

Smith William Miles

West Bromwich County Borough
Alock Eliza
Alcock Thomas

Botterill Harriet Louisa
Brookes Vera Mary

Care Eric
Care Harry
Care Jill
Care Matilda
Care Roy
Care Thomas William
Care Vera
Clare Edith Gertrude
Clarke Thomas Edward
Cook Elsie
Cook Ivy Blanche
Cook John Frederick
Cook John Thomas
Cook Valerie

Downing Eliza
Downing Jean
Downing William

Evans Joseph Brian
Evans Roger Barry
Evans Violet Alice

Ford Carol Ann
Ford Joseph Sidney

Green Joseph Higgins

Handley Frank
Harris Alfred
Harris Desmond
Harris Edna
Harris Harry
Harris Harry
Harris Mary Ann
Haynes Chrissie
Hunt Annie

Jeffries Agatha Rose
Jeffries Arthur

Kyle Edith Hannah

Lamb Ernest Albert

Parker Clara Ellen
Perry James
Perry Samuel
Piddock Hannah Betsy
Piddock John Alfred
Piddock Lillian Irene
Powell Thomas
Price Esther

Richards Gladys Maud
Richards Rose Evelyn

Stevens Annie
Stevens Nellie Jean

Watton John
Weeks Ellen Claudia

BIRMINGHAM AREA AIRCRAFT CRASHES 1939-45

This Miles Master I (N7408) hit a balloon cable and crashed onto the roof of W & T Avery in Smethwick on 28th August 1940.
Phillips & Powis Aircraft Ltd

28th August 1940
At 11:30 hours Miles Master I N7408 en-route from Sealand to Brize Norton struck a balloon cable (site Pri 22 of 911 Sqn) at West Bromwich. The aircraft crashed onto the roof of W & T Avery's factory, Smethwick. The pilot was killed but there were no serious civilian casualties.

28th October 1940
Bristol Blenheim IV R3840 struck a balloon cable (site Pri 24 of 911 Sqn) at 15:30, severing a wing. The aircraft crashed near the Warley Odeon. The machine was being ferried by the Aircraft Transport Auxiliary (ATA) which was based at White Waltham, Berkshire. The pilot was killed.

9th November 1940
Avro Anson I N9945 of the Wireless Intelligence Development Unit (WIDU), based at Wyton, Huntingdonshire, hit a balloon cable (site 3 of 913 Sqn) at Stechford and crashed onto the LMS railway track. The accident occurred at 00:15. The crew of five were killed.

10th November 1940
Hurricane I P3891 of 308 (Polish) Sqn crash-landed at Romsley, when the Polish pilot became lost flying from RAF Worcester to his base at Baginton, Coventry. The crash occurred at dusk around 18:00 hours; the pilot survived. The airframe was deemed a write-off but the engine was salvaged.

19th November 1940
Hawker Audax I K7322 of 9 Flying Training School (FTS) based at Hullavington, Wiltshire, collided with a hedge while landing at Hockley Heath airfield, Warwickshire. The pilot was uninjured.

21st November 1940
Westland Lysander II L4788 of 7 Anti-Aircraft Co-operation Unit (AACU), based at Castle Bromwich, crashed on farmland near Castle Bromwich. The pilot was unhurt.

30th November 1940
Vickers Wellington IC T2893 of 214 Sqn, based at Stradishall, Suffolk, suffered engine failure and hit trees while carrying out a forced landing at night near Elmdon.

12th December 1940
Hawker Audax I K7445 of 9 FTS crashed at 16:30, after hitting a balloon cable (site 61 of 915 Sqn) at Longbridge. The pilot was killed.

31st December 1940
De Havilland Tiger Moth II K4272 of 14 Elementary Flying Training School (EFTS), based at Elmdon (Birmingham airport), got lost and stalled in a low turn while attempting to land at Hockley Heath. Both airmen were killed.

12th February 1941
Handley Page Hampden I AD734 of 83 Sqn, based at Scampton, Lincolnshire, returning from an operational mission, hit a balloon cable (site 67 of 914 Sqn) at 02:00. All of the crew bailed out safely.

21st/22nd March 1941
Bristol Blenheim IV T1892 of 105 Sqn, based at Swanton Morley, Norfolk, whilst returning from an operational mission, hit a balloon cable (site 61 of 915 Sqn) shortly before midnight. It crashed soon afterwards at Cofton Hackett. All of the crew were killed.

10th April 1941
Heinkel He 111P (w/n 1555) 1G+KM of 4/KG27 was attacked by a Defiant and then collided with a balloon cable (site 17 of 915 Sqn). The aircraft crashed onto two adjacent houses in Smethwick at 01:40, killing seven civilians. Two of the crew were killed and two were taken prisoner.

24th April 1941
De Havilland Tiger Moth II R5178 of 14 EFTS stalled near Hockley Heath. The Royal Navy pilot was killed.

The wreck of Heinkel He 111H-8 (w/n 3971) G1+MT of 9/KG55 following its demise in the early hours of 11th May 1941.

11th May 1941
Heinkel He 111H-8 (w/n 3971) G1+MT of 9/KG55 was brought down at around 00:25 by light anti-aircraft fire at Earlswood. Three of the crew were killed and one was taken prisoner.

7th July 1941
Armstrong Whitworth Whitley V Z6476 of 10 Operational Training Unit (OTU), based at Abingdon, Oxfordshire, hit a balloon cable (site 51 of 915 Sqn) at Quinton at 01:55. The aircraft was on a cross-country exercise. The Polish crew of six were killed when the aircraft crashed on open ground at Quinton.

10th October 1941
De Havilland Tiger Moth DH.82A T8199 of 19 EFTS, based at Sealand, Flintshire, hit a balloon cable, stalled and crashed near Bartley Green at 12:40. The pilot was injured.

12th October 1941
Westland Lysander IIIA V9612 of 7 AACU hit a balloon cable (site 5 of 913 Sqn) at 12:13. It crashed at Erdington.

8th November 1941
De Havilland Tiger Moth II N9156 of 14 EFTS hit a balloon cable (site 29 of 913 Sqn) at Castle Bromwich at 15:44. The aircraft broke in two and crashed a few hundred yards from the balloon site, both of the airmen having bailed out successfully.

The wreck of Blenheim IV Z5899 following the crash at Bearwood on 20th February 1942.
Mirrorpix/Birmingham Mail

22nd November 1941
De Havilland Tiger Moth I L6946 of 7 EFTS, based at Desford, Leicestershire, stalled and crashed at Coleshill. The pilot was injured.

8th December 1941
De Havilland Tiger Moth II N6938 of 7 EFTS crashed when forced landing at Wythall.

9th January 1942
De Havilland Tiger Moth II N9158 of 14 EFTS spun into the ground at Elmdon.

9th January 1942
Vickers Wellington II W5356 of 12 Sqn, based at Binbrook, Lincs, was returning on one engine following an operation to Cherbourg, when it crashed at around 09:05, approximately two miles from No.6 Barrage Balloon Centre (HQ) at Wythall. Two of the six crew survived.

20th February 1942
At 10:38 a Bristol Blenheim IV Z5899 of 17 OTU, based at Upwood, Cambridgeshire, hit one of 911 Sqn's balloon cables which was tethered at Avery's sports ground in Edgbaston. It fell onto houses in Bearwood. There were no civilian casualties but the crew of three were killed.

7th August 1942
Vickers Wellington IC R1075 of 16 OTU, based at Upper Heyford, Oxon, hit two balloon cables in succession, site 12 at 01:37 and site 38 at 01:41 (both sites part of 911 Sqn). The aircraft crashed at Erdington. Four of the crew were killed and two bailed out safely.

11th October 1942
An Avro Tutor K3461 of 1 Flying Instructors School (FIS), based at Church Lawford, Warwickshire, undershot upon landing at Hockley Heath. Both airmen were uninjured.

21st November 1942
A Vickers Wellington crashed into two de Havilland Tiger Moths when landing at Elmdon. Tiger Moth DH.82A T7285 of 14 EFTS was written off.

10th January 1943
Newly-built Short Stirling III BK660 was on a test flight from Elmdon, with the elevators locked externally. It climbed away steeply, stalled and crashed just outside the aerodrome boundary. Both of the crew were unhurt.

17th February 1943
An Auster III (possibly MZ107) of 654 Sqn, en-route from Bottisham, Cambridgeshire (its base) to Codsall, Wolverhampton, crash-landed at a farm near Great Barr at 16:45. The pilot and his passenger were uninjured.

19th July 1943
Airspeed Oxford I HN772 of 285 Anti-Aircraft Co-operation (AAC) Sqn, based at Honiley, Warwickshire, broke up when recovering from a dive and crashed at West Bromwich, killing its crew of three.

28th August 1943
Airspeed Oxford II N4733 of 18 (Pilots) Advanced Flying Unit ((P) AFU), based at Church Lawford, dived into the ground at Wythall. The pilot was killed.

9th November 1943
Vickers Wellington III X3932 of 23 OTU based at Pershore, Worcestershire suffered engine failure and crashed at Rowney Green (near Alvechurch) at 19:40. All of the Canadian crew were killed.

10th December 1943
De Havilland Tiger Moth DH.82A T7240 of 14 EFTS hit a civilian on the perimeter track while taking off from Elmdon. The civilian was killed and the two airmen were injured.

9th March 1944
A newly-built Vickers-Armstrongs Spitfire from Castle Bromwich crashed near Elmdon while on its test flight. The test pilot was injured.

16th March 1944
Handley Page Halifax III LW413 of 425 Sqn, based at Tholthorpe, North Yorkshire, was abandoned by the crew, due to a low fuel state, near Brierley Hill, following an operational mission. The aircraft crashed onto houses, killing one civilian, but the seven-man crew bailed out safely.

19th March 1944
De Havilland Mosquito NF.XVII HK314 of 219 Sqn, based at Honiley, hit trees and crashed at Knowle, near Solihull, killing its crew of two.

22nd March 1944
Vickers Wellington IC HD987 of 105 (T) OTU, based at RAF Nuneaton (actually located in Leicestershire), suffered engine failure and crashed at Mill Lane, Digbeth, near the Midland Red bus garage. All of the crew were killed.

10th June 1944
Republic P-47D Thunderbolt 42-22518 of 552 Fighter Squadron, 495 Fighter Group (United States Army Air Force), based at Atcham, Shropshire, crashed onto the Wykham Martin Estate at Hockley Heath when it undershot the runway, killing the pilot.

19th June 1944
De Havilland Tiger Moth II N9336 of 14 EFTS crashed when making a forced landing at Northfield. The two airmen were unhurt.

19th June 1944
De Havilland Tiger Moth DH.82A T6124 of 14 EFTS stalled and hit a hangar while overshooting at Elmdon. Both airmen were unhurt.

31st July 1944
Miles Master II DL961 of 5 Glider Training School (GTS), based at Hockley Heath, crashed onto West Smethwick Park. Both airmen were killed.

4th August 1944
Miles Master II W9027 of 5 (P) AFU, based at Tern Hill, Shropshire, stalled at low level and crashed at the Parkinson Cowan stove works in Stechford, Birmingham, killing both the instructor and pupil.

22nd August 1944
Vickers Wellington X MF517 of 105 (T) OTU was on a night cross-country flight from Bramcote, Warwickshire, and crashed between Rubery and Romsley. All three of the crew were killed.

15th September 1944
General Aircraft Hotspur II (Glider) HH140 of 5 GTS undershot and hit a hedge at Hockley Heath.

22nd November 1944
De Havilland Mosquito NF.II HJ650 of 60 OTU High Ercall, Shropshire, stalled after a near miss with another Mosquito and crashed at West Bromwich, killing its crew of two and injuring a civilian.

3rd January 1945
De Havilland Tiger Moth DH.82A T6571 of 14 EFTS was blown over while taxying at Elmdon.

1st March 1945
De Havilland Tiger Moth II N9145 of 14 EFTS crashed when force-landing at Halesowen. The pilot was injured.

2nd March 1945
De Havilland Tiger Moth II DE490 of 14 EFTS hit the ground on approach to Elmdon in fog.

11th May 1945
De Havilland Tiger Moth DH.82A T5982 and T6910 of 7 EFTS collided at Elmdon. All four airmen were killed.

22nd May 1945
De Havilland Tiger Moth DH.82A T6047 of 14 EFTS hit a blister hangar on approach to Hockley Heath. The pilot was unhurt.

12th June 1945
Supermarine Spitfire IIA P8196 (used by Vickers and Dunlop for testing tyres) was written off when it accidentally became airborne at Castle Bromwich, while testing a new tailwheel design.

10th July 1945
De Havilland Tiger Moth II N6836 of 14 EFTS crashed on take-off from Elmdon. The pilot was slightly injured.

20th August 1945
North American Mustang IVAs KM113 and KM201 of 303 (Polish) Sqn, based at Andrews Field, Essex, collided near Bromsgrove. Both of the Polish pilots were killed.

The author wishes to thank Delwyn Griffith and Mark Evans (http://www.aviation archaeology.org.uk/marg/crashes.htm) who supplied much of the information for this particular appendix.

Short Stirling III BK660 came to grief immediately after take off from Elmdon on 10th January 1943.
Geoffrey Alington

ACKNOWLEDGEMENTS

In addition to those whose names appear as photo credits, the author wishes to thank the following for their assistance so generously given: Amanda Low *nee* Bodien, Andrew Gardner, Arthur Lockwood, Avery Historical Museum (Andrew Lound), Birmingham Air Raids Association, Chris Goss, David Harvey, Delwyn Griffith, Earlswood Village Museum (Val Tonks), Eddie Nielinger, Glyn Warren, Gordon Griffiths, Jean Barnsby *nee* Lockwood, John Seale, Les Whitehouse, Lloyd Penfold, Mark Blamire Brown, Mark Evans, Mary Bodfish, Mike Kemble, Mirrorpix (David Scripps), Nigel Parker, Philippa Hodgkiss, Quinton Local History Society (Bernard Taylor), Robert Johns, Royal Air Force Museum Hendon (Peter Elliott), Royal Artillery Museum (Paul Evans), Royal Observer Corps Trust (Neville Collingford), Transport Museum, Wythall (Dave Taylor and Malcolm Keeley). On the production side: Carol Thomson, Dave Heaney, David Oliver, David Westley, John Barclay, John Handford, John Hobday, John Taylor, Margaret Hill, Marie Oliver, Neil Lewis, Sue Casswell and Tony Mitchell.

Special thanks to my wife, Carole, and daughters Emma and Julie.

BIBLIOGRAPHY

AA Command, Britain's Anti-Aircraft Defences of the Second World War, Colin Dobinson, Methuen, London, 2001.

Action Stations 2, Military Airfields of Lincolnshire and the East Midlands, Bruce Barrymore Halpenny, PSL, Yeovil, 1991.

Action Stations 6, Military Airfields of the Cotswolds and the Central Midlands, Michael J. F. Bowyer, PSL, Cambridge, 1983.

Adolf Galland, The Authorised Biography, David Baker, Windrow & Greene Ltd, London, 1996.

The Air Defence of Britain 1914-1918, Christopher Cole & E. F. Cheesman, Putnam, London, 1984.

The Air Raids on Smethwick 1940-42, Peter Kennedy.

Birmingham at War Vol.1, Alton Douglas, Streetly Printing (Birmingham) Ltd. 1982.

Birmingham at War Vol.2, Alton Douglas, Birmingham Post & Mail, 1983.

The Blitz on Birmingham 1940-1943, Anthony Sutcliffe c. 1969, Research paper no. 1, University of Birmingham.

Blitz Over Britain, Edwin Webb & John Duncan, Spellmount, Tunbridge Wells, Kent, 1990.

The Blitz Then and Now Vol.1, Winston Ramsey, Battle of Britain Prints International Limited, London, 1987.

The Blitz Then and Now Vol.2, Winston Ramsey, Battle of Britain Prints International Limited, London, 1988.

The Blitz Then and Now Vol.3, Winston Ramsey, Battle of Britain Prints International Limited, London, 1990.

The Bombing War Europe 1939-1945, Richard Overy, Penguin Books, London, 2014.

Brum Undaunted, Carl Chinn, Birmingham Library Services, 1996.

A City at War, Birmingham 1939-1945, Edited by Phillada Ballard, Birmingham Museums and Art Gallery, 1985.

The Defence of the United Kingdom, Basil Collier, The Naval & Military Press, Uckfield, East Sussex, 2004.

Defiant, Blenheim and Havoc Aces, Andrew Thomas, Osprey, Botley, Oxford, 2012.

The First Pathfinders, Kenneth Wakefield, William Kimber, London, 1981.

History of Birmingham Vol.3, Birmingham 1939-1970, Anthony Sutcliffe & Roger Smith, Published for the Birmingham City Council by Oxford University Press, London, 1974.

Home Security Summaries, National Archives, Kew, London.

The Luftwaffe's Blitz, Chris Goss, Crécy Publishing Limited, Manchester, 2010.

The Luftwaffe War Diaries, Cajus Bekker, Corgi Books, London, 1969.

Most Secret War, R.V. Jones, Hamish Hamilton, London, 1978.

The Mouchotte Diaries, René Mouchotte, Panther, London, 1957.

The Night Blitz 1940-1941, John Ray, Arms & Armour Press, London, 1996.

Night Fighter, C. F. Rawnsley & Robert Wright, Corgi, London, 1966.

No Place for Chivalry, Alastair Goodrum, Grub Street, London, 2005.

Portrait of Birmingham, Vivian Bird, Robert Hale & Co, London, 1979.

RAF 1939-1945 Vol.1: The Fight at Odds, Denis Richards, HMSO, 1953.

RAF Fighter Command Victory Claims of World War Two: Part 2, 1 January 1941-30 June 1943, John Foreman, Red Kite, Walton-on-Thames, Surrey, 2005.

Roof Over Britain (The War Facsimiles), TSO Publishing, 2001.

The Second World War: Vol.2 Their Finest Hour, Winston Churchill, Cassell, London, 1948.

Solihull Air Raids WW2 – Heinkel 111 Crash at Earlswood, 11.5.1941, J. Prince, P. Kettle & G. Nall, Solihull, 1998.

A Sound in the Sky, Geoffrey Alington, R. K. Hudson, London, 1994.

Squadron Operations Record Books and Pilot Combat Reports, National Archives, Kew, London.

That Eternal Summer, Ralph Barker, Collins, London, 1990.

Warwickshire Airfields in the Second World War, Graham Smith, Countryside Books, Newbury, 2004.

Worcestershire at War, written & published by Glyn Warren, 1991.

INDEX

Index of Military Units

OTHER TITLES BY THE SAME AUTHOR

AEC MATADOR
TAKING THE ROUGH WITH THE SMOOTH

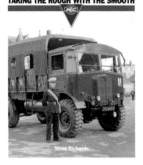

Steve Richards

ISBN: 978-1-904686-24-8
Format: Softback
Size: 280x215mm: 80 pages
Photos: 101 b/w, 69 colour
Price: £15.99
Postage: UK £2.50, EU £8.00, Rest of World £10.50 (air mail)

Midland Red
MOTORWAY COACHES

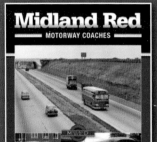

Steve Richards

ISBN: 978-0-9563708-1-5
Format: Softback
Size: 280x215mm: 112 pages
Photos: 135 b/w, 75 colour
Price: £19.95
Postage: UK £2.50, EU £8.00, Rest of World £10.50 (air mail)

More room on top

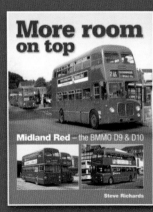

Midland Red – the BMMO D9 & D10

Steve Richards

ISBN: 978-0-9563708-2-2
Format: Softback
Size: 280x215mm: 112 pages
Photos: 135 b/w, 75 colour
Price: £19.95
Postage: UK £2.50, EU £8.00, Rest of World £10.50 (air mail)